AFRICAN ISSUES

The Front Line
Runs Through
Every Woman

T0366690

AFRICAN ISSUES

●

AFRICAN ISSUES

The Front Line Runs Through Every Woman

Women & Local Resistance in the Zimbabwean Liberation War

ELEANOR O'GORMAN
Senior Associate
at the Gender
Studies Centre &
Research Associate,
Department of Politics
& International Studies,
University of Cambridge

 JAMES CURREY

WEAVER
PRESS

James Currey
is an imprint of
Boydell & Brewer Ltd
PO Box 9, Woodbridge
Suffolk IP12 3DF

and of

Boydell & Brewer Inc.
668 Mt Hope Avenue
Rochester, NY 14620, USA
www.boydellandbrewer.com
www.jamescurrey.com

Weaver Press
Box A1922
Avondale, Harare
Zimbabwe
www.weaverpresszimbabwe.com

© Eleanor O' Gorman 2011

First published 2011

1 2 3 4 5 15 14 13 12 11

British Library Cataloguing in Publication Data

O'Gorman, Eleanor, 1968-
The front line runs through every woman : women and local resistance in
the Zimbabwean Liberation War. -- (African issues)
1. Women and war--Zimbabwe. 2. Zimbabwe--History--Chimurenga
War, 1966-1980--Women. 3. National liberation movements--Zimbabwe
--History--20th century.
I. Title II. Series
303.6'6'082'096891-dc22

ISBN 978-1-84701-040-7 (James Currey paper)
ISBN 978-1-77922-156-8 (Weaver Press paper)

Papers used by Boydell and Brewer are natural, recyclable products
made from wood grown in sustainable forests

Typeset by forzalibro designs, Cape Town,
in 9/10 Melior with Optima display

Printed and bound by CPI Group (UK) Ltd, Croydon, CR0 4YY

DEDICATION

This book is dedicated with love, in memory of my mother
Eileen O' Gorman –
mother, wife, farmer, sister, friend and much much more –
and to the women of Chiweshe
whose stories are the heartbeat of this book

CONTENTS

LIST OF MAPS & PHOTOGRAPHS

ACKNOWLEDGEMENTS

This book would not have been possible without the encouragement, friendship and academic insight of Jim Whitman, who persevered in goading me to write it. Thank you.

The John D. and Catherine T. MacArthur Foundation funded the original research that underpins this book and I remain deeply appreciative of the opportunity. I am grateful to the Department of Politics and International Studies and the Gender Studies Centre at the University of Cambridge for the intellectual base they provide for my research and writing. Special appreciation and affection is extended to New Hall (now Murray Edwards College), Cambridge, for providing an enabling and supportive environment; Anne Lonsdale, former President, has provided more support and influence than I can adequately express here.

The ideas and arguments of this book have benefited from various conversations and forums. Stephen Chan introduced me to Zimbabwe during my MA at the University of Kent and provided important advice through later rounds of fieldwork and analysis. Geoffrey Hawthorn, as my PhD supervisor at Cambridge, helped to harness the beasts of theory and fieldwork. I would also like to express my appreciation to John Illiffe, John Lonsdale and the African Studies Centre at Cambridge, Terence Ranger, Jocelyn Alexander, Diana Jeater and the Zimbabwe research group in Oxford and Vivienne Jabri and the Feminist Theory and Gender Studies section of the International Studies Association.

I would also like to acknowledge the Department of Politics and Public Administration at the University of Zimbabwe, where I was an Honorary Research Associate in 1993. In particular, I thank Hasu and Diana Patel, Treasa Galvin and Charles Chawanda for their intellectual support and hospitality. I appreciate the research support that Ishmael Magaisa and Tracy Kandeya in particular provided.

In Chiweshe, I owe heartfelt gratitude to many women and their families for their time and hospitality. I am grateful to Trust, Lorine, Juliet, Whisper and Mrs G for their interpreting skills and moral support. My debt beyond words is to Mrs C (Mai Anna) for giving me a home that only a mother could provide. The Sisters at St Michael's Convent, Harare, also opened up their home to me and introduced me to a loving and supportive network of remarkable women that includes 'Cousin Carmel'.

I also wish to thank the archivists and librarians who facilitated my search for information at the National Archives of Zimbabwe; the Ministry of Local Government Library, Harare; the Zimbabwe Women's Resource Centre and Network, Harare; and the Catholic Institute for International Relations, London. A special word of thanks is owed to the African Studies Library at the University of Cambridge.

Thanks are also due to the National Archives of Zimbabwe for the photographs of the Protected Villages in Chiweshe featured on p. 89.

Friends and colleagues supported this work in various ways and I would like to acknowledge them here: Bela Bhatia, Kate Brown, Jude Browne, Catarina Cardoso, Deirdre Collings, Ann Cotton, Zeev Emmerich, Jude Howell, Margaret Jungck, Uma Kambhampati, Mike MccGwire, Polly Mohs, Tanni Mukhopadhyay, Susie Penney Delaney, Marjan Radjavi, Rafal Rohozinski, Sanjay Ruparelia, Liz Trinder, Sarah White, Helen Yanacopulos and Dubravka Zarkov.

I would like to thank my family, in particular my father, John O' Gorman, for bearing with me and supporting me in the many journeys, not always understood, that have taken me many directions. Loving gratitude is extended to my sister Mae, my brothers Ger and Flor, and my Aunt Mae.

I wish to thank Douglas Johnson and Lynn Taylor at James Currey for their editorial advice and excellent support in guiding this book to publication and Teresa Barnes for her reader's comments. I also wish to thank Dave Clarke and Kate Kirkwood for their designs of the maps for Chiweshe and Zimbabwe and Frances Marks for her careful copy editing. I am also grateful to Margeret Cornell for her work on the index. As author I take full responsibility for any errors or omissions in the text and indeed in these acknowledgements.

ACRONYMS

AIDS	Acquired Immune Deficiency Syndrome
BSACo	British South Africa Company
CCJP	Catholic Commission for Justice and Peace
CIIR	Catholic Institute of International Relations
DA	District Assistant
DRC	Democratic Republic of Congo
FRELIMO	Front for the Liberation of Mozambique
GMB	Grain Marketing Board
HIV	Human Immuno-Virus
LRF	Legal Resources Foundation
MCDWA	Ministry for Community Development and Women's Affairs
MDC	Movement for Democratic Change
NDP	National Democratic Party
NGO	Non-Governmental Organisation
PV	Protected Village
RF	Rhodesia Front
SADC	Southern African Development Community
SRANC	Southern Rhodesia African National Congress
TTL	Tribal Trust Land
UANC	United African National Congress
UNSC	United Nations Security Council
ZANU-PF	Zimbabwe African National Union–Patriotic Front
ZAPU	Zimbabwe African People's Union
ZANLA	Zimbabwe African National Liberation Army
ZANU	Zimbabwe African National Union
ZIPRA	Zimbabwe People's Revolutionary Army

GLOSSARY

Amai	Mother (also a title of respect for an older woman)
Ambuya	Grandmother (also a title of respect for an older woman)
Auxiliaries	Paramilitary force attached to Bishop Abel Muzorewa's UANC
Baba	Father (also title of respect for older man)
Chimbwido	Female youth supporter of the guerrillas
Chimurenga	Struggle; name given to the war of liberation
Communal Areas	Administrative title for the former Native Reserves (TTLs)
Dagga	Clay used for building huts
District Commissioner	Colonial official who administered the African reserves
Dovi	Peanut butter
Gandangas	Terrorists; derogatory name for guerrillas used by Rhodesian government
Growth Point	Local township or business centre in the Communal Areas
Headman	Traditional village leader
High-density areas	Urban townships
Kabibiya	Someone who cannot keep a secret
Kapenta	Small dried fish
Kitenga	Cloth wrap or shawl worn by women
Kraal	Wooden pen for holding cattle; can also refer to a village settlement
Kwashiorkor	A form of malnutrition casued by lack of protein
Lobola	Bride price; paid by prospective husband to the bride's family
Matoros	Derogatory name used for guerrillas; terrorists
Mealie meal	Ground maize
Mhondoro	Lion; refers to the ancestral spirit of a Chief
Midzimu	Ancestral spirit
Mujibha	Male youth supporter of the guerrillas
Muriwo	Green-leaved vegetable eaten with *sadza*
Murungu	White person
Native Purchase Areas	Private land holdings located outside the TTLs for purchase by selected African Master Farmers during the colonial period

Nyama	Meat; also meat relish eaten with *sadza*
Povo	The masses
Pungwe	Night-time meeting conducted by the guerrillas in the bush; also referred to as a *morari*
RIC number	Registration Certificate number
Sadza	Very thick maize porridge, which is a staple food
Sekuru	Grandfather; also title of respect for older men, particularly a mother's brother
Selous Scouts	Counter-insurgency army unit of the Rhodesian military
Shave	Animal spirit
Simba Yehonda	Power of war
Simba Yemvura	Power of rain
Situpa	Identity card
Vakomana	The boys; familiar name for the guerrillas
Vatete	Aunt; a father's sister
TTL	Tribal Trust Land (Native Reserve)
Women's League	Women's membership section of ZANU

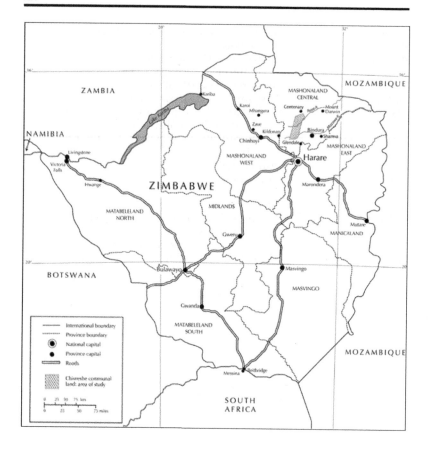

Map 1 Zimbabwe

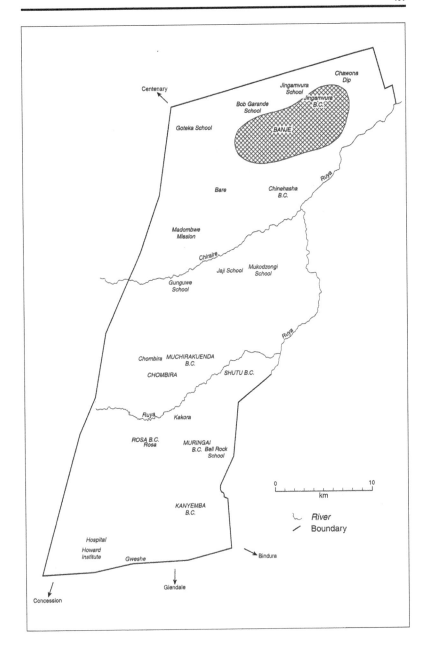

Map 2 Chiweshe Communal Land

Introduction | Women, War
Voice & Agency

In October 2010 the United Nations celebrated the tenth anniversary of the landmark Security Council Resolution (UNSCR) 1325 on women, peace and security.[1] This resolution finally acknowledged the impact of war on women across the world and set out the political imperative to protect women from targeted acts of violence and ensure the greater participation of women in all aspects of peacemaking, peacekeeping and peacebuilding. The global agenda for international peace and security had at last accepted the importance of gender in understanding violence and transforming the prospects for peace and security, or so it seemed. This framework of commitments was added to in 2008 with the adoption of UNSCR 1820, which focused on specific actions to combat sexual violence in conflict, including better prevention and protection strategies during war as well as ending impunity for perpetrators.[2] This was driven by the brutal facts on the ground coming from over a decade of war and violence in the eastern Democratic Republic of Congo (DRC), and compounding generations of such atrocities of rape in war that in some measure had been acknowledged by the International Criminal Tribunals for Rwanda and the former Yugoslavia. There is much to reflect upon from the decade of the 2000s and the progress made, particularly in Africa, where the most pernicious wars of the post-Cold War period have continued to wreak trauma and havoc on the prospects for peace and development, and where civilians, especially women and children, have paid a very heavy price.

During the campaign for Resolution 1325 in the late 1990s, I completed my PhD on the study of women and war in Zimbabwe, revisiting the anti-colonial liberation war of the 1960s and 1970s that gave way to independence in 1980. One of the last such wars in the wave of decolonisation, it pressured such hopes and expectations of democratic transformation in Africa and the end to racially divisive rule. Zimbabwe 'celebrated' 30 years of independence on 18 April 2010. Here too there was much to reflect upon in terms of the pains of transition and

---

[1] United Nations Security Council (UNSC) (2000). See also Rehn and Johnson-Sirleaf (2002) and United Nations (2002).
[2] UNSC (2008).

1

statehood, with their attendant failures of governance, land reform and human rights giving way to centralised power, pernicious violence, political intimidation, deepening poverty, weakened institutions and the betrayal of promises and prospects from a long-fought and endured guerrilla war. Following three decades of consolidation of one-party rule under Robert Mugabe's ZANU-PF, the centralisation and capture of state power and resources in a system of patronage and corruption, the repression of political opposition from political parties or civil society activists and groups and the attendant brutal political violence in villages, urban centres and on commercial farms, in 2009 Zimbabwe entered new political territory in an uneasy Global Political Agreement between ZANU-PF and the opposition Movement for Democratic Change (MDC) under the leadership of Morgan Tsvangarai. The arrangement has been beset by the overwhelming challenges of achieving the necessary conditions for a land audit as the basis for a transparent and fair process of land reform and resettlement, a new Constitution setting out the balance of executive powers between President and Prime Minister, the repeal of laws still being used to repress Zimbabweans around the country and the break of the stranglehold of a security elite on political power and patronage. Yet, despite this, there is still hope that tomorrow may be better.

Revisiting a PhD sounds a warning bell to writer, reader and publisher. However, sometimes the fermentation of the wait helps to deepen the relevance of the original research and guide its re-working for publication to reach a wider audience. This is the claim I make for this book on women and local resistance in Zimbabwe's liberation war of the late 1960s and 1970s. I carried out the original fieldwork during a 12-month period in 1993 and completed my thesis in 1999. My experiences between those signposts included a lectureship in development studies and a stint with an NGO supporting girls' education in Africa. Since 2000 life has taken me more fully into the world of aid and contemporary wars both with the United Nations and as a freelance adviser on policies and programmes in countries as diverse as Liberia, DRC, Timor-Leste, Sri Lanka and Somalia. More recently I have had cause to work on issues of sexual violence in conflict in the context of UN Security Council Resolutions that have mandated more action on women, peace and security. My experiences during this decade since the adoption of UNSCR 1325 have amplified for me the resonance of the story of Zimbabwe and the need to share it more widely. The experience of women in Zimbabwe endures, even if it seems that the political realities of war and international peacekeeping and aid interventions have changed and that Zimbabwe itself is in a different place.

New wars, old problems

Women, agency and war have been tested one generation on from the anti-colonial wars of southern Africa in Angola, Mozambique, South Africa and Zimbabwe, as new wars have proved internecine, lengthy and paralyzing to any hope of peace and development in many parts of Africa. These post-Cold War theatres of war are found notably in the Great Lakes region (DRC, Burundi, Uganda and Rwanda) and West Africa (Liberia, Sierra Leone and to some extent Côte d'Ivoire). However, their neighbours have not escaped the regional and spillover impacts of wars without borders and the debilitating impact on already weak social and economic infrastructure. Even those countries that came through earlier revolutionary wars to a new politics of independence, the legacies of revolutionary wars and the manner in which they were fought have produced legacy dynamics that inform continuing struggles of legitimacy, authority and power in post-colonial states. The experiences of Angola, Mozambique, South Africa, Zambia and Zimbabwe are testament to this. The generalised acceptance and rise of violence, often armed violence, in many contemporary African states has been shaped by a mix of global economic trends and policies, persistent poverty, demographic pressures, inequality and political power struggles. This, linked to regional and global security trends of organised criminal activity, trafficking of many kinds, illegal trade, natural resource extraction and migration fuels ongoing instability. Nevertheless, our understanding of civilian experiences of war stubbornly fails to take account of community perspectives and agency in the shaping of international policies and interventions in a range of areas – military/ peacekeeping, diplomatic, humanitarian and development assistance, human rights and law.

The academic field of gender and war has grown considerably and is a testament to the theoretical and fieldwork undertaken by a generation of activists, researchers and academics. Writers such as Cynthia Enloe and Jean Bethke Elshtain, who inspired my early questions of the failures of revolutionary politics for feminist agendas, have endured as the foundations of a field that has burgeoned in recent years. Recent works range across themes that include a fascination with women and violence, notably the aberrant roles of female suicide bombers of Palestine, the Black Widows of Chechnya and other perpetrators of violence, new workings of patriarchy and militarism in the context of the global 'war on terror' and the grassroots histories and testaments to women's civil society activism and often unacknowledged work for peace.[3] In addition, there is a surge of policy and advocacy literature arising in part from UNSCR 1325 and the attempts to put a 'gender lens' on the increasingly complex aid, security and post-conflict reconstruction operations world wide.[4] It is difficult to say what has begotten what, but the synergies of what is now known as Feminist International Relations and global political activism have never been so optimistic.

---

[3]   For examples of these themes see Sjoberg and Gentry (2007), Al-Ali and Pratt (2009), Enloe (2007) and Naraghi-Anderlini (2007).

[4]   This policy work includes International Committee of the Red Cross (2002); Rehn and Johnson-Sirleaf (2002); United Nations (2002); International Alert (2002) and Sherriff with Barnes (2008).

Zimbabwe's past and the legacy dynamics of the Liberation War

Zimbabwe too has changed. Today the country has a population of over 12 million people, of whom 50% (six million) are under 18 years of age. It is estimated that around 3.4 million people have fled the country in recent years, many to South Africa, so total population statistics are not reliable.[5] There is a HIV prevalence rate of 15%, with an estimated 1.3 million people living with the disease and around one million children orphaned as a direct result of HIV/AIDS. Life expectancies have shortened dramatically collapsed, falling from 61 years (1990) to 44 years in (2008). There has also been a marked increase of urbanisation as people move in search of work, access to services and foodstuffs. From 20% urbanisation in the early 1990s, 37% of Zimbabwe's population now live in urban areas. Unemployment is running at 90%.[6] Official statistics in February 2008 showed an inflation rate of 100,580%, up from 7,600% in July 2007.[7] This hyperinflationary environment began to stabilise when the inclusive government – negotiated with the mediation of SADC and former President Mbeki of South Africa in September 2008 –came into operation in February 2009.[8] The International Crisis Group reports that GDP grew by 4.7% in 2009, the first positive figures in a decade. The suspension of the Zimbabwe dollar and the acceptance of the US dollar and South African rand as legal tender saw inflation fall from the official rate of 231 million per cent in July 2008 to an average of six per cent in 2009. In real terms, however, poverty and economic hardship for Zimbabweans continue.

Behind these statistics and the grim picture they paint lie 30 years of complex and intertwined issues that have shaped the crisis in Zimbabwe.[9] These include land reform and farm invasions, constitutional crisis, political violence, economic meltdown, social breakdown and

---

[5] International Organisation on Migration (IOM) figures cited in http://news.bbc.co.uk/1/hi/world/africa/7304635.stm (accessed 03/03/2011); the International Crisis Group report (2010) estimates the number of emigrants and exiles to be one-third of the population, or around four million Zimbabweans.

[6] http://www.unicef.org/infobycountry/zimbabwe_statistics.html; http://www.who.int/countries/zwe/en/ (accessed 03/03/2011).

[7] http://news.bbc.co.uk/1/hi/world/africa/7304635.stm (accessed 03/03/2011).

[8] International Crisis Group (ICG) (2010).

[9] For an excellent overview of the deepening crisis in Zimbabwe and more recent prospects for a transition to stability and democracy see the chapters by James Muzondidya and Brian Raftopoulos in *Becoming Zimbabwe: A History from the Pre-Colonial Period to 2008*, edited by Brian Raftopoulos and Alois Mlambo (2009). For political updates and analysis on Zimbabwe, see the reports of International Crisis Group cited in the bibliography. In terms of further reading on the issues of squatters, land invasions, war veterans, resettlement and farmworkers see Alexander (2006; 2003) Kriger (2003), Sachikonye, (2003), GAPWUZ (2010) and UNDP (2008); on historiography as a battleground with contested notions of patriotism, revolution and who is a Zimbabwean see Ranger (2004) and Phimister and Raftopoulos (2004); on political violence see CCJP and LRF (1997), Lindgren (2003), Phimister and Raftopoulos (2007) and United Nations (2005).

resilience and the reinvention of patriotic history. The early calls of reconciliation and accelerated provision of health care and education services to the rural areas gave way quite quickly to one-party rule by ZANU-PF. The pursuit of ethnic-based policies of control against the Ndebele in Matabeleland led to a brutal campaign of violence, torture and killing from 1982–87 orchestrated by the notorious Fifth Brigade. This period is a referred to as *Gukurahundi* ('the rains that wash away the chaff') and resulted in the killing of 20,000 civilians (CCJP and LRF 1997). The Unity Government of ZANU and ZAPU (the latter then still led by the late Joshua Nkomo) in 1987 led to the absorption of the official opposition; a precedent that must haunt Morgan Tsvangirai and the MDC today as they navigate the transitional government. The MDC was born out of the social opposition and movements of civil society organisations including the trade unions, NGOs, academics and women's organisations. This grew through the 1990s in loose coalitions and became a political force in by 2000 as the Movement for Democratic Change when it successfully campaigned for a 'no' vote in the constitutional referendum of that year, stymying efforts for compulsory land acquisition and greater concentration of executive power. The elections of 2000 were also hotly contested. The violence formally and informally wielded by the government worsened through the 1990s and 2000s and elections were increasing marked by intimidation, beatings and torture.

Two particular groups have emerged as critical to political control, particularly in the rural areas: the war veterans (ex-guerrilla fighters from the independence war, although such categorisation is not easy) and the youth militia (known infamously as the Green Bombers because of the fatigues they wear and their militia-style activities). These latter ZANU-PF youth brigades are also sometimes referred to as 'youth workers'; some 20,000 militia are thought to be on the civil service payroll (ICG, 2010). They attend training camps in what has become a type of 'national service' scheme. The war veterans came to prominence as a political force in the late 1990s with increasingly violent claims for the lack of compensation for war service and their impatience for allocations of land to make amends.[10] After 2000 the state deliberately began to use the veterans as an army with which to lead the land invasions and forced acquisitions that were part of its Fast-Track Land Reform Programme.[11] Who exactly is a 'veteran' is much debated on all sides but their power and patronage as a group is undisputed.

The leaders of the security forces (the army, police and intelligence services) also gained in status and power over the period, much empowered and enriched by the decision of President Mugabe to back Laurent Kabila to take and keep power in the DRC in 1998. The emergence of

---

[10] This dissent was evident during the 1980s. The government did make some pensions and payments available at that time.

[11] See Alexander (2003) and Kriger (2003) for contestations of 'veterans'. In 2000 there were around 4,500 white-owned commercial farms; by 2008 there were only 450 (Raftopoulos 2009). Farm workers suffered as they were often treated by squatters, veterans and government officials as property of the farmers. In 2003 there were reports of 40 farm workers being murdered and 500 farm schools being forced to closed (Sachikonye, 2003). By 2008 roughly one million people had been rendered homeless as a result of the land reform programme (UNDP 2008).

a political-military elite that has benefited from land 'redistribution', diamond and gold trading and packages of support from the President is further indication of the governance crisis. In addition, a new ideology of a 'Third *Chimurenga*' (liberation war) has been crafted to create a narrative for ZANU-PF and more particularly for Robert Mugabe's entitlement to govern. This has in essence meant defining a 'patriotic history' that must be learned and understood by all Zimbabweans; it is predicated on the continued violent struggle that is needed to take on not just the settlers but their backers, internationally and locally, in the reinvention of who is a real Zimbabwean by 'dividing up the nation into revolutionaries and sell-outs' (Ranger 2004:223).

It seems timely therefore to revisit the Second *Chimurenga* – the liberation war that brought independence and consider why and how women participated in that struggle. In understanding how rural women survived and resisted within the guerrilla and counter-insurgency warfare of the struggle for liberation I believe we might understand some of what these same communities are facing today.

The focus of this study of Chiweshe

Women's participation in revolutionary struggles has been an important focus of feminist writings and politics on gender solidarity and transformation since the 1960s. Their role in revolutionary movements and the political gains and losses associated with their participation has been a bittersweet narrative. This book explores the dynamics of women's revolutionary involvement through the oral histories of women in Chiweshe, Zimbabwe, who took part in the national liberation struggle from 1966–1980. The analysis of these voices acts as a critical foil, re-considering two bodies of literature: histories of the war and feminist interpretations of women's relationship to militarism, revolution and war. The first, historical body of literature focuses on peasant mobilisation, including the defining works of Terence Ranger (1985), David Lan (1985) and Norma Kriger (1992). I argue that their focus on peasant mobilisation does not fully take account of the complexity of women's lives in revolution and that a reconsideration of revolutionary consciousness is necessary to explain women's participation in the Zimbabwean war. Feminist interpretations of women and war from the perspectives of political theory and International Relations do highlight women's involvement in revolutionary movements. This includes the foundational work of Cynthia Enloe (1988; 1989; 2007), Jean Bethke Elshtain (1981; 1995) and Maxine Molyneux (1985). However, I argue such feminist critiques often take insufficient account of differences between and within women and that the analysis of women's experiences of war has been stereotyped and leaves unasked questions and untold stories in between the polar extremes of heroic fighter and passive victim.

Thus, the question posed here is how do rural women understand and interpret their experiences of revolutionary war and it is offered as a riposte to the question of why do revolutions fail women? This perspective draws on understandings of gender identities and transformations in a setting of the revolutionary war in the Communal Area of Chiweshe, 80 kilometres north of Harare.[12] In guerrilla and counter-insurgency wars, the use of camps to contain the civilians of a region and break their contact with fighting forces is not new. From the British use of 'concentration camps' in the Boer War in South Africa at the turn of the twentieth century and the 'New Villages' in the communist insurgency in Malaysia in the 1950s to the failed attempts of the United States to create 'strategic hamlets' in Vietnam in the early 1960s, we come to the experiences of Zimbabwe in the 1970s when Protected Villages were established in the Tribal Trust Lands (TTLs) to cut off the oxygen of community support to the guerrillas of the national liberation movements of ZANLA and ZIPRA.

The local focus on revolution explored here maps out the field of possibilities and risks for women who were simultaneously surviving a war and enacting a revolution. Their stories emphasise the importance of the *context* of war in shaping their agency and consciousness as revolutionary and post-revolutionary women. An important element of this context is the social relations of war; women were constantly negotiating their relations with the state, the revolutionary forces and their neighbours. These relations were fraught with risk and required skilful handling. Support and subversion co-existed in the strategies devised by women who were both enacting a revolution and living with a guerrilla war. Women's strategies of survival and engagement were more complex than a simple model of 'consciousness raising' or revolutionary mobilisation can explain. They reflected the support and subversion and the dislocations of self, family and community that accompanied the revolutionary and counter-revolutionary aspects of guerrilla warfare. Here, the personal had no choice but to be political.

A theoretical and methodological approach of *Gendered Localised Resistance* is developed to guide this exploration of complexity and locality. This approach brings together Michel Foucault's (1978; 1979) idea of agonistic power/resistance as embedded in subjectivity and James Scott's (1985; 1976) practical consciousness of everyday resistance as embedded in local experience. What emerges is a more complex rendering of the local dynamics of women's participation and resistance in revolution. 'The front line runs through every woman' evokes this alternative narrative of women and revolutionary war that halts the pendulum of fighters or victims. The battleground drawn from women's voices and perceptions uncovers layers of agency bound up with revolutionary resistance, local resistance and daily survival. In so doing, these biographies of resistance illuminate our understanding of women's experiences of, and participation in, revolution as the triumph of survival over and through the dislocations of revolution. The struggles for everyday survival, the atomisation of community life and the differences amongst women in living through the revolution indicate the need to rescue resistance from revolution if social transformation for women is to have a post-revolutionary prospect.

---

[12]   These were formerly referred to as Tribal Trust Lands under colonial rule.

The politics of voice

Voice is central to the methodology of writing about women's experience and agency in what was simultaneously a revolutionary, liberation, anti-colonial, civil, guerrilla and counter-insurgency war, particularly rural women who are still the lifeblood of their communities. Each has a story, a life and voice that is rarely heard or recognised. The testimonies of women from Chiweshe form the basis of the story to be told here. The use of their testimonies is a political act, seeking to empower and give space to women's voices; to allow women to bear witness to their own experiences, however inarticulate or contradictory they may be compared to other sources such as archives, canonical historical works and organisational perspectives.

The use of testimonials has long been contested as a source of substantiated information, particularly in relation to the issue of rape and sexual violence in war. Susan Brownmiller (1976) exposes the ambivalence towards such testimonies during the post-Second World War military tribunals at Nuremberg and Tokyo. She castigates the military enthusiasm for using testimonies of rape as propaganda while displaying no long-term commitment to seeking retributions for victims of rape through believing and acting upon such testimonies. She is also critical of historians and journalists for their reluctance to register such testimonies as records of war. Tamara Tompkins (1995) reiterates the struggle to accept oral testimonies in respect of rape in war in the former Yugoslavia. Media coverage was part of the growing trend towards using women's voices and testimonies to push for the acknowledgement of rape as a 'crime against humanity', something which finally received recognition in 1993 in Article 5 of the Statute of the International Tribunal convened in The Hague. Media coverage and collections of cases have become more commonplace as advocacy tools for contemporary campaigns to address rape, violence against women and witness statements to human rights atrocities during times of war. Others, however, have sought to capture the story of women in war and to let women speak of where they were and what they did.[13] It is how these voices and testimonies are treated that shapes the experience and representation as empowering, degrading, indifferent, revealing, voyeuristic and even pornographic.

The analysis of life histories acknowledges women as agents in war, rather than simply as victims, and validates civilian experiences of war. The notion of voice is thus important in representing women's differentiated experiences of war to generate a more inclusive rendering of resistance in a revolutionary setting. In building upon 'peasant voices' and 'women's voices', a perspective from below involves working outward from the collected testimonies of women to map out the parameters of their participation in a revolutionary war. The importance of oral history as methodology in this study also lies in the possibility of

---

[13] For examples of oral history collections see Bennett, Bexley and Warnock (1995) (eds) and Staunton (1990).

understanding differences amongst women in the experience of revolution. Zimbabwean writer Charles Mungoshi, for example, captures the inevitable diversity of those voices for rural women in his review of Irene Staunton's collection of women's testimonies of the Zimbabwe liberation war:

> while they may have some aspects in common – like the separation of children from parents, or wives from their husbands, or the total uprooting of one's communal or social ties, or the wholesale destruction of whole villages, or the disruption of the psychological and spiritual ties of a whole people to their traditional way of life – each experience, however, is as different from the other as there are social and economic differences in Zimbabwe, and as there are psychological differences between any two individuals'. (1990:20).[14]

Ethnography is central to this presentation of voices yet this is not without tension. While mindful of the traditions of oral history and cultural anthropology, the approach here is more resonant with newer explorations to develop an ethnography of violence and war that is appropriate to the fragmented and diffuse scope and impact of contemporary conflicts that is witnessed daily in situations as diverse as DRC, Sudan, Afghanistan and Sri Lanka. Jan Vansina (1980; 1985) and Joseph Miller (1980), when writing of oral histories, distinguish between 'personal reminiscences', which they dismiss as private recollections of a recent event within the lifetime of the speaker, and 'oral tradition', in which particular memories are consciously sedimented over time to provide a public shared perspective of, say, lineage or myths of origins within a particular (usually non-literate) society. The distrust of personal memory and the need for verification are extended by Vansina (1980) in his description of the complex and subtle psychological processes that mediate the translation of experiences through the acts of remembering and speaking. Such processes include 'current self-image', emotions, blocking painful memories, reliance on images rather than events and the influence of others' versions of one's own situation and actions at the time. However, I suggest that just as historical fact and document can illuminate and challenge the remembrance of events by individuals and communities, so too can the sought-after memories, reminiscences and forgotten fragments of experience of particular events illuminate and challenge accepted fact and document. They can reveal a sentient context of understanding and belief that is important in interpreting and situating historical facts.

In the field of cultural anthropology, there is similar debate about disciplinary claims on the methodological and epistemological appropriateness of representing researchers' experiences and the words of interviewees as 'speaking subjects'. James Clifford (1988), in a post-structuralist turn, addresses the difficulties and possibilities of incorporating and representing informants' 'voices' in anthropological and sociological reconstruction. He maps out the tensions between objectivity and subjectivity in his evolutionary tale of ethnographic authority in anthropology. He elaborates on the 'complex subjectivity'

---

14   Charles Mungoshi is the author of the celebrated novel *Coming of the Dry Season* that is based on the war in Zimbabwe. This quote is taken from a review of *Mothers of the Revolution*, an edited volume of women's testimonies of war in Zimbabwe.

at the heart of participant observation that he argues emerged in various forms as the *sine qua non* of professional anthropology and lent authority to claims of knowledge and truth of 'others' made by ethnographers. This complex subjectivity, Clifford reveals, is not a direct translation of non-western cultures for a western academic audience but involves the subjective, intersubjective, dialogical and interactive activities of fieldwork, writing, interpretation and reading that shape the representation of 'cultures' and 'peoples'. He further explores the possibilities of polyphonic ethnographies that may reflect more fully the complex workings of producing and textualising accounts of cross-cultural representation. Within this, Clifford reveals the persistence of power relations that bedevil all attempts to overcome the implicit and explicit hierarchies of representation involving informants, subjects and researchers.[15]

The work of Carolyn Nordstrom (1995; 1997) and Paul Richards (2005) is instructive in turning toward a new type of ethnography that confronts and interrogates contemporary wars and political violence. Nordstrom has developed an ethnography of violent places that travels the continuum of violence inside and outside of war. In the concern of war she is interested in how individuals engage with it: 'It is in creativity, in the fashioning of self and world, that people find their most potent weapon against war' (1997:4). This interest in political violence and creative resistance informs what she terms 'ethnography of a warzone'. Richards similarly stresses a continuum of 'no peace no war' to argue for greater social engagement and understanding of war that has too often been left to security specialists. Rather than simplistic diagnoses of causality, he places the emphasis on the 'patterns of violence already embedded within society' and the need to use 'ethnography of the actual practices of war and peace' (2005:11-12). This means building knowledge and understanding from where war is experienced and how it affects those who directly participate in it.

The voices related, interpreted and shared here are many. I speak of an experiential voice and consciousness of women in a time of war. At this level, it is a voice and consciousness that bears witness to experience, a voice and consciousness that is spoken and is listened to and a voice and consciousness that is transformed in the act of speaking and listening as a different perspective on the experience of war by women. This Chiweshe perspective becomes a 'jointly constructed' exercise in interpreting the local experiences of war.[16] By this, I mean that in this

---

[15] For more on this see Clifford (1986a; 1986b).

[16] To view the events of the Zimbabwean liberation war through the eyes of women in Chiweshe is not to assume the impossible and undesirable task of stepping into their shoes. There are filters that influence the interpretation and analysis of oral testimonies of which the researcher needs to be conscious. The interpretive process of this research is influenced by a number of factors: my own thoughts and understanding of the events in question; my identity as an outsider who may observe but must accept the limitations of my identification and identity; the interviews and how information was gathered; how questions were chosen and framed; the ability of women to recall events, many of which by then were twenty-five years past; and the women's own reinterpretation of those events as they told them in light of life since the war. The fact that women speak with retrospective voices is perhaps the most significant filter of understanding affecting their accounts as memory and remembrance shape their reconstructed understandings of the war.

study of women and the Zimbabwean liberation war arises not only from the interviews and oral histories of women in Chiweshe but also from my questions, engagement with theory and the act of writing. This is to say that a 'truth' is not being advanced and neither is a mere reflection of Chiweshe women's voices. Rather, the analysis offered in this book constitutes an account of a 'conversation' in Chiweshe about the war and the practices of survival and resistance. At its centre, this conversation involves myself and a number of women from Chiweshe. In a wider sense, it is a conversation that brings in historians writing on the revolution, feminists writing on women and war and social theorists writing on resistance, subjectivity and consciousness. In its final form it is a symphony of voices that builds a lost narrative of women and war.

Observing is always key to the research work but being a participant is to overstate the ability of an outsider to become part of a community in a short space of time. Even when helping to harvest the maize, shell the nuts, or cook food, I was always an outsider and at best a guest. I could never be any of the women I interviewed or stand in their place. This was in part due to the general sensitivity of talking about the war and the feelings and fear of intimidation when discussing it with an outsider. Gossip was rife and rumours abounded of me as a South African spy, a government inspector, the daughter of a local white farmer and, most worryingly, as a Catholic nun! In a more instrumental way I was often viewed as a source of project funding and seen to have contacts with possible donors. Despite holding the requisite permits and papers, I was nevertheless questioned by the local MP and his associates, followed by members of the Central Intelligence Organisation (CIO) at one point in my field visits and reported upon from the Department where I was affiliated at the University of Zimbabwe. Some of my informants received visits and were advised not to speak with me. As a white female researcher I was entering a context where race relations had been predicated on the superiority claimed by actors ranging from District Commissioners, commercial farmers, soldiers, government officials, community development officers and missionaries. The lone field researcher, however, is a fish out of water. The power relationship was reversed when this white female researcher found herself in a situation where she was non-black, an outsider who had to explain her presence and depend on the graciousness of local contacts to help her in her research. This process of building, negotiating and understanding personal relations and coming to grips with a culture completely different from my own taught me much about alienation and voice. The most I could hope to achieve was understanding, empathy and insight; at other times frustration and ignorance. I was always going to leave and the women knew that. I was a visitor, like many others who had come before me. This awareness brought a necessary humility and pushed me to learn and understand as best I could the hardships, suffering, humour and strength shared by the women in their responses to war. Such a view is neither romantic nor judgmental. War makes for difficult choices; that the women I met continued to survive and rebuild their lives was testimony to that.

The political context is implicit in the entire research process, given the sensitivity of the war in Chiweshe. While this was often related to fear in a context where political intimidation still lingered when the field research was conducted, it was sometimes a deeper reaction against the pressure to remember what is best forgotten.[17]

The fear of discussing the war mingled with the fear of showing dissent or dissatisfaction with the government of the day. The war was still a very difficult subject for women to talk about and I assured anonymity to the women who agreed to talk to me about their lives during that time. That anonymity extended to the lettering of transcripts, the assumption of pseudonyms, and the absence of detailed descriptions of respondents that may allow them to be readily identifiable. Where the interview was held – in the kitchen, in the field, at the grinding mill – was a sensitive issue in terms of reassuring women and giving them the opportunity to feel relaxed about speaking to me. The dictaphone itself was a site of struggle to be explained and negotiated. Their own blocking and opening devices in interview scenarios included claims of forgetting the war, professions of ignorance and lack of education, talking of others rather than themselves, refusing to be interviewed, running away from an interview and seeking advice from others before speaking to me.

The women were often shy and professed themselves to be ignorant. This was often not about not wanting to speak but reflected a genuine belief that no one would be interested in what they had to say. Many claimed to know nothing of politics as this was 'the business of men'. Another issue affecting the social context of the interview was what women thought of the interpreters. Local women I befriended acted as interpreters, but this was double-edged in offering confidence on some occasions and being a source of tension on others. For some women it was a signal to trust and be open, for others it raised fears about gossip and awkwardness about talking about their lives because the interpreter was local. A related point was the status of the interpreter in the community. Sometimes it was helpful to have an interpreter such as a female teacher who carried authority. On other occasions it was a source of unease. Accessing the voices of women in Chiweshe was therefore a difficult and lengthy task as the establishment of contacts and a continual presence were necessary to build trust.

Within the fieldwork I underwent my own conversion from the view that 'The War' was central to women's lives and their understandings of post-independence realities to understanding it as a context in which women adapted their everyday lives. My search for the grand gestures, the good stories and the failed or successful revolution was constantly thwarted by an insistence upon talking about the economic and social struggles of the present. I stubbornly insisted on referring to the grand narrative of the revolution for women and nursed my continued frustrations at references to everyday matters of then and now. The realisation finally dawned that herein were the stories underlying the revolution, writ large. The subscript, when magnified, revealed a plethora of every-

---

[17] This political intimidation and fear had yet to take on the new dimensions and intensity that define political and community relations today in Zimbabwe. However, in revisiting the interviews I am struck by the continuities as much as by the changes from the war through to the 1993 fieldwork period and into contemporary accounts, of the fear and distrust and the legacies of physical and structural forms of colonial-era and liberation war-era violence. These themes are taken up in the Conclusion.

day actions, struggles and dilemmas that made up the retold experiences of living in revolution. The connections made by many women between the plights of poverty, violence and struggle during the revolution, and subsequently in response to intermittent drought, the adverse effects of aid policies, and the failures of government pointed to the continuities of this everyday terrain of local resistance. The experiences of guerrilla war by women in rural communities, I now understood, were better explained and represented through an exploration of this localised resistance. Such a focus opened up the location, nature and representation of rural women's struggles for survival and their strategies of resistance in the context of a revolutionary guerrilla war. In the excavation set out in this book there are enduring insights to understanding the experiences and agency of women in a range of contemporary wars.

Outline of the book

Chapter One explores the ways in which women's participation in revolution has been explained, firstly in feminist theoretical debates of the prospects and failures of revolutionary transformations in women's lives, and secondly in the grounded context of the Zimbabwe war and debates concerning peasant consciousness and revolutionary agency. Chapter Two develops a conceptual framework of gendered localised resistance to illuminate the complexities of rural women's struggles for survival in the context of a guerrilla war. I explore the workings of power and resistance as bound up in the women's many identities played out through the dynamics of social relations. This approach guides the reading of the following field chapters and the presentation of women's accounts of their war. I open up the terrain of guerrilla war as a place where fixed gender subjectivity and metanarratives of revolutionary resistance can be challenged and alternative local and personal narratives developed.

Chapter Three sets out the context of the field research through a descriptive analysis of the war in Zimbabwe and its particularities in Chiweshe. This chapter also elaborates upon some of the methodological issues involved in the interview analysis that underpin the following field chapters. Chapter Four analyses women's perceptions of revolution and their participation in it. The vagaries of participation are highlighted and indicate that women's motivations and actions were changeable and sometimes contradictory. The overall aim is to signify the diversity of experience and understandings that underlie gendered divisions of revolutionary labour and trajectories of revolutionary consciousness. By contrast, Chapter Five demonstrates how women, through their engagement in the revolution, were caught up in a set of community dynamics that fragmented, atomised and dislocated their sense of daily life and survival. These dynamics are summarised as surveillance, distrust, fear, silence, and avoidance. This chapter also illuminates the daily struggles of survival faced by women during the war.

Chapter Six brings together the themes of the previous two chapters (forms of revolutionary participation and unstable community dynamics) to map out a conflicted battleground of women's participation in revolution that collapses boundaries of political/non-political, public/ private and combatant/non-combatant. It does so by drawing out the interconnectedness between household economic survival and food security and revolutionary participation through food provision to the comrades. These pressures were exacerbated by the state counter-insurgency policies to curb such provision. What emerges is a terrain of participation, resistance and risk that operates around strategies of survival, resistance and the constant negotiation of identities through various and simultaneous demands and expectations made by and of women. In the Conclusion I return to the importance of reconceptualis-ing women's participation in guerrilla wars and outline the implications of this study for understandings of Zimbabwe's liberation war and cur-rent manifestations of crisis and violence in the country, as well as of the plight and agency of women in more contemporary wars and the prospects for the implementation of UN Security Council Resolution 1325.

1

Situating Women in Revolution | Battlefront Myths & Homefront Lies

The drive to explore local understandings of revolution by women to uncover how they participate in and survive revolution arises from both feminist theoretical and Zimbabwe historical perspectives. The narrative of revolutionary transformation for women that has emerged from feminist theoretical debates requires a local focus on women's experiences of revolutionary wars in order to uncover the nature and extent of rural women's participation. Similarly, the narratives of participation found in the historiography of Zimbabwe's war of liberation (1966–1980) suggest that the failings of explanation are not only confined to feminist theoretical debates but also mark historical accounts of the Zimbabwean liberation struggle.

Part I Women and Revolutions: The Quest for a Narrative of Liberation

How do rural women understand and participate in revolutionary liberation wars? An attempt to answer this question can be found in the body of literature emerged from the late 1960s onwards examining the revolutionary struggles of decolonisation that had paved the way for the newly independent states in Africa, Asia and Latin America. More particularly, writers turned their attention to the experiences of the oppressed, inside and outside of such struggles, and sought to uncover the history of subaltern or marginal groups such as the peasantry.[1] Women, as a category of social actors, have also been the subject of attention through the rise of feminist research in the expanding field of studies that explores women's relationship to war and revolution. A diverse feminist literature, ranging from politics and international relations through to law, literary criticism, social theory and development studies defines this

---

[1] For example see Migdal (1974); Moore (1966); Scott (1976, 1977); Skocpol (1979, 1982); and Wolf (1969, 1977). Norma Kriger (1992: 5-33) provides a very interesting reading of this literature as a precursor to her discussion of the Zimbabwe liberation war.

field.[2] It is perhaps surprising, therefore, that the literature is not well-equipped to frame a perspective on the question posed above; to date, the debates in what may loosely be called 'women and war' literature have revolved around two main arguments.

The early feminist focus (that is, in the revolutionary heights of the 1960s through to the early 1980s) held much promise in the potential of national and social revolutionary movements and wars to liberate women in their wake. However, as post-revolutionary realities negated women's roles in independence struggles and sought to return them to traditional domestic and non-public spaces, feminist analysts were forced to confront the question of why revolutions have failed women. Much of the narrative of this debate relies upon under-explored assumptions about the nature of grassroots-level agency, that is, about the nature of rural women's political awareness and participation in revolutions. What is absent is a grounded understanding of the everyday dimension of women's experiences, understandings and actions in revolutionary war settings. As this study on Chiweshe illustrates, this bottom-up perspective ruptures many of the neat academic narratives that 'explain' the workings of women in war by revealing the deeply complex and localised terrain of women's daily struggles for survival and resistance in the course of revolution.

Women and revolutionary wars: Out of the home and back again

Why do liberation movements invite the possibility of women's emancipation in the course of revolution? This question of 'women in the struggle' is important because of the major role women play in the success of such revolutionary wars. It is also important because of the expectations of change that are excited by the promises of an end to oppression in terms of race, gender and class. The romantic appeal of liberating women through liberating states is readily encapsulated in the iconic poster that has donned student and activist rooms and offices for decades; the strong beautiful woman with a semi-automatic rifle slung over her shoulder and a baby at her breast.

Cynthia Enloe (1988:160) and Christine Sylvester (1987:505) argue that anti-state aims and the decentralised structure of guerrilla armies pose opportunities of social transformation for women in revolutionary struggles. Thus, unlike conventional warfare involving state militaries, revolutionary struggles enable a qualitatively different experience of participation for women. Enloe argues that state armies aim 'to mobilise human and material resources for the sake of optimising military effectiveness', whereas guerrilla armies aim 'to bring about

---

2   See, for example, Brownmiller (1976); Boulding (1988); Cohn and Enloe (2003); Davies (1983); Elshtain (1995); Enloe (1988, 1989, 2007); Giles and Hyndman (eds) (2001); Isaksson (1988); Macdonald, Holden and Ardener (1987); Molyneux (1985); Moser and Clark (2001); Nnaemeka (1997); Peterson and Runyan (1999); Pettman (1996); Ridd and Callaway (1986); Tetreault (1994); Tickner (1992, 2001); Urdang (1979, 1989). See also the Introduction and Conclusion of this book, where current trends in the women and war literature are discussed.

fundamental alterations in the socio-political order' and eschew the 'gendered distinction between "front" and "rear"' (1988:160-1, 164). The revolutionary appeal of a transformative agenda arises from a text-book expectation of grassroots politicisation through education that raises women's political consciousness of revolution and the need for armed resistance. Such politicisation can also arise from a necessary military strategy of local co-operation to ensure supplies and protection from the community in the conduct of a guerrilla war. Furthermore, Enloe and Sylvester emphasise the taking up of unconventional roles by women and the politicisation of traditional gender roles as further cause for optimism. My research in Zimbabwe indicates that women's 'domestic' work assumed political importance because of the central-ity of local food supply networks to the effective conduct of guerrilla warfare. Women fighters receive particular attention in feminist analy-sis for subverting existing gender relations. Sylvester suggests that the woman warrior identity is one that subverts patriarchy by challenging the expectations of the elite, defying stereotypes of women's work and providing proof of reconfigured power relations (1987:502, 505-6).

Whilst the revolutionary vision of post-independent society often sees women's traditional roles as irreversibly politicised and taking on increased importance and recognition in the new state (Macdonald 1987:10), the more likely consequence is one where the post-revolution government adopts the structures of the previous state and reinforces the public/private split that hastens the demobilisation of many women from their revolutionary roles. The pressures for a return to normality and the embedding of new power structures mean that there is a heavy emphasis on preserving and/or reinstating gender norms and relations. This is reflected in the focus and rhetoric of stability, public order and return to community and family life as it was before the upheavals of war. The demobilisation of women and their removal from any military or paramilitary associations is part of this rebuilding period and thus the political import of their wartime actions is quickly dismantled and lost. Even those women who carried arms and fought, who lived in the bush and camps during the war years, are often denied the post-revo-lutionary status of liberation army veterans (Enloe 1988:161-9; Pettman 1996:138). The domestic-political strategy of bringing women's work into the public sphere of war is therefore one that does not necessarily ensure advancement for women through revolution; their participation in revolution is seen less romantically in the context of continuity in the sexual division of labour which leaves the way open for demobilisation of women and integration into a 'new-old' order.

Why do revolutions fail women?
The quest for a feminist understanding

In response to the frustrated narratives of transformation that have accompanied revolutionary struggles, feminists have asked 'why do rev-olutions fail women?' Three major explanations can be identified from the literature in the search for an answer.

Nationalism subsuming women's struggles
One explanation for the lack of transformation is the subsuming of women's needs, interests, or struggles to the wider national struggle. This has been described by Jo Beall et al. (1989) as the 'woman question' position wherein women become 'a bit on the side' of liberation struggles. It finds revolutionary organisations (and sometimes women's sections of such organisations) calling for women to subsume their own struggles to the cause of national liberation (Molyneux 1985). This 'state first, women later' philosophy is well-tested in southern Africa. In the promise-filled setting of pre-election South Africa in April 1994, a female ANC parliamentary candidate claimed the party to be 'the first liberation movement to link the emancipation of women to the emancipation of a country. Across Africa, it was national liberation first, women later, and, of course, the "later" never came' (*The Independent* 15 April 1994:20). A world away, this echoes the Palestinian women's plea that 'we won't be another Algeria' (Gluck 1995; Sayigh 1984). For many liberation movements the primary site of oppression is held to be national identity, and therefore any focus on women's struggles to transform gender relations is interpreted as undermining the wider struggle. The tactical value of women's participation is thus the primary impetus for their inclusion in the liberation struggle. Women are a political constituency to be mobilised for support in the way of other sub-national groups. However, a consequence of subsuming women's struggles to the national struggle is that the 'sanctioned' roles of mothers and daughters of the revolution circumscribes women's expressed loyalties and provides licence for the policing of their behaviour by the revolutionary organisations and their communities (Pettman 1996:123). It also subsumes the possibility of articulating a specific agenda for women to effect post-revolutionary change. As Enloe cautions, 'when on occasion women's liberation is wielded instrumentally by any masculinized elite as a rationale-of-convenience for their actions, we should be on high alert; they'll put it back on the shelf just as soon as it no longer serves their longer-range purpose' (Cohn and Enloe 2003:1203).

Lack of feminist consciousness
The second, and related, explanation of failed revolutionary outcomes for women is the lack of a feminist consciousness to give transformative meaning and effect to women's participation in revolutionary struggles (Molyneux 1985; Beall et al. 1989). The focus of some writers from this perspective is the importance of autonomous women's movements to articulate women's struggles in revolution and forge a post-revolutionary agenda of change for women (Peteet 1991:88). This involves separating women's gender struggles from other sites of difference and conflict, such as race, class, sexuality and generation. The shift from woman-related to feminist-related participation assumes a collective and radicalised consciousness on the part of women that may be acquired in the course of fulfilling revolutionary roles. Implicit in such understandings is that gender transformation through revolutionary struggle requires a type of consciousness that can move beyond the mobilisation of gender stereotypes to define appropriate participation and representation of women's

experiences of struggle. Such consciousness is of concern to Beall et al. (1989), who call for a fuller exploration and appreciation of women's grounded gender struggles in the course of revolution to effect greater sustainability of change in the reconstruction phase of the post-revolutionary state. Jan Pettman outlines the development of a transformative consciousness as 'a move from female consciousness, which seeks rights or safety within family and gender expectations within the nationalist struggle, to feminist consciousness, where activist women view women's liberation as an intrinsic part of national liberation and seek social transformation' (1996:125). However, this separation of woman-related and feminist-related consciousness can have the effect of reducing women's motivations, experiences and consciousness of participation to female (read 'non-political') or feminist (read 'political') categories. It also obscures the workings of difference amongst women whereby factors such as class, age and ethnicity also define women's resistance.

Revolutionary aims, militaristic means:
Men positioning women in the same old place
The third perspective on failed revolutions for women arises from feminist research on militarism that uncovers the systemic gendered processes of war and peace. Mary Burguieres (1990) helpfully describes this feminist critique of militarism and patriarchy in terms of three schools differentiated by their treatment of existing stereotypes in relation to men and war and women and peace. The first school embraces the maternal female stereotype and valorises it as a vision of peaceful society. The second school rejects the female stereotype and seeks instead to argue for some kind of military equality by proving women to be as capable as men in the defence of the state. The third school challenges both male and female stereotypes and digs deeper to reveal and deconstruct the operations of militarism as structural power. Here, the conduct of war is criticised as an alliance of militarism and patriarchy that subordinates women in particular ways to ensure the effectiveness of war. The categories of participation open to women are tied to an operation of patriarchal power that depends on a 'presence/absence' dynamic whereby 'the presence of men depends on the absence of women' such that in the conduct of war a set of male values is promoted in opposition to devalued female 'others' (Peterson and Runyan 1993:7-8). This defines a public and private space where society sets sanctions and rewards for women's aberrant actions during war. Enloe and Susan Brownmiller argue that as a result, women are more readily positioned in non-combat but nevertheless key supporting roles as wives, defence workers, nurses, drivers, administrators and prostitutes; they are the camp followers. Even as fighters of war, women's participation must be constructed in gendered ways to perpetuate male power and female subordination in support of militarisation (Enloe 1988, 1990; Brownmiller 1976). In summary, militarism builds upon and reinforces particular gender power relations that perpetuate an understanding of participation in war where 'men fight and women weep' (Pierson 1987:214).

Enloe (2002) argues that this militarised masculinity that relies on women's exclusion or 'otherness' carries into post-war public life. She also suggests that the aberrations and expectations of women's work in the militarisation thesis are not confined to state militaries. Irregular forces recruit women to ensure the effectiveness of their operations, not necessarily for the transformation of women's roles or the promotion of new forms of gender relations. Strategies of allocating roles according to gender, generation and marital status in insurgency operations often reinforce existing divisions of labour and power. The militarisation thesis of state armies with their particular understandings of femininity, masculinity and violence finds ready connection with the norms and practices of fighting insurgencies and revolutions by irregular and guerrilla forces (Enloe 1988). The politicisation of the 'domestic' work of women in such wars may therefore constitute no more than a temporary change to the status quo.

Jean Bethke Elshtain's (1995) treatise on women and war reveals and challenges the binary logic of representing and perpetuating women as life-givers and men as life-takers by asserting a complexity of identities for women in war, for example, 'Ferocious Few', 'Non-combatant Many' and 'Aggressive Mother'. Male identities are extended to include 'Militant Many', 'Pacific Few' and 'Compassionate Warriors'. Sharon Macdonald et al. (1987) draw attention to the imagery of women in war that reinforces the gendered assumptions of militarised society. The heroic image of woman as both guerrilla and mother is a familiar trope in revolutionary art and propaganda. Is this to shame men into military action, to reassure society that women involved in masculine activities are still feminine and will return to traditional domestic roles after a temporary aberration of the natural order through war? Implicit in this image creation is the ambivalence of women warriors as role models. Are they an aberration in gender terms (neither man nor woman) or a liberatory role model for women generally? (Stiehm 1988; Enloe 1988; Macdonald 1987). These multiple possibilities underscore the difficulty of creating categorical identities for women in revolutions and reinforce the artificiality of gendered public and private space in war. Enloe (1988:15) reveals the irony of women working at the front-line of war who are domesticated in their roles to ensure they remain 'home-front' women even in the line of fire. Such women include nurses, soldiers, intelligence workers and prostitutes. There is therefore a tension between the possible transformations of front/rear distinctions through guerrilla war and the continuity of gendered assumptions concerning militarised roles. These tensions and risks arise particularly in war situations where military tactics involve increased civilian involvement. This was the case for women in Chiweshe during the Zimbabwean liberation war and endures on the unbounded battlefields of contemporary wars in Africa. As I will show, women lived through a daily war of attrition along with counterinsurgent responses that involved the development of local supply and intelligence networks which implicated rural women and placed them on the front line.

Posing a different question:
How do women view their participation in revolution?

The question of why revolutions fail women assumes an inevitable transformation of women's gendered social position through revolution. However, such an assumption overlooks the complex lives and identities that women participating in revolutionary wars experience. The first two perspectives outlined above exemplify the narrative of power seized and lost as revolutions fail women by subsuming, or not enabling, a long-term agenda of change for women. This is too simplistic and ideologically-driven a narrative to account for the complexities of a war fought out in local communities where the battlefront/home front divide becomes redundant. It is also role-ascribing in the presumptions made of women's participation; women are either subservient nationalist supporters or a collectively politicised participating group focused on change for women through revolution.

The third perspective, the critique of militarism, offers some helpful systemic insights and suggests that despite the rhetoric of transformative revolutionary agendas, women are still positioned in particular ways that ensure any advances are short-lived. However, the weight of systemic explanation risks naturalising gender relations that position women outside of war or as auxiliary agents in war, defined in terms of men and masculinity. The difficulty with such a systemic analysis is not only that women may be constructed as passive victims or circumscribed actors in a male script, but that at the same time women may be seen as complicit in their own subordination. The responsibility for change thus falls to women in refusing to support the system. This identity of victim, vulnerable and protected woman has to be paid for by silence, acquiescence and the loss of an acting self that deprives women of the capability of agency. Such an explanation of women's relationship to war 'de-politicises their actions, and makes their agency or politics appear unruly, rebellious, ungrateful or asking for trouble' (Pettman 1996:99-100).

All three perspectives share a fundamental weakness: a top-down perspective that facilitates the designation of women as a unified category of social agents, constructed in opposition to men. This results in a failure to account for differences amongst women and within individual women. It also leads to misguided simplifications regarding the cohesiveness of a 'female' subjectivity with a shared sense of participation and experience in revolutionary struggles. That this is definitively *not* the case is the key contribution of the case study presented here.

Knowledge claims and the considerations of difference have been core critiques within feminist research and theory in terms of not replicating grand narratives that oppress and exclude particular women as political agents. Chandra Mohanty (1988; 1995) argues for more relational understanding of the intersections of gender, race and class in shaping power in women's lives. This is to counter what she describes as 'discursive colonialism' that is implicit in a Western feminism that replicates 'otherness' in its representations and understandings of 'third world women'. In the extreme the resulting homogenisation of women from non-western societies leads to a glib type of feminism based on the 'erasure of difference and inequality' (1995:77). Oyeronke Oyeyumi (1997; 2002; 2011) goes further in challenging the existence and utility of 'gender' as a social category of analysis, particularly in Africa. Her research among the Yoruba peoples of Nigeria leads her to challenge the very basis of feminist epistemology by disputing gender in terms of 'women' and 'men' as roles and identities; there is no word for gender among the Yoruba. Through an historical methodology she shows how the importation and impact of colonial gender categories have been integrated into contemporary representations of the Yoruba as well as in ways of retelling and understanding the past in ways that obscure and corrupt traditional knowledge and understandings. Hers is an 'historical feminism' that seeks to redress the colonialism of gender and excavate past female understandings, identities and power as a necessary intellectual and political act in breaking the existing link between the ongoing creation of patriarchy and the failure to decolonise this knowledge:

> The issue of the historicity of gender cannot be overstated, given that in the Western dominant discourses, gender is presented as transhistorical and therefore essentialist. Studies of Africa should not rely on Western-derived concepts to map the issue of gender in African societies, but instead must ask questions about the meaning of gender and how to apprehend it in particular times and places. Thus, the problem of gender in studies of Africa is fundamentally an epistemological one. (2011:1)

In her review of Oyeyumi's work, Bibi Bakare-Yusuf cautions against a type of nihilism that would seek to simply replace one unreflexive form of power analysis (seniority) for another (gender). She seeks to find some redemption in the awareness of projecting knowledge claims:

> All future research into gender outside of the west should therefore be mindful that it runs the risk of projecting into the society that which is not there at either a discursive or paraxial level. With this incessant vigilance about the threat of theoretical projections in mind, it is then possible to examine ways in which inequality may yet still exist by other means despite its absence within discourse. Or it may be that gender demarcation and discrimination on further exploration is relatively absent. In this case, the analysis of other social systems may reveal distinctive constellations of power (both as capacity and constraint) (2003:11).

Mohanty, in her riposte to 'discursive colonialism', also seeks to push forward with better understandings of power and women in their own lives: 'What matters is the complex, historical range of power differences, commonalities and resistances that exist among women in Africa which construct African women as 'subjects' of their own politics' (1988:84).

With this in mind, gender identities for the purposes of this study of women and war in Chiweshe are explored in the next chapter with an emphasis on difference and non-fixed roles that give rise to more relational categories of gender where 'other' relates not simply to a category 'men' but to guerrillas, soldiers, families and communities. Also, the dynamics of difference amongst women participating in and surviving revolution emerge to defy a cohesive category of women's responses to guerrilla war. What is striking, from the perspective of my research in Chiweshe, is the lack of immediate consensus on the roles of women and the actions they adopted on a daily basis. The agency and consciousness of women do not always conform to the militarised expectations of their roles and behaviour. In addition, my analysis will show that negotiations of power and resistance are also a feature of participation within each individual woman. This leads me to argue and demonstrate that a more grounded analysis of women in revolutionary struggle calls into question the feminist quest for why revolutions fail women. Women take up various 'roles', adopt various strategies of survival, hold various views on the politics of war and live many lives in the course of a guerrilla war. To reduce these to a neat taxonomy ignores the consciousness and resistance of women in their daily lives during revolutionary struggle, and imposes a narrative of participation that does not fully reflect these complex realities. These war experiences are also filled with contradictions whereby women may not be faithfully following the roles read off from their domestic existence or from a military imperative; a woman growing food in the face of guerrilla demands for resources and state counterinsurgency attempts to cut off such supplies cannot remain in the cosy category of the 'domestic' but is drawn into and forms part of the public reality of war. The conduct of a liberation struggle is not confined to the public realm of men in revolutionary organisations or government counterinsurgency policies but is built upon and affects the lives of women and men at local level.

The feminist approaches to women and revolution discussed earlier are basically asking a loaded question. Their search for the reasons for failure is grounded in assumptions of ideologically inscribed 'success'. This quest for the macro of *why* has ignored the micro of *how*, but until we understand how rural women experience, interpret and respond to revolutions, 'our' quest to pursue strategies for 'their' emancipation will remain elusive. How do women map out their battlefield? What are the strategies of survival and resistance that they deploy at the junctures of war and community? It is in understanding the everyday struggle for survival that we may illuminate our understanding of women's experiences and participation in revolutionary war and the opportunities and obstacles to social transformation. These everyday struggles identify and explore the dynamics of relations with the guerrillas, the soldiers and the local community that inform women's lives in war. Through a local understanding of women's resistance and subjectivity in the course of revolution, we can better conceptualise women's agency to take account of difference and to overcome the lack of representation of women who do not readily fit roles or radical agendas designed elsewhere. Far from being in need of politicisation, the awareness of women to their political context is a striking feature of their daily negotiations for survival and resistance in the course of revolution. This everyday dimension of war is often excluded from stories of revolution, armed conflict and violence.

Part II The Liberation War in Zimbabwe:
Peasant Wars and Women's Voices

The war in Zimbabwe (formerly Southern Rhodesia) was an anti-colonial liberation war fought out between 1966 and 1980.[3] Southern Rhodesia was created and colonised in 1890 when it was occupied by direction of Cecil Rhodes and the British South Africa Company (BSACo). Following the rise of nationalist politics, particularly during the 1950s, the tactics of anti-colonial resistance turned to armed insurgency in the late 1960s, and the Battle of Chinhoyi in 1966 marked the beginning of a guerrilla war that was to sweep across the country. This war involved the revolutionary forces of the two main nationalist parties: ZANLA (Zimbabwe African National Liberation Army), which was the military wing of ZANU (Zimbabwe African Nationalist Union), and ZIPRA (Zimbabwe People's Revolutionary Army), which was the military wing of ZAPU (Zimbabwe African People's Union). By the end of the war, ZANU was under the leadership of Robert Mugabe, who went on to take his party to power in the post-independence elections and become the first Prime Minister of independent Zimbabwe. ZAPU was led by Joshua Nkomo. Both movements were pitted against the then white minority government of the Rhodesia Front under the leadership of Ian Smith. Zimbabwe became independent in 1980 following a negotiated settlement brokered by Britain through the Lancaster House talks.

To pose the question of rural women's participation in the liberation war of Zimbabwe we need to revisit an influential body of war historiography that includes Terence Ranger's *Peasant Consciousness and Guerrilla War in Zimbabwe*, David Lan's *Guns and Rain: Guerrillas and Spirit Mediums in Zimbabwe* and Norma Kriger's *Zimbabwe's Guerrilla War: Peasant Voices* and examine the extent to which these histories of the war give a full and persuasive account of women's agency and resistance and review the debates surrounding peasant consciousness and revolutionary participation that have defined these histories. It is suggested that the preoccupation with guerrilla mobilisation and peasant consciousness limits the representation of women's lives in revolution.

Lan (1985) and Ranger (1985) present the reader with the romanticism of a unified peasant consciousness grounded in an assumed shared experience of cultural nationalism that at best absorbs women into the category of 'peasants', or at worst, ignores their presence in the liberation struggle. Whilst Kriger (1992) differentiates peasant experiences of revolution by exploring the radicalism of struggles that arise from within the peasantry, her treatment of gender as a site of difference and conflict is too narrowly focused and does not go far enough in taking account of women's struggles within the wider struggle for national liberation. The challenge arising from this critique is to move beyond concerns of peasant–guerrilla relations and mobilisation. A fuller treat-

---

[3]   A fuller background of the war in Zimbabwe is provided in Chapter 3. Appendix 1 provides a chronology of key dates and events of the war.

ment of the question of rural women's participation in revolutionary wars is advanced through an extension of Kriger's focus on local struggles and peasant voices to take account of women's social identities, self-understandings and voices.

'United we stand, divided we fall': The nature of peasant revolutionary consciousness

The romantic nationalism of a unified peasantry
Ranger and Lan share a common line of argument in respect of the causes of peasant resistance and the unified nature of peasant consciousness in the liberation war in Zimbabwe. Both writers give primacy to the relationship between guerrillas and peasants in explaining the nature of peasant consciousness and guerrilla mobilisation during revolution. However, there is a reversal of major and subsidiary themes in their analyses. For Ranger, the development and radicalisation of a peasant consciousness that was mobilised by the guerrillas is historically constructed within a framework of class formation that owes some debt to traditional peasant religion but is largely an outcome of the relationship between peasants *qua* peasants and the settler state. For Lan, peasant consciousness is shaped through the discourse of 'lost lands' that arises from peasant religion and draws upon cultural and anthropological understandings of leadership and land as personified by the *mhondoro* mediums who are possessed by the spirits of ancestral chiefs. The apogee of revolutionary consciousness and resistance in Ranger's study is in the peasantry becoming a class for itself, receptive to the militancy of the guerrillas, whereas for Lan it comes in the form of ancestral legitimacy through the relationship between spirit mediums and the incoming guerrillas.

Ranger's study is based in the Makoni district of eastern Zimbabwe, close to the border with Mozambique. His account of peasant consciousness proposes a spontaneous dynamic of revolution that emerged from the long years of fighting to preserve the 'peasant option' (the desire to produce above the limits of subsistence in order to sell the surplus) in rural communities and created a unified and radicalised peasant class. The rise and fall of the peasant option, as the entrepreneurial ambitions of peasants were thwarted through direct competition with white settler farmers and the coercive interventions of the colonial state, shape the progressively radicalised nature of peasant consciousness (Ranger 1985:25).[4] Land alienation and the oppressive structure of the agricultural economy that forced peasants into a scenario of small plots, migrant labour and low crop prices are the formative elements of this radicalisation process. Ranger's historical account of the erosion of the peasant option charts how the peasantry first became a *class in itself* ('self-peasantisation'), and the radicalisation of that consciousness so that it became a *class for itself* during the liberation war:

4   For more on the agrarian history of early Rhodesia see Arrighi (1977; 1970); Phimister (1988, 1986); Palmer and Parsons (1977) and Ranger (1978).

> They had to struggle and to develop a certain level of consciousness in order to become peasants in the first place: thereafter they developed another level of consciousness as they saw only too clearly with their own eyes the expropriation of land, the use of state violence and the establishment by the state of discriminatory price mechanisms. (Ibid.:21)

While Ranger acknowledges some degree of differentiation within the peasant class based on economic stratification, he argues that the unity of rural cultural nationalism prevented these tensions from being exploited or used to advance the interests of any particular group. This is epitomised by the proposed relationship between peasants and the rural elite in gaining access to the market and sharing the debilitating effects of settler policies designed to limit such access and to destroy the entrepreneurial ambitions of the peasantry. He claims that '[t]he Zimbabwean peasantry, diversified as it is, must nevertheless be regarded as a class in itself' (289).

This practical ideology of the 'lost lands' was deepened by a spiritual interpretation that helped shape the war as a people's war. In particular, traditional religion offered potent symbols for the issue of lost lands by invoking the ancestral past to vocalise present discontent. This argument is supported by the leading role deemed to have been played by spirit mediums in reinforcing and radicalising peasant consciousness:

> Spirit mediums were significant to peasant radical consciousness precisely because that consciousness was so focused on land and on government interference with production; above any other possible religious form the mediums symbolized peasant right to the land and their right to work it as they chose. (189)

For Ranger, the historical and spiritual dimensions of this radicalised peasant consciousness underpin the 'peasant–guerrilla' ideology as the hallmark of guerrilla mobilisation and strategy. This dynamic between peasants and guerrillas is also termed the 'grassroots dialectic'. The growth of peasant consciousness is charted as a cumulative process, moving from passive resistance to a more systemic understanding of state oppression, and then onwards and upwards towards more overt and militant expressions of discontent. This radical fermentation is argued to have opened the way for a more militant strategy when the war began in 1966 and peaked in the 1970s. It meant that 'very many Zimbabwean peasants had arrived at a radical political programme for themselves before guerrilla political education arrived on the scene', thus reducing the importance of political education for guerrilla mobilisation as the incoming guerrillas tapped into this pre-existing peasant consciousness and resistance to articulate a revolutionary agenda during the war (24-5). The strength of this peasant–guerrilla ideology, Ranger continues, allowed 'for a more direct input by the peasantry into the ideology and programme of the war' (14). The vehicle for the militarisation of such an ideology was the guerrilla wings of the nationalist movements, whereby the shared resistance finds its ultimate expression in 'collective action and collective suffering of peasant and guerrillas' (182).

David Lan (1985) explores the liberation war in Zimbabwe through the lens of traditional religion and writes of the influence of the past on the present and the dead on the living in an evocative account of local responses to the war in Dande.⁵ The issue of the 'lost lands' is argued to be central insofar as it was tied to ancestral grievances voiced through the spirit mediums. It is this identity that allowed the mediums to act as the voices of a peasant consciousness founded upon those traditions: '[A] strong emotional bond exists between individuals and the territory of their ancestors.... Home for the living is essentially the home of the dead. Life is good if you live where your ancestors lived before you' (1985:20); the land and spiritual attachment to the land are mutually inscribed. The main role of the *mhondoro*, as the spirit of a dead chief, is to protect his people: 'The most important characteristic of the *mhondoro* is his altruism, his profound moral concern for all the people who live within his spirit province' (67).⁶ The powers of protection include the fertility of the land, the healing of the sick, the conduct of war and the selection of living chiefs to govern the people within his spiritual province.

Peasant–guerrilla relations, in Lan's account, revolve around the role of spirit mediums in giving legitimacy to the incoming guerrillas 'when they too claimed to be "owners of the land", authochthons rather than conquerors' (112). This is argued to have paved the way for guerrillas to mobilise the local peasantry by using traditional religion with its systems of affiliation to gain popular support. The key relationship for Lan is that between the guerrillas and the peasants, more specifically his paradigm of ancestral legitimacy, which privileges the relationship between the guerrillas and the mediums in interpreting rural resistance to the colonial state. Lan develops in depth the points raised by Ranger concerning the power of local knowledge the mediums could share with the guerrillas, thus aiding their military strategy by providing hiding places and setting out protective rituals for the guerrillas. In return, 'the guerrillas offered land as renewed fertility and restored tradition' (148). The legitimising role of the mediums was also important in justifying the killing in good cause for the lost lands and removed the feared spiritual consequence of killing, that of drought. Lan suggests that:

> If you think of the ZANLA guerrillas as the warriors of the past returned in new guise, their alliance with the *mhondoro* mediums seems neither innovatory nor surprising. No more does the desire of the guerrillas to gain their permission for, or better, their legitimisation of the killing which they knew would ensue. (152)

Lan thus conceptualises a unified consciousness that was shaped by the discourse of the lost lands; this consciousness is one of cohesion, with

⁵ Dande is located on the Zambezi escarpment in the north-east of Zimbabwe and because of its proximity to the Mozambican border became an active operational area for ZANU's military wing, ZANLA. Another feature of the war in Dande, as it was in Chiweshe, was the setting up of 'Keeps' or 'Protected Villages' by the Smith government as part of its counter-insurgency operations. This involved gathering people in specific locations and fencing them in so as to cut off supplies to the guerrillas and prevent interaction between the people and guerrillas. This policy is further discussed in Chapter 3.

⁶ *Mhondoro* means 'lion' and denotes the highest status of a medium. There are other types of mediums such as *midzimu* (ordinary ancestral spirits) or *shave* (animal spirits). Neither possess the rain-making or war-making powers of the *mhondoro* spirits of the dead chiefs.

the past and the present, peasants and guerrillas and religion and revolution all coalescing to overthrow the white regime:

> The guerrillas, all the residents of Dande – Korekore, Tande, Chikunda and Dema – the poorest peasants and those who farmed about fifteen hectares, the schoolteachers, the shopkeepers, the mothers, the young women who disappeared and returned as armed fighters, the widows, the youngest children organised in their *mujiba* platoons, the elders, the headmen, the healers, the mediums – all of these and all of the ancestors, in opposition to the conquering whites, were placed in one category. (172)

Thus, the experiences of revolution by communities in Dande are interpreted by Lan as a unified, cohesive homogeneity of resistance that cuts across categories of gender, ethnicity, generation, class, past and present. All were involved in the supply networks of support for the guerrillas: young boys and girls were recruited as *mujibhas* and *chimbwidos* to deliver food and gather intelligence while adult men were appointed to lead 'secret support committees' and charged with the tasks of gathering supplies for the guerrillas. Adult women cooked food and supplied it to the guerrillas. The past and present then merged to consolidate a guerrilla strategy that was entrenched in the land and its rituals. In Lan's analysis this becomes a logical progression of events in the way Ranger's emergence of peasant radicalism becomes the logical outcome of a historically developed peasant consciousness. For Lan, ancestral legitimacy rather than a transforming socio-political consciousness guided and ruled the guerrillas. Like Ranger, the resonance with an *a priori* peasant consciousness precluded the necessity for political education by the guerrillas as part of a revolutionary strategy of transformation: 'the guerrillas were able to get their way without undertaking a programme of education that might have ensured that these advances be maintained and perhaps even extended when the war was over and they had left the countryside' (Lan 1985:213).

The radicalism of a differentiated peasantry

Norma Kriger (1992) mounts a serious challenge to the romantic peasant nationalism found in Ranger and Lan's accounts of peasant revolutionary consciousness. The district of Mutoko, located in the north-east of Zimbabwe on the border with Mozambique, is the focus of her research and was a strong operational area for incoming ZANLA guerrillas. Her focus on internal peasant struggles opens up the local dynamics of a community caught up in a revolutionary war. She argues that the political radicalism of a differentiated peasant consciousness emerged from inside the peasantry through self-styled agendas that reflected self-interest rather than collective consciousness: 'Peasants' responses suggest that gender, generational, and other structural inequities within villages may be more powerful motivating factors than peasant grievances arising from their externally oriented relationships' (1992:20). Furthermore, these are understood as *pre-existing* struggles, that is to say, they were developed before and outside the war or the influence of the guerrillas. These 'struggles within the struggle' offer a portrayal of revolutionary participation that moves beyond external explanations of peasant grievances to emphasise the formative influence of grievances within the village communities in shaping a differentiated peasant consciousness. The effect is one of harsh romanticism:

> where peasants found themselves squeezed between government and guerrilla coercion, peasants often did not behave as if they were motivated primarily by a desire to limit personal damages. Instead, peasants often took further risks to try to promote their own revolutionary agendas even when they clashed with guerrilla goals. (Ibid.)

This internal radicalism, Kriger argues, was more likely to question, challenge and create opportunities to transform rural daily life than were the politics of nationalism. This forms the basis of a relationship of both convergence and conflict with the guerrilla agenda of mobilising popular support: 'peasants had their own ideas and agendas and saw the guerrillas as potential allies or susceptible to manipulation to further their own goals' (19). She suggests that such dynamics influenced the civilian support organisations (the war committees) during the war.

The logistics of this support were shaped in Mutoko by the effective division of tasks allocated into the concerns of *parents* and *youth*. It is the accounts given by those active in the 'civilian network of organisations' or war committees that underlie Kriger's assessment of popular support. War committees were organised by guerrillas in contact with local communities to ensure a secret and accountable line of supply when different groups of guerrillas entered an area. This network was made up initially of village committees and, later, branch committees that covered the work of a cluster of villages. These committees were the concern of parents and included a chairman who co-ordinated the whole effort of supply; a secretary who kept a record of the contributions; a treasurer; a security officer who oversaw the activities of strangers in the area and generally watched out for potential sell outs to the security forces; an organiser who collected food supplies from the households and money to buy other items; a 'logistics' representative who supervised the cooking of food and finally a political commissar who was charged with political education, and in particular reporting what happened at *moraris*.[7] The turnover of committee members was notoriously high, reflecting the reluctance to take on responsibility for this often dangerous work.

Kriger places at the centre of her analysis the methodological approach of 'direct interviewing' of peasants to provide the 'empirical illustration' of the importance of village relations (19, 23-24, 31). She asserts a challenge to Ranger's work in particular, arguing that his methodology depends on an objectification and universalisation of the peasant experience such that, by emphasising the 'objective condition' of peasants, he abandons the need for them to speak for themselves:

> The almost one-to-one correspondence that Ranger posits between growing peasant consciousness and the progressive undermining of the 'peasant option' means that changes in consciousness can be inferred from changes in the peasants' objective situation. This absolves him of the need to find out

[7] *Moraris* (also known as *pungwes*) were night-time meetings held at the guerrilla base camp. Villagers had to attend and sing *Chimurenga* songs and be politically 'educated'. They were also a platform for identifying and punishing sell outs, in the manner of kangaroo courts.

what peasants consider to be central issues in their lives and how they feel about them. (1988:30)

In overcoming this 'objective' view of history, resistance and the peasantry, Kriger sees the peasant voices she presents as serving to 'valorize peasant ideas and interests in the revolution, even when they are at odds with those of the revolutionary elite, and show how peasants sought to manipulate a revolutionary organization to promote their own local objectives' (1992:29). The outcome is that '[p]easant voices suggest peasants are more likely to blame their neighbours for their woes and act on this understanding of the source of their problems' (20-21).

An important contribution of Kriger's study is to illuminate the nature and extent of guerrilla coercion as a formative influence on popular support for the war through the very real costs of war to local communities. This shatters the assumed benign nature of peasant–guerrilla relations that informs Lan and Ranger's approaches. Kriger argues that in the decline of strength and consistency of normative claims (such as the return of land and the promise of better lifestyles) by the guerrillas, coercive appeals through the threat and use of force became more prominent. These appeals took the form of beatings if resources were not provided, if people failed to attend *pungwes*, or if individuals were identified as sell outs. A scenario of generalised coercion is depicted by Kriger, as 'the categories of people who were potential targets expanded ... [such that] anyone was liable to become a victim of guerrilla coercion if they dared disobey guerrilla commands' (104). From the viewpoint of civilian committees, the experience of guerrilla coercion was one that 'often appeared arbitrary and unreasonable' (155). The issue of sell outs is the most salient illustration of guerrilla coercive appeals that Kriger highlights. She demonstrates how the 'stratification-related conflicts' arising from a differentiated peasantry were expressed as envy and grievance held by the less well-off peasants against better-off peasants and the rural elite. The war committees are seen to have entrenched these divisions (187). Such envy found legitimate expression in the guise of aiding guerrilla security in the identification of sell outs; teachers, missionaries, shopkeepers, nurses, agricultural extension workers and migrant workers in town were all potential targets. The issue of sell outs, particularly the death of many innocent people because of jealousy and mistaken identity, is one important feature of the war which Lan and Ranger glide over. It might also explain how 'official figures show that guerrillas killed more African civilians than regime force members' (Kriger 1992:157).[8]

---

[8] For Lan, the issue of sell outs during the war is bound up with ideas of witchcraft and the role of mediums in the process of witch-finding. His benign line of reasoning asserts that the identification of sell outs and witches 'demonstrates ... the profound degree to which the guerrillas, and by extension the nationalist politicians, had become identified with the *mhondoro*' (Lan 1985:170). This seems a somewhat idealistic presumption which does not take account of the strategic benefits to the guerrillas of gaining local support by generating and acting upon envy and fear within communities. Sell outs were often named by *mujibhas* and *chimbwidos*, giving the latter much power in communities as substantiated (and unsubstantiated) claims of helping the government led to beatings, torture and death by the guerrillas. Kriger's analysis suggests such a view and my research in Chiweshe supports some of her findings. See Chapter 5 for a discussion of guerrilla coercion and sell outs in Chiweshe.

Guerrilla coercion, Kriger argues, was intensified by the inability of the guerrillas to offer immediate material benefits to the people. The outflow of food and money to the guerrillas from the local communities contributed to the impoverishment of the people; giving with one hand and taking with the other is the pattern that Kriger presents as the costs for parents increased in the form of demands for supplies from the guerrillas. These costs included food, money and labour paid as a 'war tax'; the loss of cattle, goats and chickens, which meant that the youth and guerrillas (because the youth often cooked and ate with the guerrillas) ate relatively better than the parents; collective fines of cattle and money imposed by the government as punishment for aiding the guerrillas; and the loss of government services such as transport, marketing, cattle dips, health clinics and schools. Kriger's arguments of guerrilla coercion and costs to peasants raise uncomfortable questions about the accepted pervasiveness of cultural nationalism and the ability of individuals to challenge the state.

'Add women and stir': Situating women in Zimbabwe's peasant war

Wanted: Peasants and spirit mediums – women need not apply
The narratives of revolutionary consciousness offered by Ranger and Lan share a theme of romantic nationalism. Whilst providing histories of class formation and peasant religion that appear to explain the inevitability of peasant revolution, their understandings of peasant agency and consciousness are a primarily male experience that subverts, and at an extreme, ignores the experiences of women as peasants and as participants in the revolutionary struggle. In both accounts, cultural nationalism is assumed to demonstrate a shared peasant consciousness that provides the radicalism of resistance for the armed struggle. Not only is it supposed that there was a single peasant consciousness and that it was revolutionary, but also that it found a single, seamless (and internally non-contradictory) consciousness of national liberation.

Whilst Ranger assumes 'a substantial continuity of peasant consciousness', he cites the challenge to gerontocratic power by young women in particular to be one of the 'substantial discontinuities ... which made it difficult for there to be immediate or total collaboration between the peasant elders and the young guerrillas' (1985:206). The disturbance to an otherwise seamless male authority in the radicalised peasant consciousness of war is described in the following scenario:

> Men in their fifties, who had hitherto dominated Makoni peasant radicalism and who were used to controlling a flock of dependent women-wives, daughters, daughters-in-law, now found the initiative had passed to young men with guns. These young men called upon the unmarried women of Makoni to act as their cooks, informants and messengers and in these latter two roles teenage girls were able to exercise a great deal of power, for the first time in Makoni's history. (Ibid.:206-7).

More often, however, women appear in Ranger's work as assumed participants in the peasant family with the appropriate divisions of labour. They become bit players in the war drama and, at best, subsumed into the general category of peasant consciousness.

Elizabeth Schmidt (1992) in her exploration of the colonial period from 1870–1939 genders the 'peasant option' that is at the heart of rural society depicted by Ranger and Lan. In *Peasants, Traders and Wives*, she opens up the notions of peasant and peasantry to allow a closer examination of the experiences of women. Her critique also implicitly challenges Ranger's notion of women's subversion as a discontinuity rather than a continuity of a consciousness of resistance. In effect, Schmidt creates new categories of historical subjects and agents and helps us to move from an analysis of men *qua* peasants to women *qua* peasants. Her central critique of Ranger is that he perpetuates the myth of the 'peasant option' as a *male* option. Such an exposition, she argues, is flawed because it fails by its very definition to acknowledge the very important contribution of female labour to the peasant option:

> Ranger ... discusses the 'peasant option', the choice to produce commodities rather than send household members into wage work, as an exclusively male option. Explicit – and unique – in his definition of the peasantry is the notion that a significant amount of agricultural work must be done by men. The choices, decisions, and strategies made at household and village levels are presumed to be made by men, while innovations in crops and tools, as well as modifications in the gender division of labour are assumed to be the result of male initiative. (1992:3)

In fact, what Schmidt demonstrates is that a feminised peasant option is a more realistic picture of the colonial period:

> one can hypothesize that the agricultural surplus produced by the Shona in some parts of Southern Rhodesia during the early twentieth century, the flourishing peasant trade with the mining industry, and the resulting competition with European farmers was the product of a predominantly female-based agricultural economy. (Ibid.)

The process of self-peasantisation in the first decades of colonialism is revealed as a gendered process. The innovation of women peasants contributed to the creation and marketing of agricultural surplus and involved the use of 'domestic skills' as a basis for petty trading activities. Women were at the forefront of diversifying income through activities such as beer brewing, the making and selling of pots and crafts and the sale of grain and vegetables in the European areas of mines and commercial farms.

Schmidt reveals how male migrant labour placed heavier demands on rural women's labour and adversely affected the gender divisions of labour within the household. The increased burden of work for women became tied to the declining status of agricultural production as a primary source of income. Women were left with all the chores, including traditionally male chores such as threshing the grain crops, ploughing, herding cattle and clearing the land for planting. The more widespread introduction of maize as a staple crop also had implications for female labour as it was a more labour-intensive activity than that of growing sorghum. This, together with attempts to increase cultivation, meant that women and children's tasks such as hoeing and weeding became harder and more time-consuming. Unlike women, men benefited from technological innovation, particularly plough-led cultivation which eased their main task of preparing fields for planting. Men were therefore able to promote extensive cultivation with the use of ploughing and in so doing increase the intensive labour burden of women and children. The gendered impact of settler policies also meant more work and declining status for women in agriculture. Due to the Maize Control Acts, '[n]ot only were poorer women forced to carry their maize long distances and sell it for lower prices in the reserve stores, frequently they could not obtain cash for their product' (Schmidt 1992:80).[9] Other state policies such as the dipping of cattle and payment of dipping fees added more to the unpaid labour and assumed the persistence of the eternally resourceful rural African woman. The gendered impact of the decline of the peasant option also adversely affected women in a more immediate way; they themselves became a more valuable resource in terms of bridewealth as male elders attempted to access the cash earnings of younger men who were now working in European areas (Schmidt 1992:84-6, 113; Barnes 1992:594).

Women are also particularly placed in Lan's (1985) study of revolution. His spiritual discourse of the 'lost lands' reflects religious knowledge and rituals that are highly gendered. This history allocates to men the powerful primal role of straddling the past and the present: 'By contrast with women who give life to people, men give life to the *mhondoro* who brings the rain which confirms the ownership of the land by the *mhondoro's* descendants, the chiefs' (1985:100).[10] A theme of what can be termed 'female pollution' also pervades this spiritual realm. One aspect of the possession ritual of spirit mediums is that of 'pleasing the *mhondoro* ... by praising their bodiless but eternal life by keeping themselves free of the polluting power of female sexuality' (162). This theme carries over to the restrictions on diet and behaviour that applied to the guerrillas as 'sons of the soil'. These 'ritual prohibitions' were to ensure the protection of the ancestral spirits but seem contradictory to any agenda of empowering women; for example, not seeing blood, including menstrual blood, and not eating food prepared by menstruating women or pregnant women. The devaluation of the 'female/life' and the valorisation of the 'male/spiritual' realms is therefore central to the construction of ancestral continuity and power. For Lan, the temporary nature of the upheaval of social categories (particularly women and youth) during the war occurred precisely because the notion of ancestral legitimacy and thus guerrilla legitimacy is tied to the denigration of 'woman':

[9]   The Maize Control Acts of 1931 and 1934 legitimised discriminatory pricing mechanisms aimed at supporting settler agriculture through the removal of African competition coming from the Reserves.

[10]   With the notable exception of the *mhondoro* Nehanda, spirit mediums are usually men; '[T]he famous *mhondoro* Nehanda is known to have the *simba yehonda*, the power of war and the *simba yemvura*, the power of rain' (Lan, 1985: 72, 5-7, 159-60). In the 1896 rebellion (or the First *Chimurenga*), the medium of Nehanda was executed by the colonial government and her martyrdom served as a potent symbol for the Second *Chimurenga*.

The glory of the ancestors requires that women be thought of as expendable and worthless. By this denigration, the containment of women within the private, domestic sphere is made to seem inevitable while male domination of the key institutions of the society goes unchallenged. (213)

For Lan, the argument that 'the notion of femininity is made up of equal parts of weakness and danger survived intact into the post-war world' defines women and their war experiences (213). The agency of change remains with male guerrillas and peasants and the benevolence of male elders. Although Lan seems almost apologetic in his closing chapter as he gives voice to this failed opportunity, he preserves the version of romantic cultural nationalism grounded in local spiritualism and traditionalism; he eloquently voices the silence of women's experience while at the same time valorising the framework of that silence. It is understandable therefore in Lan's explanation that 'the guerrillas fitted themselves into a structure of authority that had existed before they arrived and which has survived their departure' (113).

Lan echoes Ranger's finding of the challenge posed to the power of elders by the guerrillas and says of the female guerrillas that:

By transforming themselves into warriors, the archetypal male role, and by wandering far from their fathers' homes with neither husbands nor chaperones, the women achieved a dramatic break with the past and they were fully conscious that they had done so. (1985:212)

However, the number of women who made such a break and realised a longer-term transformation would appear to be few. Both Ranger and Lan construct a traditional radicalism; Ranger's emerges from the historical grievances of a predominantly male peasantry whilst Lan's is grounded in the religious strength of ancestor worship and attachment to the land. The receptivity of local communities was effected through the idioms of a traditional radicalism that holds particular implications for women; any transformations in gender power relations or improvements in the position of women in the economy and society were not a necessary part of this radicalism. Given such parameters of radicalism, it is not surprising that the transformation of women's lives is not a theme of peasant consciousness in these accounts. In the crucible of war, the rural communities – the more traditional networks – rather than revolutionary rhetoric are argued by Lan and Ranger to have been the mechanisms of mobilisation. How then could any longer-term transformation for women beyond the necessity of war roles be envisaged? Such traditional radicalism may also help explain the tensions between socialist revolutionary ideology and claims to tradition that pervaded the fabric of the independent state.

Wanted: Peasant voices – some vacancies open for women
Due to the emphasis given to peasant differentiation and voice by Kriger, one would expect to find a fuller and empowering treatment of rural women's experiences of revolution. However, her discussions of gender and women are constrained by a preoccupation with guerrilla coercion and lack of women's voices as evidence of such coercion. While Kriger exposes the cross-cutting cleavages of peasant identities, she does not

explore sufficiently the differentiating nature of gender relations within rural communities and the part they played in structuring women's responses to the war. In other words, neither the relationships in which women were involved through the war nor their location within the peasantry and within the local community are mapped out in any detail. In particular, the differences *amongst* women are not explored either. These reservations are important because of the centrality given to peasant voices of revolution in Kriger's work.

Kriger, however, makes an important contribution to the inclusion of rural women in the history of the war in her exploration of women's motivations and gender agenda for participation. She argues that the self-styled agenda for women is not collectively derived: 'Like *youth*, women protested as individuals rather than in an organized way' (1992:196, emphasis in original). The participation of women is thus a consequence of individual agency and consciousness. This gendered context of participation includes the social restrictions of tradition, parental control and the influence of elders that marked the low status of young women. She thus uncovers the individuated and personal motivations for women to participate in the struggle and acknowledges the formative influence of such personal decision-making on women's revolutionary consciousness. Motives for joining the guerrillas are argued to have 'changed with changing circumstances', including following a husband/lover, responding to local attacks such as the burning out of a school or the killing of a relative, responding to the excitement generated at guerrilla meeting, answering the promises of escape from the drudgery of village life and the promises of education at the camps. In some cases it provided an escape route from domestic violence (Kriger 1992; see also L. Scott 1990). I argue in later chapters that these actions were, in effect, sites of local resistance.

Household tensions in particular shape the agenda of women in Kriger's account of war and she highlights the 'important initiatives of married women to change gender relations' (1992:194). These initiatives emphasise the ability of the women to influence guerrilla appeals to men 'to stop beating their wives and drinking excessively' (Ibid.). As a rule, women are seen by Kriger to not engage in direct violence; rather, they 'relied on guerrilla violence to express their anger towards their husbands' (Ibid.:186). She therefore argues that the moral appeals of the guerrillas were influenced by the individual initiatives of women. In response to women's complaints, the guerrillas encouraged the banning of beer drinking, wife-beating and adultery in some villages; Kriger cites cases where guerrillas threatened or beat a husband to 'warn' him against committing further acts of violence towards his wife. However, as with other normative claims, their effectiveness declined over the course of the war as the resistance of men to guerrilla interventions in household affairs proved antagonistic to guerrillas, who needed their support in the rural areas. The agenda of women is therefore a story of gains that were quickly lost over the course of the war. The primacy of popular support, eroded by the realities of the costs of guerrilla demands and the coercive nature of those demands, meant that issues such as the ban on beer drinking and the emphasis on sexual discipline gave way to a more erratic scenario of guerrilla intimidation and the flouting of the guerrillas' own codes. Any empowerment of women was transitory, as guerrillas themselves 'had difficulties accepting gender equality in practice' (Kriger 1992:164). One could conclude therefore that women were trapped not only by patriarchal power in household relations inside communities but also by the declining discipline, degrading attitudes and sexual and physical threats of the freedom fighters.

The use of peasant voices to understand the revolution from the source is central yet double-edged in Kriger's methodology. She draws heavily on the war committees for her peasant voices and seems to rely on the testimonies of male chairmen in particular. The references to the voices of '*parents* and *youth* active in the civilian network of organizations' often results in the analysis of women's voices being summarised and dissolved into those two categories of agents. Kriger's reliance on the ungendered categories of parents, youth, and villagers obfuscates rather than clarifies women's agency in the war. In addition, her notion of 'peasant' narrows and broadens, depending on the context of her argument. If it is socio-economic, it seems to refer to all cultivators within the Tribal Trust Lands whilst also interchangeably referring to 'parents' within the war committees. To set out the debates on a self-styled gender agenda for women, she relies on male elites to criticise the stand taken by some women in complaining to the guerrillas of their husbands' behaviour. The general impression gained is that of a distinctly *male* sense of voice.

However, by excavating local peasant structures, the effects of guerrilla coercion, and the importance of voice, Kriger provides very important openings to address more fully the nature and extent of women's agency in the war. What Kriger does, and to devastating effect, is reveal the hidden, divisive and opportunistic workings of political violence within a local community caught up in guerrilla war. This has profound effects for any romantic narrative based on assumptions of a unified consciousness:

> A focus on what factors might produce a mutually supportive relationship between guerrillas and civilians diverts attention from civilian relationships during a guerrilla war and how these might produce strong reasons independent of the guerrilla cause for participating in a national liberation war. (Kriger 1992:169)

In moving to a more disaggregated peasantry Kriger does, however, argue for a dominating effect of guerrilla coercion and swings the pendulum of explanation to another extreme:

> In interpreting behaviour as resistance, there is a risk of overstating or overdetermining the significance of locally based popular struggle. Even if internal peasant grievances and resentment toward the rural African elite have been overdetermined in this study, it does not diminish the case for their importance. (Ibid.: 208)

This self-confessed overdetermination of coercion and resentment prompts us to return to questions of resistance. Can these local struggles be seen as separate from anti-colonial resentment and forming their own dynamic? Her conclusion that 'peasants experienced resentment against those closest to them rather than the more distant white state' overstates the discourse of envy within local communities and the exclusivity of coercive appeals (Ibid.). Similarly, Kriger's treatment of gender risks underestimating the capacities of women to offer a discourse of resistance that is framed by more than guerrilla coercion and marital conflict. Her emphasis on guerrilla coercion requires the counterbalance of the terror imposed by the counterinsurgency operations of the settler state. In the absence of equal focus on government oppression, not only through the long history of agricultural and administrative intervention as pointed to by Ranger and Lan, but also through the local dynamics of counterinsurgency strategies during the war, she overdetermines the instrumentalist nature of peasant consciousness and agency; guerrilla coercion simply displaces and replaces peasant legitimacy as the nexus of peasant–guerrilla relations.

Life during war may be more complicated than that. The insecurity and ruptures in societies create their own moral economy that is volatile and short-lived and often has consequences for post-war reconstruction and community development. Community tensions are one aspect of war, as is the use of coercive appeals and the variety of responses to such appeals. Whether we can infer radical agendas from such actions and agendas is contestable. I suggest that in Chiweshe a tense co-existence of legitimacy and coercion, support and fear, better reflects the Daedalian maze of insecurity and opportunity that confronts local communities in guerrilla war. Rather than offsetting internal and external factors, we need to consider the two levels together to understand the operation of power and resistance in a local community during a guerrilla war. The case of Chiweshe suggests that women are as likely to blame soldiers and guerrillas as they are their neighbours for the woes of war. Kriger's focus on the war committees as the civilian point of contact with the guerrillas is also challenged in this study of Chiweshe, where more informal networks and individual contact with guerrillas and soldiers were found to be more characteristic of women's participation as food providers to the guerrillas. Civilian relations will be shown to interact and impact upon a series of key relationships in which women were involved in the course of the war. It is the interplay of combined local relations that marks the shift beyond Kriger's exploration of a differentiated peasantry in a context of guerrilla coercion. Such a focus reveals a terrain of struggle for women that cannot be simplified as mutually exclusive determinations of romantic nationalism or the opportunism of promoting pre-existing community grievances.

How women view their participation in revolution: The gender analysis of narratives

If the why and how of revolutionary struggle for women remain centred on mobilisation, the consciousness and actions of women's agency remain secondary to the organisational concerns of revolution and the use of personal stories or witness accounts loses its political saliency. In privileging the voices of women in a revolutionary war, the exploratory question also has to be turned on its head to view the *how* of living through revolution to yield up aspects of war, identity and resistance that revolutionary organisations or historians have not considered. What does it mean to be a 'peasant voice', a 'woman's voice' or 'a child's voice' in such a war? What does daily life mean beyond the rhetoric of revolution? Such considerations yield up the lives of women as being beyond subjects awaiting mobilisation, and beyond roles read off from domestic space and political necessity. The idea of a defined 'woman' or 'peasant' experience is ruptured as the axis of explanation is shifted from peasant–guerrilla interaction to women and their daily experiences of war.

The exploratory question of this study concerns the nature and practices of resistance enacted through women's participation in revolutionary struggle: how do women in a rural community understand their experiences of revolution as guerrilla war, and what does the variety of their experiences tell us about women's agency and participation in revolution? Posing this question has involved the critique and extension of feminist accounts of failed revolutionary transformations for women and historical accounts of peasant revolutionary consciousness in Zimbabwe's liberation war. The lives of women lived between revolutionary resistance and survival are at the centre of an alternative narrative of gender struggles in the liberation war of Zimbabwe; this is a narrative of self, relationship and community. The war accounts of women from Chiweshe open up the modalities of revolutionary resistance and suggest the existence of other forms of resistance and struggles of survival that provide a more complex rendering of agency and participation in revolution than the exclusivity of explanations tied to particular forms of peasant consciousness.

How women react to war is grounded in context and experience; their own accounts tell us this and provide the evidence of experience. The form of gender analysis developed here goes beyond social categories of difference and similarity to propose a narrative analysis that stresses context and change. Such narrative gender analysis does not rule out the use of categories to explain certain dimensions of experience, but it does provide a richer analysis of women's experiences of war. It also circumvents the top-down tendencies of classifying women's experiences according to pre-determined categories of social identity. Through women's own accounts of context and experience we can reconceptualise their participation in revolution as embedded in a volatile context of relationships and struggles for survival.

It is this perspective of day-to-day interactions with the immediate context of war that frames women's accounts of their lives. The impact of the war on the community is just as important as the roles taken up by women in explaining their political participation. This understanding of the context illuminates our understanding of the dynamics of identity that inform the agency and consciousness of women in the war as 'localised resistance'. The conflicted context involves the breakdown of public and private space and action through the intimate involvement with war on a daily basis; participation was often not a matter of choice but a necessity of survival. Women facing different struggles and issues responded in different ways to revolutionary war. The resulting narrative is not a clean one; it reflects the many dilemmas that women faced in the rural communities as survival and resistance became intertwined. This is the story not only of a war against a colonial state, but also of a war for and against the state and the revolutionary armies, and a war played out within a community itself. Not alone do these wider relations collide and contradict from the perspective of women's voices, but in their own understandings of themselves women had to constantly renegotiate their identities in a war situation.

2

Re-framing Women's Revolutionary Lives

Women, Gender & Local Resistance

Moving on from the notion of revolutionary resistance tied to a unified peasant or feminist consciousness, an alternative framework of Gendered Localised Resistance is developed in this chapter.[1] It involves rethinking revolutionary resistance to better understand rural women's experiences of guerrilla war and shifts our understanding towards individualised and localised resistance by women as a major feature of women's participation. Localised resistance is discussed in the light of James Scott's (1985) work on 'everyday forms of peasant resistance' that highlights the personalised and class dimensions of consciousness and actions in the context of South Asia and the Green Revolution in agricultural production. I challenge his impermeable boundaries of the local context of resistance through the use of Michel Foucault's ideas of power and resistance as tied to subjectivity and the creation of identities. Building on this critique, I suggest and explore the modalities of localised resistance as practised by women in the forging of identities in this study of Zimbabwe's liberation war. These discussions broaden the field of possibilities for the agency of women and shift the focus to understanding the complexity of women's social relations and self-identifications in the course of war. The agency and participation of women in revolution is interpreted through their subjectivity – their agency of being. Resistance and survival are highlighted as two key aspects of that subjectivity. How important these dimensions are for any particular woman is suggested to be a matter of context and her experience of identities through everyday social relations. The struggles of survival and identity in a context of revolutionary war thus give rise to the reinterpretation and expansion of resistance to illuminate women's experiences of, and participation in, revolution.

Rethinking revolutionary resistance as localised resistance

From the critique of feminist narratives of revolutionary wars and the historiography of Zimbabwe's liberation war, I see a reconsideration of

---

[1] See O'Gorman (1999) for the origins of the argument for Gendered Localised Resistance.

revolutionary resistance as 'localised resistance' as a necessary conceptual shift to open up the full terrain of rural women's participation in revolutionary conflict. My central claim is that by shifting our theoretical focus to women's identities, resistance and survival in revolution, we are able to redefine the realm of the local as the most illuminating starting point for understanding women's revolutionary lives.

Three core aspects of the analytical framework of Gendered Localised Resistance are interwoven in creating an understanding of resistance to enable such a shift. *Localised resistance* brings together Foucauldian ideas of power/resistance as embedded in subjectivity and the practical consciousness of James Scott's everyday resistance as embedded in experience. The *gender* aspect focuses on the socially constructed meanings attached to women's identities and location in revolution and war. Gender is interpreted in two ways, referring to male/female relations and relations amongst women. It is so interpreted to highlight the differentiation within and between women's accounts of their war experiences. The lives of women in Chiweshe can be considered *local* in two senses: the first refers to the geographical sense of Chiweshe as a rural area and community; the second understanding is discursive in the sense that women exhibit no sharp division of understanding between what others might distinguish as the 'public' and 'private'. In other words, the war is demonstrated to have penetrated all aspects of their lives and vice versa.

Women's own stories of revolution challenge the assumptions of peasant and revolutionary subjectivity and provide rich insights into the differentiated, personalised and conflicted nature of their participation in revolution. Through the looking glass of women's perceptions and responses to the various demands placed upon them, we can understand the collapse of neat categorisations of women as a coherent, collective and mobilised group of revolutionary supporters. In their place there is daily engagement with risk. In a grounded interpretation of resistance by women, even in war, the radicalisation of internal struggles is tempered by an understanding of resistance that is localised and embedded in the impetus for survival. War is disruptive, bringing into sharp relief the relations, survival struggles and resistances of daily life. Yet what emerges, particularly from the stories of the women of Chiweshe, is the continuity of everyday struggles, even in a time of crisis. The strategies and coping mechanisms that women call upon and create are intimately familiar to them.

The juxtaposition of resistance and survival in a revolutionary context is the concern of this study, wherein survival and resistance interact with and contradict each other in considering unbound and bounded forms of resistance. The unbounded nature of resistance in the course of revolution requires the recognition of struggles of survival and identity as a key feature of extended revolutionary resistance. This extension of resistance highlights the 'everyday' in contrast to the 'exceptional', the exceptional being in thought and deed part of a wider set of actions, real or imagined, that is implied (or assumed) by those who talk about 'revolutionary acts' or acts in the wider 'revolution'. One cannot simply assume the parameters of agency and consciousness that define acts as 'revolutionary'. The complexity of oppression and resistance arises from the nature of guerrilla warfare and the collapse of military/civilian categories of behaviour and space. The meaning of 'civilians' is often defined by a struggle involving state and revolutionary organisations for the 'hearts and minds' of the people; they will control the bodies too if given the chance. Localised resistance, as set out here, challenges the notion of resistance as bounded within the dyad of oppressor and oppressed and illuminates the unbounded nature of resistance effected through a wider set of social relations and identities that are constructed and enacted on a daily basis in the midst of a revolutionary war.

Defining the context of localised resistance

In his influential work *Weapons of the Weak: Everyday Forms of Peasant Resistance*, James Scott (1985) maps out a terrain of resistance that he argues lies outside of the great struggles and movements and, in a sense, is their precursor in the shape of everyday forms of peasant resistance.[2] He reveals a cornucopia of strategies and actions that lie beneath the surface of open revolt. Such 'everyday resistance' is marked by 'passive non-compliance, subtle sabotage, evasion and deception' (1985:295). These 'weapons of the weak' include 'foot dragging, dissimulation, false compliance, pilfering, feigned ignorance, slander, arson, sabotage, and so forth' (29). The nature of such resistance means it does not require strategic co-ordination; it avoids direct confrontation with the authority of elites and it encapsulates some notion of 'individual self-help' (29). The evidence of resistance for Scott lies in the realm of intentions as read from consciousness – 'the meaning they [peasants] give to their acts' – not actions (38, 290). Such intentions of resistance may, however, be so embedded in 'taken-for-granted struggle to provide for the subsistence and survival of the household as to remain inarticulate. The fish do not talk about the water'. To that extent, 'intentions are inscribed in the acts themselves' (301). There is therefore an unconscious dimension to everyday resistance that is bound up in the struggle for survival and the personal level of experience.

The interpretation of resistance is problematic when everyday resistance, in the context of self-interest and survival, is often read as passive compliance, co-option, collaboration and quiescence. Scott counters this through an emphasis on self-interested acts of survival and suggests an on-stage/off-stage character of everyday resistance: 'Deference and conformity, though rarely cringing, continue to be the public posture of the poor. For all that, however, backstage one can clearly make out a continuous testing of limits' (21). This public/private split is closely linked to the element of risk-avoidance that lies at the heart of Scott's everyday resistance. In this way, he discounts the notion of a 'mystified' peasantry plagued by false consciousness and argues instead for a more calculating subject, one who is aware of the room for action within local parameters, 'within the narrow limits created by the fear of repression and the "dull

---

[2]   The context of change and conflict for James Scott is the impact of the Green Revolution through mechanisation and double-cropping in Sedaka – his named South-East Asian village study.

compulsion of economic relations'" (304). Self-interest and compliance therefore become part of the calculus of everyday resistance through the constraints of local realities. These constraints of survival give everyday resistance its covert, clandestine and often atomised actions.

Scott has also argued, however, that not all acts of survival are acts of resistance. The importance he gives to the shared values of the moral economy in framing peasant intentions leads to a specific interpretation of what is resistance and what is survival. While self-interest and self-help are defining features of everyday resistance, when they are pursued at the expense of a neighbour, they are, for Scott, no longer resistance, but 'predatory behaviour' (1986:1-2). Hence survival is not resistance unless it is geared toward the appropriating superordinate classes; principled selflessness at some level would still seem to be required to define resistance, or at least a presupposed 'imposed mutuality', which means the oppressed will not undercut each other (1985:261-5). This is a rather virtuous claim, however, as such actions can be as much about displacement and self-seeking as they are about the limitation of exploitation. In Chiweshe, for example, labelling women as sell outs, prostitutes and witches was not always about 'acceptable limits', it also became a weapon the weak used to beat each other in a war that at times became each against all. In resisting the powers that be, those who resist are as often as not engaged also in opposition and hostility to others subject to those powers; 'resistance' divides as well as unites. Such 'predatory behaviour' is therefore accepted as part of the landscape of survival and resistance portrayed in this study.

Whilst Scott uncovers the workings of everyday resistance, he underplays its political force by describing it variously as pre-political, infrapolitical,[3] pre-revolutionary, a feature of peasant life 'in-between' revolt and as an inevitable precursor to revolution (1985; 1990). Everyday resistance is marked as a piecemeal, gradual process rather than an overt, confrontational style of resistance. Localised resistance, as understood here, eschews this tendency of viewing revolutionary resistance and everyday resistance as separate entities and thus defining them as political and apolitical categories of behaviour respectively. The struggles of women in Chiweshe defy such delineation; their everyday struggles within revolution opened up a terrain of resistance marked by acts of everyday resistance and struggles of survival. Localised resistance is not a discrete entity, it rather imagines a host of resistances that embraces overt and covert resistance, avoidance, compliance and the tactics of simple survival.

James Scott also assumes a homogenous subjectivity of 'peasant' and does not address the multiple subjectivities that may define peasants through class, gender and ethnicity.[4] Bina Agarwal (1994) redresses this imbalance somewhat through her gendering of local resistance that opens up the spaces for women's agency and illuminates the strategies

---

3   The infrapolitical nature of everyday resistance refers to 'a wide variety of low-profile forms of resistance that dare not speak in their own name'; however, the presumption remains of a 'shared hidden transcript', 'a shared critique of power' (Scott 1990:19-21).

4   Scott's definition of the peasantry as a class is problematic as he collapses the rural stratum into the categories of rich/poor. He has been criticised for his neglect of gender in differentiating the peasantry (Hart 1991:94, 116; Kriger 1992:23; Agarwal 1994:83). While

adopted by women to survive and resist change in the context of land rights for women in South Asia.[5] Here, resistance by women is understood as 'ranging from individual acts of covert non-compliance to overt confrontation by women's organisations, with varying degrees of covert group action and overt individual action in between' (1994:84).[6] Like Scott, Agarwal's forms of everyday resistance concern resources and meanings of the struggle. The latter involve challenging the understandings of women's identities and actions and shifting the analysis of everyday resistance to the gendered positions from which women resist: 'How we characterise women's consciousness and perceptions is of considerable importance, since it impinges critically on how we assess the prospects for change in women's situation and identify what the most effective forms of action would be' (Ibid.:83). Her understanding of risk in resistance is tied to an understanding of the material conditions within which women operate. The material context of the local, and in particular the household, is thus an important determinant of the context of resistance and the possibility of change. Women contest the material/resource inequalities through actions that pose a challenge to the actual male authority governing the household including truculence and foot-dragging activities such as the use of silence to denote disapproval or anger towards a husband and his family, the naming of children as an outward sign of dissatisfaction, the use of work songs as a subversive valve of discontent, playing male relatives off against each other, with-holding sex from husbands, humour and silence. Agarwal asserts that open shows of apparent compliance can merely reflect the strategies for survival adopted by women within understood constraints. The local context is also influenced by 'women's notion of "family" needs' that affects decisions to act in ways that may be both self-interested and altruistic; both sets of motivations, she argues, may be self-aware actions rather than actions of false consciousness or an outcome of socialisation.

In further gender critiques of Scott, Deniz Kandiyoti sees potential in his work for understanding women's bargaining strategies in household and intimate relations, but she is critical of his lack of understanding of the workings of gender power relations and his emphasis on the 'feudal landlord–peasant relationship' as the focus of resistance (1998:141). In

---

4 (ctnd) he acknowledges other local identities in terms of ethnicity and kin, he does so to argue that they constitute an obstacle to overt collective action along lines of class (J.C. Scott 1985:12, 43, 244). Apart from the lack of differentiation another problem with his concept of the peasantry is the presumed shared worldview of peasant justice as articulated through the moral economy. What results, despite his criticisms of other works, is a conservative image of the peasant as a social actor and historical agent. (J.C. Scott 1977:237, 246).

5 Gillian Hart (1991) also offers a gender critique of Scott and opens up the locations of the labour process, the household and the community as interconnected sites of resistance for women. she views everyday resistance as compliance, not resistance, and as properly practised by men in the public sphere. Women, on the other hand, are viewed as well-placed in the private sphere to build collective resistance.

6 This is also a caution against over-romanticising individual everyday resistance and over-estimating its effectiveness for change (Agarwal 1994:83, 95). Agarwal, even in her extensions of everyday resistance, claims that genuine resistance is located in collective, overt action centred on women's organisations.

seeking to explain the hegemony she sees as limiting the possibilities of James Scott's everyday resistance, Kandiyoti revisits her own formative arguments on 'patriarchal bargains' and raises questions regarding her strong view on agency within set constraints, outside of the purview of hegemony. She does this by repositioning kinships and household structures as institutions through which hegemony is produced rather than fixed constraints within which people act rationally to secure their medium- and long-term futures.

The exploration of perceptions, consciousness and acts of resistance by women is at the heart of this study in uncovering rural women's experiences of revolutionary guerrilla war. However, Gendered Localised Resistance extends the discursive limits of the local context beyond fixed class or household parameters by exploring the mobile resistance implicated in the construction of women's social identities. Whilst a gendered understanding of everyday resistance provides a clear sense of a local context infused with the struggles for survival that inform the actions and consciousness (or unconsciousness) of women's resistance, a discursive understanding of resistance and subjectivity moves us beyond local snapshots of resistance. This discursive understanding creates localised moving pictures that capture the contradictions and negotiations which limit and extend the boundaries of women's agency in war and affect their abilities to support revolutionary resistance whilst also surviving within a war.

Michel Foucault, in *The History of Sexuality* (1978) and *Discipline and Punish* (1979), offers us two readings of power that extend our thinking of resistance by opening up understandings of power that are not tied to institutions or a necessary sense of public space and performance. He challenges our understandings of the location, extent and exercise of power. He does not offer a theory of liberation but more pervasively challenges us to conceive differently of power. His engagement with and challenges to notions of subjectivity are useful in re-framing the working of resistance as personal and local. The first reading of power is *agonistic*, that is to say, embedded in the social relations of subjects. The subjectivities of acting subjects are not fixed, but de-centred and mobile in the construction of a field of possible actions that define the operations of power/resistance. The second notion of power is *disciplinary* power that serves to normalise subjects through the internalisation of the surveillance of social behaviour. The specific context of the Protected Villages (PVs) as the site of revolutionary struggle for women in Chiweshe involves both these understandings, and resistance is mapped out in this context.

In the first account of power, the workings of power/resistance are inherent in our personal and social being. These refer to practices of power and resistance that are in mutual tension as a dynamic struggle defined as *agonism*: 'It would not be possible for power relations to exist without points of insubordination which, by definition, are means of escape' (Foucault 1982:225). This challenges a binary notion of oppressor and oppressed in offering a fluid rendering of power as more circulatory and less fixed. It is this which Foucault articulates in the agonism of a 'relationship which is at the same time reciprocal incitation and struggle; less of a face-to-face confrontation which paralyzes both sides than a permanent provocation' (Ibid.:222).[7] The possibility of resistance is itself inscribed in power relations. As a result of this constant provocation of power and resistance the subject (the person who acts) and subjectivity (forms of identity and acting through identity) are themselves in a constant state of negotiation and renegotiation, being made, unmade and remade. Foucault describes this dynamic as 'a struggle ... against that which ties the individual to himself and submits him to others in this way', such that '[m]aybe the target nowadays is not to discover what we are, but to refuse what we are' (212, 216); Jana Sawicki (1991:26) terms it *resistant subjectivity*. I argue that women, in the case study presented here, resist subjection in two ways: not only do they resist the daily forms of oppression that shape their lives in war but the nature of their resistance also negates the way that feminist or historical narratives form them as 'subjects'. From these two perspectives, their biographies are inevitably a kind of resistance and, as the testimonies from Chiweshe reveal, they resist every classification.

Such continuous struggle is linked to the many identities women may be assuming at any one time, for example, revolutionary, mother, farmer, Zimbabwean, woman, daughter, friend. The strategies of power/resistance involve subjects producing a field of possible actions through a negotiation of various social power relations. Through Gendered Localised Resistance, I argue that these practices of power/resistance can be described as a practical engagement by women in creating their subjectivity not only in relation to others through social representation, but also in terms of internal struggles of self-representation and how they see themselves. With respect to the strategies involved in such perpetual struggles of power/resistance, Foucault suggests the following hypothesis: 'I would say it's all against all. There aren't immediately given subjects of a struggle, one the proletariat, the other the bourgeoisie. Who fights against whom? We all fight against each other. And there is always within each of us something that fights something else' (1980b:126). I suggest that the power/resistance dynamic therefore not only functions as resistant subjectivity, but also as *differentiated subjectivity* in relation to the self and others. This challenges the idea of revolutionary resistance as tied to a unipolar subjectivity of 'peasant' derived from a particular location of class struggle:

> The points of resistance are present everywhere in the power network. Hence there is no single locus of great Refusal, no soul of revolt, source of all rebellions, or pure law of the revolutionary. Instead there is a plurality of resistance's [sic], each of them a special case: resistances that are possible, necessary, improbable; others that are spontaneous, savage, solitary, concerted, rampant or violent; still others that are quick to compromise, interested, or sacrificial; by definition, they can only exist in the strategic field of power relations. (Foucault 1978:95-6)

This negates the notion of a fixed or static revolutionary subject, a knowing and acting person, a unified identity of being in revolt that is at the heart of the peasant histories of revolution that were discussed in

---

[7]   See also n3 on this page, where an image of 'combat' involving 'mutual taunting' is suggested by the translator to clarify the understanding of agonism.

Chapter 1. As Sawicki argues, '[t]he practical implication of his [Foucault's] model is that resistance must be carried out in local struggles against the many forms of power exercised at the everyday level of social relations' (1991:23). Resistance is therefore inherent in particular histories and relations. This understanding of power/resistance opens up the discursive spaces where power and resistance are creating, defining and defying each other in a tense dynamic of renegotiation. In such a fluid context of power/resistance relations, difference and differentiation become both conditions and effects of power. Localised resistance, as constructed here, suggests the proliferation of the field of possible actions that is entailed in the struggles over subjectivity, that is to say, definitions of self and others, and provides an entry point to exploring the instability of guerrilla war as a context of resistance for women.

The second understanding of power developed by Foucault (1979) is that of disciplinary power as forms of power/knowledge; these are discourses and relations of power that are bound up in the simultaneous development of knowledge concerning power and subjectivity that, in the extreme, become a form of social control that may be unquestioned. Disciplinary practices 'secure their hold not through the threat of violence or force, but rather by creating desires, attaching individuals to specific identities, and establishing norms against which individuals and their behaviours and bodies are judged and against which they police themselves' such that the danger is not always coercion but normalisation (Sawicki 1991:68). This production and reproduction of 'docile bodies' require methods of surveillance to be effective. Eighteenth-century English philosopher Jeremy Bentham's Panopticon, through Foucault's theorisation of it, has become the visual essence of disciplinary power. Bentham envisioned an architectural design for prisons whereby the authorities could maintain a view of all prisoners without prisoners being able to view their jailers. This was achieved in its simplest form by building a central tower (for the watchers) within a circular building that is carved into separate cells of units (for the watched). Individuals are thus isolated from each other and aware only of the tower, uncertain of who is watching and when. This structure thus creates a climate of surveillance wherein prisoners police themselves by internalising the physical weight of the gaze of the ever-watching, unseen jailer at the centre of the panopticon. The essence of such surveillance creates in the inmates 'a state of conscious and permanent visibility that assures the automatic functioning of power' (Foucault 1979:201). It is this 'anonymity' of disciplinary power that is important in understanding subordination.

Disciplinary power is particularly relevant to the case of guerrilla and state surveillance in Chiweshe.[8] In the case of the state, disciplinary power was intrinsic to the counterinsurgency policy of incarcerating people in PVs. For the revolutionary organisations, the use of surveillance to gain people's support and protect the presence of guerrillas was more informal but no less disciplinary. In Chiweshe the extreme physical reality of the PVs created panopticons where the internalisation of

---

8   Chapter 3 provides a fuller description of Chiweshe and Chapter 5 includes a discussion of surveillance and its implications for women in the Protected Villages during the war.

surveillance meant that women policed themselves. In such an environment the idea of sanctions moves away from simply coming from an individual – father, husband, state official and guerrilla – toward the idea of a disciplinary power that is 'dispersed and anonymous; there are no individuals formally empowered to wield it; it is ... invested in everyone and in no one in particular' (Bartky 1988:80). The conduct, compliance and resistance of women are partly shaped by this context. As well as the diffusive and almost ephemeral way in which discipline can manifest itself, there is the process of internalisation: 'Resistance from this source may be joined by a reluctance to part with the rewards of compliance' (Ibid.:76-7).

The argument made here is that even in the case of a Foucauldian carceral society there remains the promise and practice of agonistic power/resistance. Agonistic and disciplinary power thus shaped the landscape of Gendered Localised Resistance in the context of the war in Chiweshe. A discursive understanding of power/resistance does not mean having to ignore the very oppressive effects of power as exercised through and by institutions and practices which frame women's room for manoeuvre. This is a tension that is revealed in the attempt to interrelate disciplinary and agonistic power through the testimonies of women in Chiweshe during the war. Resistance is shown to be both bound and unbound; bound by the desire for resistance and change in the oppressive effects of power and unbound by the daily struggles of survival and resistance enacted from a number of responsibilities, fears, desires conducted through the fluid parameters of social relations in war.

Pace James Scott, the understanding of the 'local' sphere is a filter of understanding rather than an opaque barrier of parochialism, such that outside practices and ideologies are negotiated and impacted upon through interaction with the local communities.[9] In bringing together everyday resistance, power/resistance and resistant subjectivity, we imagine both a geographical and discursive sense of the local for women in Chiweshe. While everyday forms of domination mark the terrain of everyday resistance (and indeed, in this interpretive framework, they are seen as being mutually constitutive and also highly gendered), it is the experience of that domination that maps out the location and possibilities for action. It is not simply the imposition of power over but also the ways in which policies are taken up, subverted, challenged and changed with varying degrees of success and failure. That is not to deny the power inherent in state institutions and revolutionary organisations to coerce a desired outcome, but rather to deny the passivity of women who experience those policies and in so doing effect and affect those policies in practice. I argue that in a discursive rendering of resistance

---

[9]   The primacy of the local as a level of analysis arises from Scott's conception of the peasantry as somehow autonomous and sharing a unified worldview. The local in this setting is distinct from the national – 'it promotes a distinct and parochial set of political perceptions, and it forms a local unit of moral obligation' (J.C. Scott 1979:110). The peasantry therefore becomes a class that is bound geographically to viewing the world through a local lens. This lens however is restrictive in the social horizons it envisages – being defined by the confines of the 'village', 'standard marketing area' or 'market town and its hinterland' (Ibid.:111). The view is further restricted by the notion of shared values of the past acting as the glue of possible solidarity.

we can appreciate a local context where, despite force and fear being a constant presence and structural realities seemingly immutable,[10] women were constantly positioning their actions and relations with a mixture of resistance (to the state, to the guerrilla forces, to local insecurities) and survival (physical, social, moral), which ultimately have to be taken together in any understanding of everyday resistance. The woman who does not tend her fields for fear of meeting guerrillas and their demands for food is both resisting and surviving, but it does not mean she colludes with the colonial state. In fact, in other instances, she will resist against that state by carrying messages from the guerrillas to other villages. The nature of oppression and the spaces for action generate an individual consciousness of avoidance and survival that is also underpinned by a sense of resistance – in the instance above, resisting the dangerous demands of guerrillas which place her in a situation of risk. A reinterpretation of local resistance in this way leads to a mapping of actions that reflects the continuous and sometimes contradictory intentions and outcomes of everyday actions. Rather than tying those actions to some shared sense of the past, a unifying nationalism or a generalised explanation of guerrilla coercion, the context of power/resistance and gender identities is argued to inform the actions of women and the meaning they give to those actions. The problematic of interpretation is approached through accepting self-interest and survival as part of the repertoire of actions constituting and arising from local relations of power and resistance.

Practising localised resistance:
The forging of women's identities

Gender identities in the approach of Gendered Localised Resistance involve aspects of roles, subject positions and subjectivity, and it is the understanding and performance of women's identities as incorporating these aspects that is of concern in mapping out women's experiences of revolutionary war in Chiweshe. 'Roles' refer to the narrow definitions of activities and identifications of the acting subject. They incorporate a fixed idea of expectations and structural assumptions of performance through a gendered delineation of the public/battlefront – private/ home front spheres. Chapter 1 showed the extent to which the roles of rural women in revolution tend to be guerrilla-defined in fulfilling the logistical needs of revolutionary organisations. However, roles are not treated here in a purely functional sense of sexual divisions of labour and value but are reinterpreted as 'subject positions'. These can refer to defined activities but suggest greater mobility and creativity on the part of the subject than does the notion of roles because of the dynamic of positionality attached to them. The forging of identities through relationship with others draws the subject into a series of self-represen-

---

10   These include the intervening powers of the state on the back of an interventionist and destructive colonial history and the coercive efforts of guerrilla forces to secure peasant support.

tations and representations to 'others' and of 'others'. These identities
are given meaning and explanatory power through the agency which
infuses them: the everyday performance and experience of identities
that arise from and respond to an immediate social context. This allows
a dynamic sense of agency through 'positionality' whereby women take
up certain subject positions or seek to subvert and avoid others. Henri-
etta Moore speaks of such a consciousness of gender identities 'forged
through practical engagement in lives lived' (1994:53-4). We can therefore imagine a practical consciousness where the practice of generating
fluid identities is based on *intersubjectivity* and *subject positionality* in
pitting each against all and against oneself in daily interactions. Intersubjectivity implies acting and defining oneself in relation to others and
in relation to one's own self-representations, while positionality implies
the taking up of different identities through adopting changing subject
and speaking positions in the practice of identity:

> The notion of positionality allows us to examine how we are all subject to
> discourse and to the various subject positions which are opened up to us
> in discourse. Such subject positions can be resisted, both consciously and
> unconsciously, but it is in terms of these positions, even in contradiction to
> them, that we construct our sense of ourselves as selves, as individuals and
> as persons. (Moore 1994:48)

In the context of localised resistance such positionality illuminates
the different subject positions in women's revolutionary identity, for
example, sell out, mother, food provider, collaborator, good citizen and
community worker. Multiple positioning allied to intersubjectivity
creates gender identities that are discursive, that is to say, provisional
and subject to reinforcement and/or resistance. Women in revolutions
can be seen to take up a number of 'speaking positions' that are established through relation with self and others. Their positionality is also
reflected in actions that may, from different subject positions, be actions
of compliance (with the state, the guerrillas, with neighbours) or resistance (against the state, against the guerrillas, against each other). In
practice, therefore, we can speak of internally contradictory actions of
resistance within a revolution. Such interplay of intersubjectivity and
positionality has also been expressed as 'conflicting loyalties' and 'incoherent identities' (Sawicki 1991:41; Sylvester 1987:507).

Furthermore, gender identities are not simply the passive outcome of
socialisation but are constructed through processes of practical and discursive knowledge involving agency in the forms of resistance and
compliance which reproduce and/or resist dominant discourses and
categories. As Sawicki suggests, '[i]n such a relational view of personal
identity, one's interests are a function of one's place in the social field
at a particular time, not given. They are constantly open to change and
contestation' (1991:42). The question is how do individuals choose their
subject positions, and indeed, how much choice is there? The room for
manoeuvre, I argue, is both material and relational. In the first instance
the impetus for survival affects women's abilities to take up or refuse
subject positions. In a relational context, attempts to position oneself
can be thwarted by struggles within the self and with others arising
from the 'inability to sustain or properly take up a gendered subject

position, resulting in a crisis, real or imagined, of self-representation and/or social evaluation' (Moore 1994:66). It can arise from the tension of taking up and maintaining multiple and contradictory subject positions; the failure of 'others' to fulfil their subject positions in relation to one's own, for example, husband/wife, government/good citizen, revolutionary organisation/revolutionary cadre; the failure to accrue benefits from adopting a particular subject position, for example, compensation for former food providers from the independent government for cattle seized and food given to the guerrillas. It is also the case that subject positions are not always equal and this affects and is affected by choice in a context where social and material rewards and sanctions are in operation (Ibid.:65). There are thus short-term considerations in the adoption of subject positions such as Sylvester suggests:

> In fragmented fields of identity, which often include identities of mother, food producer, and party member, the armed woman warrior may be an emergency identity only, one which proves transient next to the historically more practised consciousness of deference. If so, this speaks to the importance of women becoming comfortable with incoherent identities, and resisting the temptation to seek a master reconciliation. (1987:507)

Localised resistance is therefore held to be both conscious and unconscious. The implicit warning here is that while forswearing the false consciousness of a passive, fixed subjectivity, we have to avoid the other extreme of presuming a fully knowledgeable and aware social actor who is fully engaged in a conscious realisation of constructing gendered subjectivity. Rather, the subject is implicated in a practical and discursive knowledge in the construction of such identities. The general understanding here is that there is not always a clearly understood object of resistance. In other words, acts of resistance can have personal resonance but may not be framed in a wider political framework, despite any political consequences which may be interpreted by an observer. However, I do not wish to assert that such actions are the actions of a false consciousness but rather that they are the actions of a personalised, specific consciousness which is not fixed but is temporally and spatially constructed and can also be reactive.

The implication of subjectivity in the localised operations of power and resistance means that general categories cannot hold; no one identity can capture the changing kaleidoscope of powers and resistances that define Gendered Localised Resistance. The category of 'peasant' has been demonstrated to be ineffective in this regard. We must also be cautious of categorising 'women' as homogenous in the same way. This arises from the argument that subjectivities (ways of being) are in themselves constructed through and bound up in exercises of power and resistances to power; the struggle therefore is within *and* without. In terms of Gendered Localised Resistance such resistant subjectivity invokes recognition of difference amongst women and within 'woman' as political agents. Gendered resistance is therefore properly understood not only as local but also as wholly particular; hence the focus on individuated consciousness grounded in everyday experiences of guerrilla warfare. The consciousness of resistance understood here is that of practical engagement in the everyday as the impetus to inten-

tion and form of action informed by manipulations of power/resistance
played out through negotiating identities in the form of various subject positions. This is an 'individuated consciousness', referring to the
understanding of political consciousness as grounded in the ebb and
flow of particular incidents of personal experience in a context of everyday social relations.

The practical consciousness of resistance in a liberation war derives
in part from women's long experience of deprivation under colonialism:
'Deprived of their husbands, forced to take over the man's work as well
as their own, rural women need no one to tell them they were living in
an unjust society' (Weiss 1986:45). Not only did women's colonial experiences provide the consciousness of oppression for rural women but it
also forged forms of participation women would adopt in revolution:
'The woman, left to fend by herself for the family and the land, took on
the roles that had previously been the preserve of the male. Ironically,
it was the hand of colonialism that prepared her for the vital role she
played in the Second *Chimurenga*' (Ibid.:44).[11] However, the contention
here is that such consciousness must not commit the methodological
fallacy of Terence Ranger's peasant consciousness by assuming it to be
unified, binding women together in collective consciousness. On the
contrary, whilst the historical fight for the peasant option may well
have influenced women's consciousness of oppression, an individuated expression and concept of political consciousness is argued here to
better reflect women's experiences of revolutionary struggle.

In the case of the women in this study, I identify three dimensions to
women's political consciousness that form the basis for extending the
consideration of their participation in revolution beyond assumed revolutionary identities and a radicalised revolutionary consciousness. The
first element of political consciousness is that arising directly from the
ideological context of revolution, namely, the anti-colonial sentiments
derived from the language of revolution and disseminated through processes of politicisation by the revolutionary forces. The second element
refers to the anti-colonial sentiments that arose from women's felt injustices and experiences of oppression under colonial rule, as told in their
own words. The actual context of living through a revolutionary war
suggests a third dimension of consciousness. This arises from the practical engagement with the context of war through various and conflicted
relations, old and new, as well as the emergence of new felt oppressions
and personal struggles for survival. This context includes personal
struggles that were not directly or necessarily anti-colonial, for example, family and household tensions. In some instances, these struggles
pre-dated the war and continued as a feature of life during the revolution. Although these latter reasons are not conventionally considered to
be politically motivated, I understand them to be 'political' (with a small
'p'), as they interacted with and shaped the women's understanding and
experiences of anti-colonial revolutionary consciousness. I also define
such reasons as an element of 'political' consciousness because the
struggles from which they emerged were often conflicts of power with

11 The liberation war in Zimbabwe is also known as the Second *Chimurenga*. The First
Chimurenga was an insurrection by the Shona and Ndebele peoples against the colonialists
in 1896.

individuals or within households, as well as poverty-related struggles of survival. These themes of consciousness are taken up in Chapter 4.

Whilst imagining different understandings of the local context, both Scott and Foucault also emphasise the context of immediate struggles (such as those suggested in the third dimension of consciousness above) as informing the nature and consciousness of resistance. For Scott, the 'texture of local experience' is such that '[f]or the victims as well as the beneficiaries of the large abstractions we choose to call capitalism, imperialism, or the green revolution, the experience itself arrives in quite personal, concrete, localised, mediated form' (J.C. Scott 1985:348). Foucault argues that '[i]n such struggles people criticize instances of power which are closest to them, those which exercise their actions on individuals. They did not look for the "chief enemy" but the immediate enemy' (Foucault 1982:211); and so it was for the women in Chiweshe, participating in a revolutionary war.

Moving towards Chiweshe

In opening up an understanding of resistance and subjectivity we must beware of creating another untenable position to counter the fixed identities of revolutionary resistance; namely claiming all agency to be resistant. The exercise of subjectivity is in certain circumstances more resistant than others, but resistance is not the only agency involved; there is also compliance, avoidance and the tactics of survival, as well as the forming of new ways of life and new relationships. It is by specifying the contexts of resistance *and* survival that we may escape the pendulum of an alternative orthodoxy. This also allows us to explore the specificities of women's participation in revolution and illuminate the contestations of identity in such a crisis situation. The extension of resistance to incorporate resistant and differentiated subjectivity allows us to explore women's contested identities in revolution in response to the various pressures they encounter. The testimonies from Chiweshe demonstrate that the subjectivity of women was affected by having to survive and resist the pressures placed upon them from various sources – the state forces, the guerrillas, their communities, neighbours and families. In such a context, where they had to survive and were resisting, their sense of themselves was revised and fed into their subjectivity. In moving beyond revolutionary resistance to localised resistance, the stories of women from Chiweshe demonstrate that rather than fixed identities as the explanation of participation in revolution, what actually occurs is that identities are thrown up for redefinition in the struggles of resistance and the struggles for survival. The understanding of resistance is shifted from any unipolar identity of the revolutionary subject and the fixed identities attached to such a position. In doing so, the explorations of subjectivity reveals a host of identities or positions managed by women in the course of revolution. The tensions of these identities find expression through the conduct of everyday relations. Such negotiation of relations and identities are embedded in the sometimes opposed desires of revolutionary resistance and personal and familial survival.

The argument developed from this point is one that asserts Gendered Localised Resistance as women's struggles for survival in a revolutionary context. It asserts that the 'objective' conditions of oppression or revolt are not so distant or external to the lives of women. Everyday resistance is not a pre-political or pre-revolutionary category of behaviour but is part of an ongoing struggle in a life-historical context. This suggests that even in a violent revolution, revolutionary resistance, everyday resistance and acts of survival are intermeshed. Within this local context, women's negotiations of identity in war involve self and other understandings (how women saw themselves and others, and how others saw them) of roles, responsibilities and relationships in a context of risk, uncertainty and fear. There are various degrees to which different women in Chiweshe felt bound or unbound by the impositions of the guerrilla war, or their roles and responsibilities in that war. The personal/political axis is not only clearly undefined but is in itself a site of struggle amongst women and within woman herself as an individual subject/agent. These interstitial workings of localised resistance are mapped out in the following chapters. What emerges is a more complex rendering of the local dynamics of women's participation and resistance in revolution. The analysis of the next chapters reflect the negotiation of identities by women by illuminating the ways in which women positioned themselves in a range of everyday relations that bounded their agency during the war in Chiweshe. The exploration of local relations, transformed by war, highlights the way in which revolutionary resistance is bounded by the everyday physical, social and symbolic locations of women in relations with the state, the revolutionary organisations and interpersonal relationships in the community.

3

**Setting the
Fieldwork Context** | Zimbabwe as Arena,
Chiweshe as Locale

Zimbabwe has undergone great change since independence in 1980 with a worsening of the situation in terms of abject poverty, economic collapse and a crisis of governance and human rights marked by brutality and political violence. These trends are assessed in the Introduction and Conclusion of this book to reinforce the lessons from the liberation war period and the continuities of some of the struggles that rural women in particular face. What is telling is that the testimonies of the women of Chiweshe I gathered in 1993 already reflected a sense of disillusionment and resentment with government's failure to deliver on promises made at independence, years before the crisis of the 2000s emerged in its worst aspects. In this chapter, I set out the historical context of the liberation war in Zimbabwe, and more particularly in Chiweshe, and take the story through to the years immediately after independence. This frames the context for the women's testimonies of war in Chiweshe that occupy the next three chapters. By way of background, the first section outlines the history of Zimbabwe's war of independence and women's participation in it. The second section looks at the specific features of Chiweshe as a site for research. Finally, I outline some methodological issues that help explain the ways in which the women's testimonies were gathered and analysed.

Women and the *Chimurenga* (1966–1980)

In 1890 the British South Africa Company (BSACo) of Cecil Rhodes moved to acquire the territories that were to become Southern Rhodesia. A 'Pioneer Column' paved the way northward. In 1893, Chief Lobengula led the Ndebele in a war against the incomers and lost. In 1896 another offensive was launched and the Ndebele and Shona came together to fight a common enemy, but failed to defeat the colonisers once again. This struggle – the First *Chimurenga* – smouldered to provide impetus for the rise of nationalist movements and the liberation war that is now known as the Second *Chimurenga*. The settler hopes of a 'second rand' to equal the mineral wealth of South Africa were soon quashed and led to the alternative strategy of large-scale agriculture under settler control. As a result, the colonisation of Zimbabwe was characterised by a long history of land alienation and the construction of a de facto apartheid order to uphold white dominance in agriculture, mining and industry. The indigenous pastoral way of life suffered constant attack as people were moved from the fertile plains to reserves in poorer land areas that were named Tribal Trust Lands (TTLs).[1] Stock and crop prices were controlled to force African families into subsistence livelihoods of peasant farming. Such coercive state interventions created a migrant labour system whereby many male household members sought work in the towns, farms and mines of the settler economy, leaving mainly women, children and the elderly to eke out a living from the land.

This study takes as its historical focus the war of liberation that started in 1966 and was at its most intensive between 1972 and 1979.[2] The white Rhodesia Front government under Ian Smith was in power and declared a Unilateral Declaration of Independence in 1965, marking the break away of Rhodesia from British rule and influence of the Parliament in Westminster. The late 1950s and early 1960s had seen an increased militancy in the resistance to colonial rule and the government's discriminatory agricultural policies and the emergence of nationalist organisations. The Southern Rhodesia African National Congress (SRANC) was founded in 1957, but was banned in 1959. It was quickly replaced by the National Democratic Party (NDP), which was banned at the end of 1961, but quickly re-emerged in the form of the Zimbabwe African People's Union (ZAPU) under the leadership of Joshua Nkomo. When ZAPU was banned in 1962 the struggle for independence went underground. The party split a year later and the Zimbabwe African National Union (ZANU) was formed under the leadership of Ndabaningi Sithole. In 1974, two years into the liberation war, he was replaced by Robert Mugabe, who went on to become Prime Minister of the independent government in 1980.

The Battle of Sinoia (Chinhoyi) in 1966 marked the first significant military engagement between guerrillas and government forces and signalled the beginning of the war. During the war, ZANU benefited from the support of Samora Machel's FRELIMO in Mozambique and from the People's Republic of China. Its military wing, the Zimbabwean African National Liberation Army (ZANLA), operated mainly in Shona-dominated areas including Mashonaland and was particularly strong in the north-eastern part of the country. ZAPU and ZIPRA, its military wing, operated mainly in the Matabeleland with support from Zambia and the USSR. This political profile gave the war its socialist revolutionary basis. A guerrilla bush war, it was fought along the line of classical Maoist strategies of mass mobilisation and peasant support to ensure the free movement of guerrilla groups in carrying out surprise attacks

[1]   The Land Apportionment Act of 1930, for example, put in place the effective removal of African peasants from fertile agricultural land into the impoverished areas of the reserves. The white settler minority took ownership of nearly 20 million hectares of land and allocated nine million hectares for the African majority. Native Purchase Areas, located on the outskirts of the reserves, were plots of land allocated for purchase by African peasants who had trained as 'Master Farmers'.

[2]   See Appendix 1 for a select chronology of the war.

on commercial farms and government forces. In December 1972 the incursions of ZANLA in the north-east of Rhodesia marked an intensification of the war; an attack on a white settler farm near Centenary, on the border with Chiweshe, sparked this more intensive phase of both guerrilla and counterinsurgency operations.[3] The guerrilla war lasted nearly 15 years, ending in 1979 with the Lancaster House talks brokered by Britain.[4] Zimbabwe finally achieved independence on 18 April 1980.

The bittersweet narrative of women's participation and empowerment in revolutionary struggles, outlined in Chapter 1, was a strong feature of the war in Zimbabwe. The political romanticism of female participation in the struggle painted a picture of women gaining equality through the performance of normally male-defined tasks. Women 'had been able to take advantage of opportunities given by the war and move into areas that were traditionally closed to them', for example, as fighters and political educators (L. Scott 1990:34). The potency of women guerrilla fighters as a propaganda tool was not lost on the revolutionary organisations.[5] As a result the actual number of female fighters tended to be exaggerated. Figures for ZANU vary from one-third of the total fighting force inside Zimbabwe (which, at the height of the war in the mid 1970s would have translated to around 6,600 soldiers) to accounts of 1,500 to 2,000 female fighters (Kriger 1992:191). There may well have been this number of recruits, but many simply attended camp schools in Mozambique. Figures in 1978 show that 75 per cent of women fighters and workers in ZANU camps in Mozambique were between the ages of 15 and 24 while the remaining 25 per cent were in the 25-29 age group (Kriger 1992:46-7). After 1977, ZIPRA began training women to form a separate battalion, while ZANLA were incorporating women into existing battalions (Sylvester 1991:50). The earliest indication of ZANLA having active women combatants was in Centenary in 1973 (L. Scott 1990:28). Ruth Weiss (1986:80) views this optimistically as men and women sharing the 'shedding of blood together' in the struggle. Leda Scott (1990), however, sees it as a logistical issue due to the shortage of male recruits rather than a pro-active policy of integrating women into the fighting armies. Military strategy and necessity rather then agendas of social transformation seem to have pushed the increased recruitment and training of female fighters.

There is also conflicting opinion as to the degree of equality achieved in the camps with respect to training and task allocation. The reality for many women going to training camps in Mozambique and Zambia was very different from the empowering narrative of female fighters. Some assumed the ultimate military task of combat, but for the most part unmarried women in the camps 'performed militarised though still feminine tasks, serving as cooks, nurses, and laundresses for the guerrillas' (Enloe 1988:164). Josephine Nhongo-Simbanegavi (2000),

[3]   On 21 and 23 December Altena and Whistlefield farms were attacked (NAZ:MS 735).
[4]   See Caute (1983); Kriger (1992); Lan (1985); Martin and Johnson (1981); Ranger (1985); Sylvester (1991); and Bhebe and Ranger (1995; 1996).
[5]   There are examples of African women being used by both the white state and the guerrilla movements as part of their propaganda, with the former manufacturing images of abnormal animal-like behaviour and the latter focusing on the imagery of 'mothers of the revolution' or comrades-in-arms (Weiss 1986:147-8; L. Scott 1990:33).

in *For Better or Worse? Women and ZANLA in Zimbabwe's Liberation Struggle,* outlines the key war-related roles for women as guerrillas, porters, nurse and teachers, among others, and analyses the official practices whereby these roles were subsumed to those of the male guerrillas. Her analysis of ZANLA archives and interviews with women at the rear base camps in Mozambique reveals the gap between revolutionary rhetoric and the actual 'use' of women in supporting the war; 'Women were being recruited for specific functions and to serve male needs in ZANLA. They were left out of military training programmes until they demanded inclusion, especially in view of the dangers they were exposed to as carriers of war materials' (2003:82).

However, most Zimbabwean women experienced the war in the theatre in which it was played out, namely, the reserves inside Zimbabwe. Village life was dominated by women at the peak of the war, as many of the young men had left to fight or were migrant workers in urban centres. A front line was fought by rural women as they played a crucial role in supply networks. The necessity of providing the guerrillas with food brought traditionally perceived domestic chores into the political framework of the war. Women of all generations were involved. *Chimbwidos* were young girls whose tasks varied from cooking, cleaning and generally 'domestic' chores to more openly 'political' roles of intelligence-gatherer, lookout and courier between camps. Along with their male counterparts, the *Mujibhas*, they were involved in the identification of 'sell outs' during the war and cases abound of the abuse of this power. For many young women their participation was a challenge to tradition but the benefits of perceived independence of action and increased status are offset by the opprobrium of elders and difficulties of working with the guerrillas. There was also much tension about the sexual relations between *Chimbwidos* and guerrillas and the pregnancies that resulted. Parents were often too frightened to complain and indeed not all such encounters were voluntary. Older women organised the cooking and dispatch of food to the comrades and also aided in the purchase of clothes, cigarettes, shoes and soap. Leda Scott claims that '[t]he power of the provision of food also gave older women power within the political sphere' (1990:46). Buses were subject to searches by government soldiers so that great courage and ingenuity were required and forthcoming in keeping these channels of supply open. The *ambuyas* (grandmothers) were effective heads of household in many cases, given the context of male migrant labour. Gaining the support of these women was important to the guerrillas in winning the trust and support of the locals. However, persecution as 'sell outs' and accusations of witchcraft and prostitution were just some of the problems women faced when out of favour with the guerrillas or subject to community suspicion and jealousy (L. Scott 1990:51-3; Sylvester 1991:146).

Despite the political mobilisation of women in rural areas, when one examines the tasks they were assigned there was little change in traditional perceptions. The guerrillas 'expected women to supply cigarettes, soap, food, and clothes and handed few leadership positions to women during the war' (Sylvester 1991:51). Leda Scott concludes that revolutionary change for women was not an inevitable outcome of their participation:

Given an opportunity women challenged stereotypes, often by assuming domestic tasks in relation to the war and thus forcing recognition of these and then building upon them to the extent of engaging in physical combat themselves. However unusual or new women's war roles may have been, though, they were still conditioned by traditional norms and were normally supportive. Moreover, any real challenge to gender inequality was avoided by both ZANU and ZAPU because they also needed the support of the men and to support the struggle of women would be a diversion that they could not afford in the war situation. (1990:64)

Nhongo-Simbanegavi (2000; 2003), in her excavation of the women's roles and functions within ZANLA, reveals the very clear distinctions of 'front' and 'rear' that defined a gendered hierarchy of revolutionary status and power. In doing so she disturbs the romantic nationalist mythology of equality and emancipation for female comrades: 'The women were trapped "on the inside" and the voices of the educated few who strove for equal opportunity and challenged sexism were muffled through intimidation and deceptive political sloganeering' (2003:81).

Post-independent realities: The immediate aftermath

Expectations are never greater than at the eve of independence following a protracted war.[6] Speaking at a ZANU Women's Seminar held some months prior to the Lancaster House talks in 1979, Robert Mugabe declared:

> The Party has, by waging an armed struggle created ... a process generative of forces that will result in the total liberation of the woman. But the Party has also a specific and distinct organic structure to ensure the full enrolment of women and their active participation in a struggle they alone will reap a double reward – national liberation and in its context, their own liberation. (Mugabe 1983:85-6)

In its place what emerged in the early years of the new state was the entrenchment of essentially a traditional party building upon a nationalist victory. As in other post-colonial countries, a mythical past was reconstructed as a vision of post-independence society. The clash of tradition and change was epitomised by the 'clean-up operation' in 1983 when a vagrancy law that had existed under colonial rule was enforced to allow the random arrest of women. According to the government, the aim of the exercise was to curb prostitution. In reality, unaccompanied women were arrested and held in large centres such as Rufaro football stadium in Harare. Failure to produce a marriage certificate or work documents amounted to a charge of prostitution. This affected a section of young women who, having participated in the liberation war and had no desire to return to the rural areas, relocated to urban areas in

---

6   For overviews and analysis of the situation of women in the early post-independence period, see Barnes and Win (1992); Batezat, Mwalo, and Truscott (1988); Batezat and Mwalo (1989); Kazembe (1987); Bond-Stewart (1987); Chimedza (1987); Ncube (1987); Seidman (1984); Stewart and Armstrong (1991); and Zimbabwe Women's Bureau (1981; 1992).

search of work. Returning home after the war proved particularly difficult for women who had crossed the gender divide and been fighters. One reported problem for such women in the immediate post-independent period was reintegration into their communities as they were often treated with suspicion and fear. The tension was also seen in terms of the demobilisation of female combatants, as witnessed by a newspaper debate in 1981 that questioned whether such women would make good wives (Seidman 1984).

The romantic appeal of women's liberation through revolutionary struggles waned when harsh realities saw women demobilised, neglected and disillusioned. Most of the women involved in the supply networks were demobilised from the political significance of these roles at independence and returned to an agricultural economy in which land ownership was problematic for them. The continuity of sexual divisions of labour into independence provided a sober counterpoint to the wartime romantic visions of social transformations (Enloe 1988:165). Others argued that any progressive gains made by women in subverting the traditional divisions of labour simply did not return to the rural areas:

> Today the majority of the women who had acquired practical experience of living and fighting alongside men as their moral and intellectual equals are either in the army or the towns and are not available to share this experience with the women who stayed behind. (Lan 1985:212)

Even for the women who believed the liberating premises of revolutionary Marxism and the promised withering away of gender, this was a disillusioning experience:

> Attempts to discuss this struggle, especially the struggle of women to confront their oppression, as something separate from and beyond the national struggle (or socialist struggle) has provoked a torrent of invective and sometimes crude sexist sentiment from various sections of Zimbabwean society, making it difficult to define a clear socialist, pro-woman position. (Batezat, Mwalo and Truscott 1988:167-8)

The promises of an end to bride price, access to land and other social goods became muted and the rallying cries were soon forgotten.

On the formal public level, some changes to the law in the immediate post-independence period were favourable to women. The most notable piece of legislation was the Legal Age of Majority Act (1982), which granted majority status to African women over the age of eighteen. Subsequent years witnessed the resurgence of opposition to this law and renewed the controversy about its responsibility for social ills (Armstrong 1987; Ncube 1987). Issues such as *lobola* (bride price) and claims for seduction damages by fathers became the subject of judicial review. Findings in such cases have resulted in the legal acknowledgement of the rights of African women to act on their own behalf and remove (at least on paper) the property-based relations between father and daughter/husband and wife.

The setting up of the Ministry of Community Development and Women's Affairs (MCDWA) in 1981 was supposed to be government's acknowledgement of the contribution of women to the independence struggle. In mid 1982, it adopted an adult literacy programme focused on women who had been denied education but the programme was suspended at the end of the year due to lack of funding. In 1983 the ministry received only one per cent of its budget from the government and was otherwise dependent on foreign aid to support its programmes. The decade after independence was marked by the ever-decreasing size and importance of this Ministry. In 1989 it was tied to the Ministry of Political Affairs, which dealt mainly with the internal affairs of ZANU-PF. Sylvester argues that '[t]his move seem[ed] calculated less to strengthen pro-women forces in the country than to whip women's groups into political cheerleading sections for the ZANU PF government' (1991:150).

In the rural areas, traditional powers re-emerged, if they had ever gone away. Chiefs, headmen and party officials (almost exclusively men) took back the spaces that opened up during the war and set themselves up as the brokers with the independent state structures. As Jocelyn Alexander (1996) observes:

> Though existing power structures in rural areas were challenged during the war, the conditions were not yet created for new structures to become firmly established. Women and young people, in particular, were unable to sustain the enhanced status they had achieved during the war. (1996:190)

This reflected a wider national context where the structures of the colonial economy and state remained largely intact and the central grievances of the war, notably land, remained unaddressed.

Since independence in Zimbabwe there has been a withering away of the socialist ideals that had shaped the ideology of the revolutionary movements. Over the past 30 years there has been a deterioration of early gains and hopes giving way to the poverty, violence, insecurity, corruption and ungovernability that define Zimbabwe today. As outlined in the Introduction and Conclusion, what is striking is the continuity of violence and political struggles, some of which find their origins in the liberation war and guerrilla warfare.

Chiweshe: A time and a place

In 1993 I conducted field research in the Communal Area of Chiweshe that nestles within the former heartland of white commercial farming. Part of the Mazoe District, roughly 80 kilometres north of Harare.[7] Chiweshe had a particular identity during the war as one of the first areas targeted for 'Operation Overload', the government counterinsurgency operation that was initiated in 1974. Rural communities were devastated by this forced resettlement of over 48,000 people into what the

---

7 'Communal Areas' is the post-independence administrative term for the former 're-serves' or TTLs. See p. xv for a map of Chiweshe. The local knowledge map is reinforced by and builds upon the work of other researchers who have spent time in this area (Bessant 1985, 1987, 1994; Hamilton 1964; Johnson 1964; Kesby 1994, 1996; Manungo 1991; Marangwanda 1986; Muringai 1990; Musikavanhu 1989; Weinrich 1976/77). The Catholic Commission for Justice and Peace (CCJP) also produced important investigative reports on Chiweshe during the war (CIIR, CCJP (Rhodesia) 1975; NAZ, MS 311/17).

government termed 'Protected Villages' but what many people in Chiweshe called the 'cages' or the 'Keeps'.

The narrow strip of land that is Chiweshe runs approximately 45 kilometres from south to north and 20 kilometres from east to west. It had long been a strategic location in terms of soil quality, progressive farming techniques and access to markets. The farming of maize and tobacco was particularly prominent. Land tenure was a mix of traditional authority from the Chief through village headmen, as well as through local government administration. Three chieftaincies configured the traditional structure of Chiweshe: Chief Makope (North); Chief Chiweshe (South); and, Chief Negomo (Central). For the purposes of local government administration and elections Chiweshe was divided into local wards. Traditional village structures operated under the authority of a headman. Clusters of villages included up to 300 people. Private land holdings comprised fields for women to plant and harvest crops and a 'garden' or field controlled by women for growing vegetables for their own consumption and for local sale. Such lands were differentiated from public grazing areas where cattle were herded. In addition to their agricultural work, women also had many domestic chores, often shared with children, that included cooking, grinding maize (by hand or at the grinding mill) and fetching water and firewood. Beer brewing was as another source of income for women as were crafts (knitting, sewing, pottery).

In 1993 a tarred road was the obvious symbol of independence. At that time this meant effective public transport and the development of commercial 'growth points' near the main road. West and east, there were well-maintained farm roads leading into the commercial farming areas. Modern houses stood alongside traditional kitchen huts as a mark of the relative prosperity of Chiweshe compared to other Communal Areas. Migrant remittances also built these houses. The proximity to Harare impacted on this prosperity through the prevalence of migrant labour, where men and women worked in town but kept a home in the rural areas. Women tended to return to the rural areas after marriage; migrant labour was a markedly male form of life.

The topography of Chiweshe was (and is) striking. Much of the lower part of the area was open territory, with few trees. The lack of firewood was a frequent complaint of women living here. Moving northward the terrain became more rugged and pronounced, with much scrub, forestry and impressive rock formations that stood like sculptures against the sky. These formations were dispersed throughout Chiweshe but provided more cover further north. The strategic implications of this diverse terrain for guerrilla infiltration during the war are easily appreciated. Various conversations in Chiweshe helped me understand its military importance during the war. Supply routes often determined the ability of guerrillas to operate in the area, as did the presence of police and army personnel. As one moved south these factors became important as supply routes were not always feasible and the police presence intensified, particularly towards Gweshe, Howard and Glendale in the direction of Salisbury (Harare). The southern part of Chiweshe was also difficult for guerrillas to penetrate because of the lack cover compared to the north, north-west and north-east parts of Chiweshe. The central cross-strip of Chiweshe was largely impenetrable due to heavy regime presence, particularly at Nzvimbo, where the main police station was located and from where security operations were run. This limited guerrilla activity in the south-east part of the lands. The south-west was also insecure because of the predominance of neighbouring commercial farms, which prevented easy access for the guerrillas. I learned that Chaona and Bare (in the north) were 'hot' areas, as guerrillas entered there from Madziwa Communal Lands and the Dande Valley through the commercial farms. The terrain around Bare and Goteka (in the north-east) lent itself to effective guerrilla warfare due to rocks and vegetation and was a launch pad for attacks into nearby commercial farms.

The landscape of Chiweshe made it vulnerable (in the eyes of the Rhodesian government) to guerrilla infiltration, and its proximity to settler farms, towns such as Glendale, Cenentary, Concession and Bindura and to Harare made it a threat to commercial farmers and white urban dwellers. Civilian rewards and sanctions informed the counterinsurgency policies of the Smith government prior to the setting up of PVs; leaflet distribution, rewards for information on guerrillas, collective fines for supporting guerrillas, confiscation of cattle, and arrest and torture were the hallmarks of a policy that failed to arrest guerrilla infiltration. The march of guerrilla activity toward the seat of settler power in Harare and the white settler commercial farms prompted the increased militarisation of a campaign to fight the guerrillas for the hearts and minds of the local people. Ranger quotes a police superintendent with charge over Chiweshe during the war, on the perceived strategic importance of Chiweshe to guerrilla operations:

> within weeks of their first attacks on European farms (in the north-east) the guerrillas had established themselves in the Chiweshe Tribal Trust Land. This area was a crucial importance for their operations. Surrounded by the Umvukwes, Centenary, Mtepatepa and Mazoe European farming areas, it provided nearby operational targets while at the same time serving as a safe retreat. Rocky outcrops, often densely covered with bush, are spread through Chiweshe, making it ideal territory for guerrilla hide-outs; moreover, the local people willingly offered what support and protection they could. (Ranger, 1985:282n106)

It was for these reasons that Chiweshe became the target of 'Operation Overload' and the control of space and bodies in PVs the route to preventing the advance of the guerrillas. Early attempts at 'consolidated villages' had been instituted in the Zambezi valley in the north-west of Zimbabwe in 1973. When the policy was then extended to Chiweshe, it was done so in a more exacting manner. The government propagated the lie that people had requested these centralised locations for their own protection and had been consulted as part of government policy. In parliament and government newspaper reports the protection of 'natives' from the guerrillas was the line taken (MLG Archive, Rhodesia Parliamentary Debates 1974; *Rhodesia Herald*, 1974 a-c).

The real motive for establishing PVs was one of white security; to halt the spread of guerrilla networks sweeping across the country (Weiss 1986:75). The strategy was to separate the guerrillas from their supplies of food and information. With no warning, the resettlement of Chiweshe's 48,960 people was initiated on 25 July 1974. It was completed within three weeks and was the largest operation of its kind (Weinrich 1976/77). This was the largest operation of the war involving Protected Villages. Twenty-one such PVs existed in Chiweshe from 1974 to 1979. People were uprooted and left in large fenced areas to build huts of poles and dagga (clay). Gathered in trucks, the people, and their possessions and what they could harvest of their crops, were dumped in large, high-fenced areas approximately 100 acres in size and left to build pole and dagga (mud) huts. Each family was allocated a space of 15 by 15 yards. On this they had to build basic accommodation, often dismantling building materials from their former homes. Sanitary conditions were abysmal; toilets had to be dug near dwellings. A water pump was situated outside the PV, as was a communal cattle barn. Huts were built in lines to facilitate control and at the centre of the PV was the strongly reinforced administrative centre that housed a European officer and ten to twenty African District Assistants (DAs).[8] These centres were called 'Keeps'.[9] The wire fence was topped with barbed wire and had a perimeter of floodlights facing outwards. Two exits marked the perimeter and were guarded round the clock.

The people of Chiweshe were not being protected by the state; rather, they found themselves under its intimidating gaze. Surveillance and control were the hallmarks of this policy and the immiseration of the people its effect. This constant security presence made the support of the locals for the incoming guerrillas more difficult but did not extinguish it.

The field study: Some methodological notes

Sources, sampling and interviews
The analysis presented in the following chapters rests primarily on a raft of 64 interviews conducted in 1993 in Chiweshe, Zimbabwe. The core focus of repeat interviews was a group of 35 women of different ages, social backgrounds and educational status who lived in Chiweshe during the war. Annex 2 provides biographical profiles of the women, outlining their backgrounds, similarities and differences. The interviews were supplemented by my observations and field notes that I documented during the 12-month period of visiting and living in Chiweshe. I also conducted interviews in Harare with women's organisations, churches and members of parliament to assess their opinion of women's experiences of independence. Additional interviews were conducted in an 'opportunistic' approach to sampling when travelling to different villages and when making contacts for Chiweshe in Harare. Over the course of the year I developed a strong base in five villages around Chiweshe. The interviews and fieldwork were supplemented by research undertaken at the National Archives in Zimbabwe and Library and Registry of the Ministry of Local Government (also in Harare) to

8   The DAs were often brought in from urban areas.
9   The term 'Keep' was used generally by the women in the study to refer to a PV. The terms are used interchangeably throughout the field analysis.

examine parliamentary, newspaper and non-governmental organisations' (NGO) records of the war as it was experienced in Chiweshe.
Through the Catholic Institute of International Relations (CIIR) Archive
in London I was able to access the papers and work of the Catholic Commission for Justice and Peace (CCJP) in Chiweshe during the war, where
it was a rare witness to life inside the PVs.

Women were asked to evaluate their own lives as much as was possible through interviews. The themes ran along a life-scale from their
childhood until the present. Historically marking this timescale is
the war of independence (1966–1979) and independence itself in 1980.
This process primarily involved the use of structured interviews and
in-depth or narrative interviews. The structured interviews focused on
personal details such as age, marriage and family. The in-depth interviews involved the collection of narratives to allow women the space
to recount their experiences of the war period. These were conducted
over a number of months and were supplemented by social visits and
chance meetings at the shops and the grinding mill. The building up of
trust, the development of a sense of timing with questions and learning
to respond to reluctance were all features that required practice and
patience on my part.

The sampling of women proved to be a random and snowballing
exercise. My main contact was a widowed teacher and shop owner
whom I met through the Catholic Church. She was very supportive and
the starting point in a web of contacts and friends. Another point of
contact was a local community development worker who helped out
on various projects in Chiweshe. She introduced me to three women
whom I later interviewed. Yet another area was entered with the help
of an NGO worker I met in Harare. He introduced me to a builder he
knew in Chiweshe. This man and his family became another base from
which to make contacts. As Chiweshe is a small area, my contacts soon
overlapped and I found that in some parts I had more than one contact. Contacts who I stayed with introduced me to family, neighbours
and friends and thus the circle of respondents grew quickly once I had
stayed a while in each of the areas.

The women I interviewed had very diverse socio-economic backgrounds.[10] Only two (a teacher/shop owner and a community
development worker) would fit into the category of the rural elite used
by Kriger. Other women had worked in town before marrying, many
had come straight from their home areas to Chiweshe after they had got
married. Few women, outside of the relatively well-to-do widows who
managed to maintain possession of their late husband's property, had
legal ownership of the land they work. Some women were divorced;
to leave their husbands, in most cases, meant to return to their father's
land and leave behind their children and the years of labour invested
in their husband's home area. Two others were married to teachers but
I did not take this to mean they were of the elite themselves, as their
educational backgrounds and household struggles placed them differently. Some women worked on small areas of land and lived in modest
conditions of one or two huts. Others did not have the luxury of arable

---

[10] See Appendix 2 for biographical profiles.

land and simply had a plot of land on which they had built a home. They depended on getting work from their better-off neighbours during the planting and harvesting seasons. Many women's husbands worked in Harare or one of the nearby local towns like Bindura or Mvurwi (formerly Umvukwes).

Such an amalgam of women was not the conscious result of any attempt to have a representative sample. It came rather from the trials of chance as I became enmeshed in the social fabric of Chiweshe. The network of women whose paths crossed at various junctures, be it the local shop, the women's club or the church meeting, was not a homogeneous one. In the local growth points/townships and villages the socio-cultural dynamics of society in Chiweshe are not to be found in the isolation of socio-economic groups but rather in their very co-existence. In terms of identifying women in relation to the war, I did not distinguish between participation and non-participation along military lines but took all women to have been directly or indirectly involved in and affected by the conflict. In terms of generations, the majority of the Chiweshe sample was made up of women who had been aged between 14 and 30 at the height of the war and thus at the time of their interviews fell into the 34-50 age group. These women are in essence 'the *Chimurenga* generation'.

The themes pursued in the following chapters are ones that arose during the course of interviews and were developed through the initial open coding of the transcripts and memo-writing to shape Gendered Localised Resistance as an analytical approach to understanding women's lives in war. The primacy of local relationships as a context, defining women's room for manoeuvre, came through in this process. The relationships of war highlighted included women's relations with the incoming guerrillas; women's relations with the DAs and soldiers who defined the state presence in the Keeps; and women's relations with other family members and neighbours. This last set of relations included women's relations with each other. In this context the following themes of revolutionary resistance, local resistance and daily survival were established:

- Food security – for themselves and for the guerrillas in the context of deliberate government strategies to control farming, food, markets and supplies to the guerrillas

- Surveillance – life in the PVs surveyed by the state, the guerrillas and by each other

- Economic survival – strategies and constraints related to farming, income-generation and prostitution

- Consciousness and politics, self-understanding about the war, expectations of the government and the guerrillas and about their own part in the war

- Emotional and psychological welfare – the social tensions within the community and the sense of loss relating to home, a way of life and material possessions.

Some of these themes emerged from direct questions based on background information, for example, the issue of surveillance. However, my discussions and conversations with women also yielded unexpected modalities. In relation to the experience of surveillance, for example, the atomisation of the community meant that neighbours were often at war with each other in a bid for survival. The issue of women having affairs with the DAs was one that came up by chance in one interview when the respondent commented on the moral decline of the Keeps. I took this up and asked other respondents for their reactions to this issue.

The second stage of the coding process involved a closer internal coding of these five themes, and mapping out the commonalties and differences of experience. The explanatory potential of food security to encapsulate the complexities of being 'caught in the middle' came about through the constant juxtaposition between the demands of family food provision and guerrilla supply networks that surfaced through the various readings and codings of the interviews.

The analysis of the war in Chiweshe from here on draws upon women's testimonies of war to shape thematic narratives. This involves a combination of substantiating quotation and the presentation of particular personal profiles. The assurance of anonymity, which was key to accessing interviewees and ensuring interviews were as open as possible, influenced the specificity of information that was possible or ethical to present in full.[11] The politics of the voice and memory were discussed in the Introduction in terms of the challenges of representation of the women's testimonies in providing an account of Zimbabwe's liberation war. In the following chapters extended quotes have been carefully chosen and analysed to reflect the varied personalities and characters with respect and without judgement. Some women were schoolteachers, community workers and well-educated businesswomen. Others had little formal education; in Elizabeth Schmidt's words they were 'peasants, traders and wives'. This use of direct quotation therefore leads to an inevitable unevenness in expression and fluency of English as a result of interpretation and translation infused with a desire to remain close to the vernacular. Variations in language are partly attributable to different interpreters and translators. I conducted the interviews in Shona with assistance from a network of local women who provided some interpretation in interviews that were often extended and involved sensitive questions and issues. The selection of and relationship with interpreters was thus very important, with the choice often dictated by the comfort respondents would or would not feel with someone older, younger, of different social standing or just a friend being present. The tapes were transcribed with the help of graduates and staff at the Uni-

11 In the course of my research I respectfully addressed older women and mothers in the traditional way of 'mother of X' for example, Mai Tawanda means 'mother of Tawanda'. However, in recounting their stories I wanted to give a more individual sense of them as they would have been as young women and mothers during the war, and so I chose a list of first names to assure their anonymity and yet preserve a sense of individual identity. Many of the older women I spoke to had anglicised names, reflecting the influence of colonialism as settlers such as farmers and missionaries often named children born on farm compounds or mission stations. In choosing names I have drawn on some of the actual names of women interviewed, but not in reference to the specific woman being quoted.

versity of Zimbabwe, which created another potential filter of language. In keeping with conventions of using oral testimonies I sought to be as true to the expression and vernacular as expressed by interviewees.

An analysis of women's participation in revolution
Gendered Localised Resistance is explored hereafter through an analysis of women's participation and agency in revolution that illuminates the struggles of resistance and survival in which women were engaged. This analysis deconstructs guerrilla-defined roles, collapses the public and the private spheres by exploring the impact of guerrilla war on the lives of women and highlights food provision as a site of struggle that constituted a terrain for women where they were 'caught in the middle' as they resisted and survived through many identities. The tensions of a food axis (feeding the guerrillas/feeding the family-self-community) are explored as a theme running through the data analysis.

The narratives of the women revealed conflicting relations and identities that defy the rigid categorisation of political participation in terms of activities and location for women in war. They take us through a series of themes that emerged from the data that cumulatively establish the importance of viewing women's self-identifications and differences as central to developing a fuller interpretation of gender identities and participation in war for women. These include:

1. The terrain of participation through women's perceptions of revolution and their contributions; this establishes the parameters of revolutionary resistance through the activities and consciousness of women in support of the struggle.

2. The community dynamics of living in revolution that challenge the primacy of collectivity and group consciousness as a major trope of political understanding and political action by women in the liberation struggle; this highlights the everyday struggles for survival that defined women's lives within the revolutionary context.

3. The modalities of resistance and participation by women wrought through the struggles around food security; these discussions reflect the interactions and contradictions of resistance and survival through an understanding of the dilemmas women of Chiweshe faced in withstanding the many pressures they faced during the revolutionary war.

4

Women's Perceptions of Revolutionary Participation | Understandings of Agency & Consciousness

Overview

Mapping the context of revolutionary participation for women in Chiweshe and the parts they played in the liberation struggle begins here, with the discussion of how and why they became involved in an anti-colonial war. A central theme emerges of overt revolutionary resistance and the dynamics and differences exhibited by women participating in such resistance.

The first aspect of participation refers to women's performance of guerrilla-defined roles; the types of participation required for the military effectiveness of the guerrilla war. These roles included the part played by women as fighters and providers of food. Yet an explanation of the gendered divisions of revolutionary labour only takes us so far, as what emerges is a much richer and complex rendering of participation by women. Their testimonies reflect the conflicted nature of participating through particular roles; these differences occur between women and can also be found within individual women who were ambivalent about how and why they participated in the war. In particular, there was positive consensus amongst many of the women about their important contribution in feeding the guerrillas. However, women participated in this revolutionary act in a context that was also shaped by their differing motivations, their conflicting and consenting relations with the guerrillas (support, fear, promises and threats), the government soldiers and DAs (collaboration, protection and intimidation) and, finally, their own mixed perceptions of participating in a revolutionary war.

The second aspect of participation addresses the thorny issue of political consciousness and motivations for women's participation as recounted by them. Once again, a rich complexity marks women's understanding of why they participated; the nature of women's political consciousness was differentiated and varied from slogan-led politicisation to grounded experiences of felt oppression. These women's understandings of the politics of war emerged from their own local experiences in the main and involved a language of resistance that is predicated on limited life choices, the degradation of poverty voiced as anger or the wordless lassitude of clapped hands to denote hopelessness. Because the motivations for women to participate were varied, they were not necessarily voluntary or consistent and question the extent to which a politicised collective consciousness underpinned women's participation. This opens the way to exploring the practical consciousness of women's struggles to develop strategies of survival and resistance in their engagement with a wider battleground of revolutionary war. In locating women's different experiences and motivations for participation, I suggest we need to understand the context of relationships and the daily struggles for survival which bounded women's lives as effectively as the wire fences of the Protected Villages.

Part I Forms of Revolutionary Participation

Defining women's participation in terms of roles provides a starting point from which to challenge tendencies in the feminist and historical literatures to reproduce a gendered division of labour analysis; it also extends our understanding of the battleground drawn by the women in Chiweshe. The predominant contribution cited by the women of Chiweshe was feeding the guerrillas and sustaining the food supply networks. I begin by exploring these women's perceptions of female fighters to illuminate the very contradictory opinions that surround this potent role of gender transformation in revolutionary wars. I conclude that forms of revolutionary participation (with respect to female fighters and to the generational groupings of women participating as food providers inside Chiweshe) are far from agreed on amongst and within women in terms of necessarily shared perceptions or expectations. This lack of an agreed understanding of such roles also defies the stereotypical embodiment of women in war as either heroic fighters or passive victims.

Female fighters: Women of a different kind

Perceptions of female fighters
Here, female fighters refer to women who left Chiweshe to train in Mozambique and to the incoming female comrades encountered by the women who stayed behind. A variation of this fighting role for women was working as arms and munitions carriers. This involved them going to Mozambique and carrying out the dangerous task of trekking from the training camps to the border with military supplies for the fighters inside Zimbabwe. The contradictions of female fighters as empowering role models or aberrant women that are a feature of feminist writings are also to be seen in the accounts of the women who remained in Chiweshe of their encounters with the comrades. There was no obvious or inevitable affiliation felt towards women who had broken the mould by taking up arms to fight alongside the male guerrillas. Instead, there was a range of reactions including admiration, fear, pity and revulsion.

Florence, while acknowledging the war as an unusual context that prompted challenges to gender identities nonetheless saw the female comrades as familiar:

[They were] just like us .... We were expecting different. We thought they were smaller than us because they were said to be terrorists .... They were putting on long trousers not female dresses .... We thought they were interested in war .... At that time they liked it because of the life we were living .... It wasn't usual .... Time was ripe for that.

Pardon was full of admiration for the women fighters:

People said the female comrades had gone to fight for the country .... I thought they were courageous. They were fighting the war.

There were, however, many voices of disapproval and fear with regard to the female comrades. On one level it concerned women being unsuited to war, on another it was expressed as fear of the dangers to which these young women were exposed:

Women were only there to help them (men) when they were fighting. They were helping them through giving them bullets and also carrying them. (Dorothy)

It wasn't good ... ah no, for a woman to walk such a long distance, it was difficult. Some were to die on the way, some were to die because of no food. (Ellen)

I felt they were risking their lives. The people in general took the women as prostitutes. (Lorine)

We felt that it was not the right thing to do. They had to be brave. (Farasia)

I felt it was risky for them. In general, people felt it was dangerous for women to go to the camps. (Juliet)

Phyllis's feelings of admiration were tinged with a sense of loss and sacrifice these women had made by stepping into unconventional roles that removed them from their families:

They were dressing like men and carrying guns and bags full of bullets .... We were feeling pain because they were women who were supposed to have been married and have their families but they had sacrificed their lives in order to free us, their parents .... We actually admired them. We were actually wishing if we were young we could have gone to Mozambique as well.

However, Tendai demonstrated internal dissonance around the issue of female comrades in her assertions of sameness and difference. In terms of appearance and tasks undertaken, she saw male and female comrades as the same:

They were just looking like male comrades because their way of dressing was the same. They were both wearing trousers. In the end it was very difficult to tell who was a male and who was a female .... There were no specific duties for female or for male comrades. When the struggle started they would start fighting. They had the same responsibility in the war.

Yet in terms of the propensity to violence, she saw female fighters as unfeeling and violent. Her descriptions of them suggested that they possessed hyper-masculine traits:

These female comrades were more violent than the male comrades .... The

male comrades were afraid of the female comrades .... Female comrades had
no patience at all. Once they saw the soldiers passing, they would not let them
pass, they would start shooting. Unlike male comrades who would sometimes
say 'No, do not shoot them. Let them go'. Male comrades had feelings unlike
female comrades.

These views co-existed with an open admiration for women fighters that
made Tendai want to join them:

> When I saw the female comrades, I was very much interested and I actual-
> ly wanted to go to Mozambique. But the problem was that my brother also
> wanted to go and the comrades said they could not take both of us and also my
> mother had twins and I was looking after the other baby. Therefore, if I was to
> go, the baby was going to have problems missing me. The comrades said they
> could not take me on those grounds. They said my mother was going to be
> disappointed and as a result I was going to die before I arrived in Mozambique
> .... I just admired other female comrades carrying guns so I wanted to carry
> a gun as well. Also, through the politicisation which we received, I found it
> necessary to go to war and fight against our enemy and force the masses from
> the bondage of oppression.

Judith's perceptions were equally complex, with admiration, disapproval and exaggerated violent traits being directed at the women fighters:

> They were courageous and never retreated. At our place when forced to go in
> to the Keeps, women like Amai Teurai Ropa[1] fought bravely and this resulted
> in the death of many soldiers.

Yet she also claims that:

> We disliked it. We thought it was not very important for women to go to war.
> [The elders] disliked it because they did not like war in general. They thought
> women would be easily killed because they did not know how to handle a
> gun. Men thought [that they] were hard-hearted so that if comrades were
> accompanied by female comrades, they would have the courage to kill ....
> Because most of the people who died in our area, their deaths were caused by
> female comrades.

Challenging this latter image of extreme and violent women, Margaret
saw the female fighters as less violent than their male comrades:

> They were dressed like men and the guns were the same and even their dress-
> ing. You could only tell she was a woman because of breasts .... We were
> happy because it showed us that all our children were fighting for us. Also
> women's voices were soft unlike men's voices, which were always high and
> harsh.

These variations of gendered perceptions with respect to the identity of
female fighter illustrate the complexity within such a categorical depic-

---

[1] Teurai Ropa Nhongo was the *Chimurenga* name given to Joyce Mujuru, who is now Vice
President of Zimbabwe. Her *nom de guerre* meant 'spill blood'. She is the wife of Solomon
Mujuru (Rex Nhongo), who was Deputy Commander to Josiah Tongogara and lead the ZAN-
LA guerrilla forces in Mozambique. Today, they are powerful members of the ZANU-PF
elite.

tion of women's actions in war. Such perceptions indicate the lack of consensus on the place of women fighters in the war and the challenges they posed to traditional gender relations and identities.

A tale of two comrades: Sarah and Taurai
The different experiences of the female fighters I interviewed also highlight the difficulties of making an agreed assessment of the possibilities of transforming women's socio-political position through such participation. Taurai and Sarah came from very different socio-economic and educational backgrounds, were recruited in very different ways and after independence lived in entirely different conditions.

Sarah: Sarah was 12 years old when she and her sister were *Chimbwidos* for the comrades. She lived with her sister, brother, father and stepmother in one of the Keeps and they struggled to grow enough food to feed themselves. In October 1978 she was caught in a crossfire between soldiers and guerrillas and was taken by the guerrillas for her own safety. Sarah's sister had already decided to join the comrades. Her brother wrote to their mother and informed her of this. In an effort to prevent her daughter from going away with the comrades, Sarah's mother informed the Rhodesian soldiers and was arrested along with Sarah's sister. They were severely beaten and forced to reveal the location of the guerrilla base camp. By this time, Sarah was actually at the camp, having taken food to the comrades. The soldiers attempted to ambush the guerrillas, who fled, taking Sarah with them on the long dangerous trek to Mozambique. Of this, Sarah said:

> We were in the Keeps. So when the time came, I go outside the Keeps to the fields, that is the time. We were used to give them food. At that time they [comrades] heard that my sister is now at the soldiers. And they said, 'you are not going back to the Keep. If you go there, they are going to kill you.' Since my sister had told them 'my young sister is there with the comrades' .... I was thinking of going back to my family, but there was no chance .... But people, it was not fair .... I was out. We were supposed to go together with my sister. Then her mother tell the soldiers. At that time I was out and the mother go to the camp and tell them. Then the soldiers beat her and she told the soldiers that we are going to the base to meet comrades today. And at that time we can go to the comrades; there is action we can do there to let out the comrades near the base. Just chop a tree; the time we chop a tree can see the comrades around. And then that my sister told the soldiers that tip. Anyway, then they phoned to Centenary, [to] all Keeps, and the soldiers come to that place, that mountain, Banjke [near Jingamvura] .... Then they started to fire there. And I was there. I just wake up and I didn't know what can I do. The soldiers said 'shoot there'. They started to fire. When they fired some bombs there I managed to run away from the place and the comrades followed after me and we came to that Mapuya mountain in Chinehasha. We footed from Banjke to Chinehashe and we stayed for seven days without food, without drinking water .... We started six o'clock, then we reach near that mountain at 6 a.m. Then we started to climb that mountain from six up to 12 only – top of that mountain, same day ... we are just walking. They say 'there are soldiers, they can follow us', so that we can walk faster. Then we rest and arrive to

Muzarabani at 6 p.m. Then I was tired again, the whole body was full of fluid. At other times they were happy to carry me, to carry me up. Then we reach there; we stay there two months in Muzarabani. After that two months we go to Mukumbura, near the border [with Mozambique]. Then we crossed the border. On the border there were many land mines ... and anti-personnels. So they used these spades to move the land mines and you put it on the side, but you put it carefully. If you shake you are going to die so you walk carefully.

After her training in Mozambique, she carried weapons up to the border. Despite promises of an education, Sarah had to wait until the war was over to return to primary school:

They [the guerrillas] said, 'At the Keeps, you are not going to school so that at Mozambique you are going to school'. But I did not manage to go to school. Others they managed to go there .... At the time, other kids, they go there. I was not around at the camp; I was out carrying weapons so that I didn't manage it .... Others, they were used to carry weapons over a short distance; others, long distances .... According to age .... Other times, there was seriously fought war in this country so that they can say 'no one is going to stay in the base, you are all going to carry weapons to Zimbabwe'. Since they don't have weapons at that time. So everybody, you can carry weapons but in different ways. They can leave two or three people on the base .... We used to carry the rounds .... We used to carry them by road, just use the trees, then you lift and put on the back like a baby and then move .... We took them from Chitima. Actually it is very far ... to the border. But there were different groups where you can move up and down .... [It took] about a week to reach the border .... You would bury them and the other group can take from that point.

As well as shortages of food and clothes in the camps, Sarah and the other girls faced problems of hygiene in the limited availability of soap to wash clothes and cotton for sanitary protection:

Life was difficult. About clothes, they came from Beira. We were given the clothes but it was not enough. The shoes, others we can find one pair, two with one leg! About the food, it was not enough.[2] We go to the village. So I can take my jersey and give for food. So if I don't mind ... no soap for bathing, you're just using some trees, outside of the tree [bark] .... The girls faced problems when they are menstruating. They don't have cotton; they don't have soap to wash their clothes. They just use water only. And sometimes we cannot find water. We spend almost three or five days with no water.

Sarah says the comrades were sympathetic to their problems and tried to get supplies for them. Despite training and collective politicisation, a sense of isolation and fear came through in Sarah's experiences of political education in the camps:

We were many girls there, but you talk about life? At that time we used talk about politics only. The time we can go in groups talking about politics .... It is only that I learned about leaders. I know the names and positions of the leaders and their use in the struggle .... To sing *Chimurenga* songs when we

[2]   In fact, Sarah had a funny encounter at an Assembly Point at the end of the war. As she was waiting to be demobilised she met a woman who was wearing the matching shoe to hers!

were on the parade .... It was not allowed [to talk about home]. When you talk about the home, you are thinking about going back so it was not allowed. If you talk about your home, you can go back to your family[3] .... At that time, we were not interested [in talking about home] since the politics they were getting inside our brains so that we are not thinking about our families .... People, they were used to that life so that they are happy, they are forcing their matters to be happy. If they saw you quiet, there was other person called PC, either it is a girl or a man. She can come at your place ... then she start to question you or she started to sing some songs for you to disturb your mind .... That's why they decided them to go to school. They go there and do some drama and some plays there .... That time it was a difficulty for a person to be interested but you make it just to force yourself to be happy. Just to sing some song, a *Chimurenga* song, and doing some plays.

Before leaving Chiweshe the comrades told local people to inform Sarah's father that she had gone with the comrades and not to worry about her. She was not reunited with their family until 1980, when the long process of demobilisation and reintegration brought her home to face the task of rebuilding her life. Sarah had attended school to Grade Three and being able to go back to school was part of her demobilisation package. By 1993, when I met Sarah in Chiweshe, she was a single mother living with her father and struggling to rear chickens and undertake informal trading in order to support her family. Sarah's story reveals a host of war identities in her situation as daughter, sister, *Chimwido* and comrade, and in the mixed motivations of fear and support that placed her in the wrong place at the wrong time.

Taurai: Taurai's father was a schoolteacher and unlike many fathers at that time actively supported the education of his daughter. She was 15 years old and in Form Two at a boarding school in the eastern part of Zimbabwe when she and four other girls decided to join the war. Unlike Sarah, hers was a positive decision of voluntary support influenced by her father's political activities and reinforced by the political education of the camps. Taurai's self-identification as a politico and fighter is more confident than that expressed by Sarah:

> We were five, three died and two came back. They died in the struggle. These were five, five *young* girls and we had to walk about 200 kilometres! It was not a joke .... We knew they would be hurt but what we actually said [was], 'We are going to fight for our country, we don't care. We will see our parents when we come back with the guns' .... When I was growing up, I began to see it. I began to see it when my Dad was detained in 1967, that's when I felt it. I was wondering why. My Dad was detained and he was the only breadwinner; my Mom would work and see what she could do and so forth. He was detained because he was participating in politics. So from there I don't know why it just grew. I used to see women in high-density areas. They used to plough patches and you would see them being chased by the police and so forth. You know it touched me from then. I said okay, these people are trying to make ends meet. They want to fend for their families and by so doing they

---

[3] If they talked about their families they were taken further away from the Zimbabwe border.

are trying to go and do this ... ploughing so that whatever yields they get they subsidise their families. Very few women, you know, during the colonial period worked; the majority were men. So if a man didn't get employed then, as the father was the breadwinner, the family would suffer .... Now having gone to that situation and having thought as well when we received our political classes, political orientation, that there was a need to fight for our country, and actually I agreed with some of the things that were taught because of my experience.... You would actually see there was a discrimination in terms of there was racism; you would find a black [person] is not allowed to go to a certain place and so forth ....

I was 15 when I received my military training in 1976. After my military training, I was also trained as a nurse. I stayed in various camps in the Operational Areas [in] Mozambique. Actually, I was treating all those combatants who would have been wounded in the battlefield .... All duties that were supposed to be done by a human being, not [just] a woman now, because we were treated as equal so we actually played a vital role. From there that is where I learned the tough time and I thought that is what pushed me to be in politics. This time when we were in the struggle, life was not easy. In terms of accommodation, I'm talking of a person who was staying in the bush. In terms of food we used to get food from different countries. And you would find that ... we had to go for two or three weeks without food and so forth; life was very difficult, there were a lot of diseases and you know we didn't have shelter, we used just take grass and make a bed out of grass because there were insects which would actually bite and you could end up having wounds. Some lost their fingers; it was a terrible situation. It was a situation for one to grow through. Being a woman, and at my age, it was very difficult.

Taurai was very adamant about the equality of the struggle, which she saw as a key part of the socialist platform of the revolution. Looking back, she says, 'I still feel that I went to the liberation struggle to fight for these women's rights ... that women should also be treated equal with other people because the role played by women is not that different from what men are playing.' Taurai's account of the war, with all its dangers and suffering, portrays it as a formative experience that shaped her commitment to socialism and her involvement in politics. Sarah, on the other hand, has a fatalistic attitude about her war-time experiences and now has little interest in politics. Her main concern is finding ways of making money to support herself and her son. This is not to say that Taurai does not face difficulties herself in her chosen path, it rather illustrates that two women can have very different experiences of the same role in a revolutionary war. It is in understanding and appreciating such differences that we may begin to realise the unrealistic expectations of women hoping to transform their subordinate status through the mere act of participating in a national liberation struggle. The next section explores such differences for the majority of women in my sample who remained in the Chiweshe area and were central to maintaining the guerrilla war through food provision.

'They would have died of hunger': Feeding the comrades

Food provision emerged as the major theme of self-identification for many of the women when they talked about their participation in the liberation war.[4] There was an apparent self-consciousness and confidence amongst the women that they had contributed to the success of the liberation war through food provision. Food provision to the guerrillas included a wide range of activities carried out by women in support of the struggle:; purchasing supplies such as soap, cigarettes, clothes and meat; cooking large quantities of sadza; requesting and organising supplies from neighbours to share the costs; killing their own chickens and goats; sneaking food out of the Keeps to the fields; bringing supplies from Salisbury [Harare]; contributing money for goods; organising with other women and young girls and boys to co-ordinate supplies and delivery; and washing clothes and providing warm water for bathing. In addition to requests for food, women whose husbands were working in town were asked to provide money to the comrades. These tasks, individually and collectively, were the basis of the food supply networks organised by local war committees. Parallel to these material needs was the constant request for information on the soldiers' whereabouts and the activities of neighbours who might be sell outs. The varied perceptions women had of their contribution and highlight the mixed motivations for such participation is explored below. Whilst most women saw their participation as essential to the ultimate victory, there were others who view it less strategically, as simply part of the confusion of being caught up in war.

A revolutionary contribution?
Alice, Victoria, Emily and Stella were just some of the women who claimed the comrades would have 'died of hunger' if women had not cooked for them and delivered food supplies to them. Ellen, however, did play down the situation of women in the Keeps as well as food provision as a contribution to the war. Such perceptions of their own actual contributions are mixed for a number of reasons. One reason is a gender-defined value of contribution. The relative importance of women as food providers was stressed by Florence, who said that '[w]omen contributed better [than men] because comrades could have died if they were not given food'. In opposition to this view, Joanne fully appreciated the value of women's role as food providers, but set it in a gendered context of contribution where men, because of money, gained greater respect even in the area of supplies:

> You know what, in the war women had to work. I can say they had to participate in the cooking. The cooking was very important for the comrades because they had to find someone to cook for them, to get the power to walk these mountains, climbing up. Someone cooked for them .... Women, they contributed but they didn't get more. The men then got more because the

---

4   The participation of women in the revolution as food providers is taken up in more detail in Chapter 6.

money they had they would give them, the clothes, the shoes. Whereas the women were just there for cooking, I can say.

Within the apparent consensus of food provision as a proper contribution by women to the war effort there is dissonance with respect to motivations for such support. Victoria was conscious and proud of having made a significant contribution to independence. Yet, at the time, her account revealed that she had been very uncertain of victory and feared retribution by the comrades if she did not provide food. Her words convey pride, uncertainty, fear and her ambivalence and mixed feelings lead to an underestimation of her contribution. When first asked if she played a role in the struggle she said: 'I never did anything'. But, almost immediately, when we talked about food provision she said, '[m]yself, I just gave them food but I was not quite sure whether we were going to win the liberation struggle. Also, I was scared so I had no choice but to give them food'. Following the end of the war and with the benefit of hindsight, she said '[y]es, I realised that I had contributed to the achievement of independence because I was giving them food. If they were not being given food they should have died of hunger. And also they should have killed me'.

Desperation, fear, war fatigue and hopelessness marked Florence's motivations for providing food and defined the contradiction of support and coercion in her actions:

From our experience in the Keep we thought they would not win .... We wanted the war to come to an end [and] .... We thought if they do not eat they would die before the end of the war and so feeding them was important in order for them to become strong .... [If women refused to feed the guerrillas]. They were going to punish us.

Emily voiced apparent support and political motivation but also fear of the guerrillas. While she said 'they treated us well', she also claimed that '[w]e were scared that they could not understand our situation'. Veronica said she continued to supply food to the comrades from inside the Keeps 'out of sympathy'. Her story reflected different experiences and reactions to her relations with the guerrillas and DAs over food. She seemed largely willing and proud of her role as a food provider to the guerrillas but still expressed fear and anger at the demands this placed on her. Veronica also saw the contribution of women as food providers as based on women's gullibility in the face of guerrilla demands: 'Women supplied food which was very important .... Women are gullible, if asked for anything they just give in quickly. So when we were asked for food we readily gave it'. It is in this context of mixed motives that any understanding of guerrilla support through food provision has to be explored.

Their different perceptions and experiences indicate that their roles were not necessarily agreed in terms of a shared understanding of what role they were playing and why, and that the situation in which they found themselves was new in many respects. These women shared no expectations of what they should do or how they should participate. This poses a serious challenge to the assumption in some feminist approaches of a causal link between the roles taken up by women in revolution and a simultaneous emergence of political consciousness for women. Far from this expectation (or thwarted expectation, as some of the literature claims), the forms of these women's participation and their political consciousness are in reality deeply conflicted and certainly not a collective phenomenon. In the next section, I identify the elements of an individuated consciousness that may help explain why women's participation and consciousness yielded such differences in their personal narratives of living through revolutionary war. I suggest it is to the daily engagement of women with the context of war that we must turn to better understand their participation in and experiences of revolutionary war.

Part II Consciousness and Context: Narratives of Practical Engagement

What motivated women's participation in, and support for, the struggle? What were women's understandings of the anti-colonial struggle and to what degree are such understandings a result of reflexive experience or guerrilla mobilisation efforts? I draw upon the schema of consciousness, outlined in Chapter 2, to highlight the formative influence of the daily engagement with the context of revolutionary war on women's participation and perceptions of participation in revolution.

Elements of political consciousness

Anti-colonial consciousness: Speaking in revolutionary tongues
The first element of women's revolutionary consciousness is the anti-colonial sentiment that reflects in large part the experiences of politicisation by the nationalist parties and the guerrillas and political education through newspapers and radio for those who had access to such media. From this perspective we find strong voices of political sloganeering. *Pace* Kriger, I do not dismiss the significance of the political slogans used by women because often they are supported within the interviews by life experiences voiced in terms of felt oppression. If in Chiweshe the women found the language of Marxism suitable to their cause, then should that be questioned so harshly? This, of course, is tempered by the influence of political education by the comrades that was often channelled through fear. Polly, a *Chimwido*, lapsed easily into such slogans, interspersing them with insights from her own life:

> They were talking about the oppression of the blacks by the whites. They wanted their country back from the whites .... They wanted the blacks to have equal rights as the whites. The whites were selfish because they were exploiting us in our country .... The inequality also affected me since all the means of production were controlled by the whites. Because of this the blacks rebelled against the whites .... Blacks were working very hard for the whites. [They] were given very little money which ... could not buy anything. But the whites were being paid more.

Hilda and Victoria gave voice to similar pronouncements:

> I also looked forward to win so that we could govern ourselves because [the] white government was oppressive. (Hilda)

> They said their aim was to overthrow the colonial regime so that we could have black government and become free from the bondage of oppression by the whites. (Victoria)

Women's expectations were raised through the promises made by the revolutionary movements concerning land, living conditions and, for women specifically, transformations in gender relations and inequality. In terms of living conditions, expectations of change centred on access to and ownership of fertile land (Hilda; Margaret) that is articulated by some women as the taking of land from the white settlers (Dorothy; Veronica; Phyllis; Joanne; Tendai); black self-rule (Judith; Tendai); better pay for black workers (Victoria); good houses (Dorothy; Margaret); increased crop production (Hilda); better crop prices (Polly); no taxes on dogs, cattle or huts (Judith); free education (Sarah); tarred roads (Phyllis); lower prices of goods (Pardon; Phyllis); and money and compensation for the costs of war (Hope; Joanne). Many women assumed, or were told, that the farms of the whites would simply be taken and given free to the people. These promises encouraged women like Polly to participate:

> They [guerrillas] had a lot of discussion that is why they were cooking food for the freedom fighters. They wanted independence to come and see changes taking place .... We talked about farming projects, to have more land and to be free to do what we wanted .... We expected changes in the price of our crops because during the colonial regime our crops were being bought at a very low price. We also expected to see change on the side of women. We wanted women to be employed .... Some of the promises have been fulfilled even though some have not.

Sarah's understanding of such promises reveals the almost utopian effect they engendered:

> After independence, they promised us to stay at the farms; those things that belong to the whites, they say 'they're going to be yours. You are going to sit in that town, Harare. You are going to chase away the whites and you are going to school free, you are not going to pay'.

Specific promises to women included opportunities for education and income- generating projects (Veronica; Polly), employment opportunities for women (Polly) and equal work opportunities with men (Judith). Another set of promises involved changes in the law to benefit women in terms of equal pay (Phyllis; Florence) and entitlement to a husband's property in situations of inheritance and divorce (Judith; Veronica). However, Ellen, who was a community worker with women, saw the changes for women to be a demand that arose after the war was over rather than part of the revolutionary agenda. In her words, 'There were no promises .... but after the war when women started saying "we fight the war being together and we were equal in the war so we need our rights"'. In the main, the women expressed discontent and disillusionment about the delivery of these promises in the first decade of the post-independence period:

> Women were promised to use machines for knitting jerseys and there were some areas which were promised to be under the leadership of women but today nothing has taken place. (Polly)

> They [comrades] promised land. 'People will have enough land for plough-ing. People will have jobs and you are going to stay freely'. But nothing has been done, you know. You should compare what has been said and what has been done this time and print because we are staying where we were. Very few things have changed but what you have seen I can say, the country still belongs to the whites. Because we don't have even the land. (Ellen)[5]

These promises were often discussed at meetings held by the guerril-las to encourage local support for the war and to open up the chains of supply. There was a distinction between the *pungwes* held at night in the bush and the afternoon meetings held in the fields once people moved to the PVs. Some women claimed to have attended more meet-ings when they were in the PVs because it was easier for the guerrillas to target groups when they went to the fields outside the curfew limits (Agnes). Others say such gatherings became impossible because of the surveillance of the DAs and sell outs (Phyllis). The late-night meetings were focused around songs and slogans through which the guerrillas politically educated local people. They were also a forum for planning and receiving food supplies. However, it seems that as the war went on, the political education of the *povo* became less of a priority. This is partly due to the effectiveness of the PVs in separating the people and the guerrillas; they could only meet for brief periods in the after-noon when people were tending their fields. These exchanges involved requests for food and information rather than any express attempt to politicise the people.

Tendai, a *Chimbwido*, was enthusiastic about the meetings, saying that 'Every time they came we had to have a meeting. But the meetings were not frequently held. We were used to the comrades to the extent of missing them when they were not around. We were actually enjoying their meetings'. Polly and Veronica described themselves as cheer lead-ers at these meetings:

> We were morale boosters at meetings though singing and dancing. (Veronica)

> 'They [women] were also giving advice regarding the war and motivating the freedom fighters .... We were encouraging the comrades, *Mujibhas* and *Chimbwidos* and also the masses in general to be strong in the war. We were

---

5   By the late 1990s the issue of land redistribution was at a crisis point in Zimbabwe as the government initiated a programme of reappropriating some of the white-owned commer-cial farms. The post-independence period was marked by intermittent pushes on this issue, though it has been questionable the degree to which there has been a clear, consultative policy to ensure a peaceful and successful transition that will not adversely affect the na-tional economy (which is dependent on the commercial agricultural sector) and will fulfill the criteria of fair redistribution among Zimbabwean farmers. This issue is taken up in the Introduction and the Conclusion in the discussing the legacies of the liberation war and the contemporary crisis in Zimbabwe.

motivating one another not to turn back. 'Forward with the War' –'*Pamberi ne Chimurenga!*' – were our words of encouragement. (Polly)

Agnes and Dorothy stressed the comrades' attempts to explain the purposes of the war at such meetings:

> When they first came we did not know what their motives were but later they explained that they were fighting against the oppression. The comrades did not only explain their motives ... but they would use every opportunity available to explain to people, *especially to men*. (Agnes, (my emphasis))

> When they [comrades] came at our place they asked us about our life history. When they discovered that someone's life was tough they would advise you to go with them .... They could go to places like schools and force the students to go to war. But first of all they had to motivate you, telling people what was wrong with the Smith regime, highlighting all the negative aspects. After that they would ask you to go to war. (Dorothy)

There were shortcuts, however, in the politicisation process, whereby political awareness became secondary to considerations of security and the need to access supplies:

> They were just coming without having *pungwes* .... They could only come on rare occasions and they were not coming in large numbers .... They were only asking for food. (Victoria)

The links with the people in the villages were a strategic necessity to win support and food. Yet the balance between the giving of food and the understanding of politics was far from clear. Sarah gave an interesting explanation of this exchange of food for politics between local people and the guerrillas:

> They [comrades] said, 'We are your brothers, can you cook sadza for us? We are now fighting for our Zimbabwe', and they started to give us politics .... We were able [to understand them] because they give us politics and sing some songs there .... It was not difficult for them [people] to refuse. The comrades used to tell them politics first, to know why they are fighting, why they are against the soldiers. Then people feel to give them food .... Sometimes they can use force but that force can make the people get to their side.

Political education was therefore marked by a tense backdrop of fear and force. *Pungwes* were often a difficult setting as people felt captive to the discussions of guerrillas even if they sympathised with their aims and the politicisation of oppression resonated with their own experiences. Tecla articulated this captive feeling, saying that 'During [the] *Chimurenga* war the comrades used to call us for meetings during the night and they would dismiss us whenever they feel like it, even after midnight.'

Both Tendai and Ellen highlighted the forced attendance at meetings and forced 'selection' of supporters:

> They were not selecting. Everyone who was still a boy and a girl was a *Mujibha* and a *Chimwido*' (Tendai)

> Ah, there were no chances. There wasn't any chance of saying no. You have to go whether you like it or not. (Ellen)

Such incidents reflect the limited room for manoeuvre that some women and girls faced. The meetings placed them at risk as they had to find their way home after the curfew, where anyone moving around after dark could be shot on sight:

> We feared the comrades .... If people dismissed late they could meet soldiers and get killed. But sometimes the soldiers ran away .... A friend of mine's sister was killed. When my friend came home to report, she too was killed. (Judith)

Another focus of such meetings was guerrilla security and the issuing of summary justice to reported sell outs, a strategy that was often counterproductive in terms of gaining local support.[6] Local people were constantly warned that punishment or death would be the price of selling out comrades to the Rhodiesan soldiers. When Sarah was a *Chimwido*, between the ages of eight and twelve, she attended afternoon meetings with the comrades at their base:

> Comrades, they wanted to hear from many people. If many people tell them this is a sell out, the comrades will call [him/her] to the base. Then he first give politics; if he refused, then they can do what they want.

Anti-colonial consciousness: Remembering the bad times
The second element of women's revolutionary consciousness is that of personal awareness and experience, whereby the women recounted stories from their own lives to explain their political understanding of the armed struggle. The political slogans of the revolutionaries appealed and endured not only because they were used at meetings but also because, in many cases, they tapped into the felt grievances of black women living under colonial rule. The stories of the women I interviewed are just as 'political' as revolutionary slogans in creating a consciousness of oppression and resistance:

> I thought it was possible to get independence. We just believed that [the guerrillas] were not lying because [of] what they were telling us; the hardships they were talking about were true. We were actually being ill-treated by the whites. So when they came saying they wanted to fight against the whites, we believed that it was going to happen and that we were going to attain independence. (Susan)

Some believed that the injustices arose in direct response to the agricultural policies of the settler state that demanded more and more of peasant farmers by way of taxes, land, farming methods and soil conservation policies:[7]

> It was difficult for us to speak out on the issues at that time. It was painful to us and we felt very much cheated. This in the end made people realise that we were oppressed. (Agnes)

These intrusions of the state met with growing acts of civil disobedience

---

[6]   The detail of sell outs and information-gathering is addressed in the next chapter.

[7]   This has some resonance with Terence Ranger's concept of peasant resistance, though in this analysis it is just one element of women's differentiated revolutionary consciousness. See my discussion of Ranger (1985) in Chapter 1.

and resistance. Hilda recalled the slashing of tobacco crops in the commercial farms around Chiweshe that marked this increased militancy during the 1960s:

> ZANU once came when people destroyed tobacco in the farms .... Because the people were fighting against the whites in the farms .... Only white farmers were allowed to grow crops for sale. They also allowed whites only to use fertiliser while blacks used manure only.

Such tactics were part of wider acts of civil resistance taking place in urban areas and reflected a groundswell of anti-colonial sentiment. Anna, a trainee teacher at the time, recalled that '[i]n those days you find so many strikes at companies for wages and schoolchildren were also striking because many of the colleges were run by whites'. The perceived power of the colonial state gave rise not only to feelings and actions of anger and resistance but also to a sense of futility in terms of possible change. Rachel remembered that the elders 'talked about what they had experienced. We couldn't expect that anybody could rule this country except Smith .... Even the whites never thought or dreamt the situation would change'. Maggie saw the comrades as the only option in a situation that offered little hope of change, saying that 'they [the people] like that one that fights for the people. If you treat me hard and someone says "I can take care of you", then of course you will listen to that one .... That is why people said it was better to vote for the comrades'.

Hilda attributed her awareness of economic exploitation and racism to working on the commercial farms around Chiweshe harvesting tobacco:

> I was picking up tobacco. We were working the whole day and then go to school in the evening. We were getting money for our school fees from the farm .... The difference was in language. The rural people could not understand English. At the same time, they [settlers] could not understand Shona. The white people did not want the black person near them when they were having their meals. Also, the food which the black people was eating was very bad as compared with that of the whites. The type of food which was given to the blacks was not suitable to be eaten by a human being, maybe to pigs or dogs .... The life was hard but we could not think of any solution because we were oppressed .... I knew that blacks in Zimbabwe were oppressed by the white government. People were not talking about it but one was in a position to tell that we were oppressed because people could work very hard but be given six or seven dollars at the end of the month .... It was actually taboo for a white man to shake hands with a black man. They were not coming into the communal areas. They could only come to the Administrator's Office and Magistrate Court at Concession .... You could only see them when you have gone to the white farms.

This dehumanising experience of racial oppression is reinforced by Phyllis, who said '[i]t was true that the whites were richer than us. And because of that, they were looking down upon us. They actually saw us as dogs'. Like Hilda, Polly did not need to be enlightened by revolutionary slogans to know she was oppressed:

> I was aware that we were oppressed, [but] not because somebody told me about the oppression. Even though some women were not aware of the oppres-

sion, myself, I was aware and I think this differed because thinking differs. What one might think to be bad, one might look at it as good or not so bad.

This latter point is illustrated by Judith's experience, where her awareness that the racial divisions of wealth and the structure of society were not as natural an order as she once supposed increased with age:

> Long back we did not know that it was bad. We just thought that the white men's lifestyle was like that and not meant for the black men .... I was aware the whites were rich whilst the blacks had to live a life of struggling because they did not have enough resources. The blacks were poor .... Comparing our rural life with their life in towns, it was different. The rural life was tough, while the life for the whites was just too good. People were living in good houses in town and having good food whilst those in the rural areas were having poor health services and they had nothing to feed themselves.

These interrelated workings of i) revolutionary political and ii) experienced personal consciousness still leave us with the fear and uncertainty and the internal contradictions voiced by the women of Chiweshe in their perceptions of the war. This uncertainty suggests another form of consciousness forged through the allegiances and relationships of war that that affects, adversely or positively, their political understanding and experience of the revolutionary struggle.

The consciousness of context
This third dimension of consciousness arises from the practical engagement with the context of war through various and conflicted relations, old and new, as well as the emergence of new felt oppressions and personal struggles for survival. Gendered localised resistance (as outlined in Chapter 2) establishes the basis for this claim by extending local resistance to include interaction with struggles for survival and advocating 'resistant subjectivity' as a premise of political agency. This claim is further substantiated in the next two chapters in respect of the importance of the context of war in affecting women's agency, consciousness and identities in the course of revolution. What emerged from the women's testimonies is the strong sense that their motivations for participation were mixed and very much embedded in the uncertainty of day-to-day life in war. The desperation of life in the rural areas, both before and during the war, buttressed by promises of liberation, underpin the variegated nature of their revolutionary consciousness. The consciousness of such a context included personal struggles that are not directly, or necessarily, anti-colonial, for example, family and household tensions. In some instances, these struggles pre-dated the war and continued as a feature of life for women during the war. They often reflect the desperate home situations that prompted girls and women to join the struggle.

For example, Dorothy (a *Chimwido*) was equivocal about her own political understanding at the time but was adamant that she was desperate to escape her terrible home life: 'I was young .... I had no negative attitude towards the comrades. Actually, the comrades were staying at our house during the evenings and it was better to be with them. I did not care if I was going to die'. This fatalism may be linked to her deprived childhood where she lived with a drunken grandmother and had to look after her brother and sisters from an early age. By the age of 19 she had a broken marriage and a child of her own.

The context of war was also marked by a complexity of nationalist politics that was played out in conflicted local relations. Rosy suggested an 'us and them' division between leaders and followers in understanding the politics of revolution.[8] She also claimed that a lack of understanding on the part of the followers reduced politics to a simple matter of hating those who were not in your party:

> There wasn't much change, but the problem was that most of these young people didn't have full understanding of what politics is. Those are the people who sort of harassed others. For those who knew politics and understood it, all these political leaders never harass each other. They did gather at times, they talked to each other, giving each other ideas. But we, through our not understanding what is going on, just hated somebody because they are supporting the other party. So all those who were supporting the parties which did not win, some were with their houses burned, some were beaten'. (Rosy)

This context is clearly defined by women in their relations with the guerrillas and the Rhodesian soldiers and DAs.[9] In part, it was the situation in the Keeps and the struggle to survive the uncertainty of war that prompted women to support the guerrillas. Emelda joined the struggle in 1976 when she was 13, having already served as a Chimbwido:

> It [joining the struggle] depended on human judgment of the situation we were faced with. The soldiers were beating us. The way of living was just too hard. Because of this we realised that going was the only way we could free ourselves and our people .... The way the people in Zimbabwe were being treated forced us to go to war. We were being told not to walk after 6 p.m. in the evening and before 6 a.m. .... My intention was to get a gun from Mozambique and fight against the oppression who was mistreating us.

Ellen explained the inconsistent relations between local women and the comrades by the fact that some incoming groups were simply nicer than others. 'It depends on the type of comrades who visited that time .... You know when I say type of comrades I mean to say someone has got his own attitude. Some wants to beat people, some wants to teach people. So they were different,' she said. This basic difference affected interactions and had to be considered by women in their responses and actions. It also undoubtedly affected their perceptions of the guerrillas and their own participation in the war. This co-existed with the treatment meted out by the DAs who were policing women's movements and actions inside the PVs.

For Stella, her harsh experiences of the soldiers informed her support for the comrades by whom she felt liberated and avenged:

[8]   Rosy felt that a political understanding of the war was only achievable for the privileged few who were literate and had access to the media: 'Just a few understood what was going on. It was for those who could read and listen to the news and had a full understanding of what was going on'. However, others highlighted the importance of radio, particularly for getting news on the war that was available to all. The 'Voice of Zimbabwe' radio programmes were broadcast from Mozambique by the fighting nationalist forces (Hilda; Judith; Polly; Monica).

[9]   Chapter 5 maps out this context of relations and the struggles to survive during the war.

The soldiers were beating us. They once beat me and I had to go to Bindura Hospital to have my blood drained. But comrades were not troublesome. They never gave us problems as what the soldiers did. The soldiers were inhuman .... They wanted me to tell them where the *gandangas* [terrorists] were. Yet, I had not seen them before. They wanted me to tell them where the comrades were, yet I did not even know them. I told them I did not know the *gandangas* .... People couldn't think of anything since they were oppressed by the Smith regime .... The comrades had good relations with the people. They never beat us. Also they did not stay with people since we were staying in Keeps. The soldiers were staying together with the people and mistreating them.

Joanne and Ellen voiced the fearful dilemma that many women faced in engaging with the uncertain and conflicted context of the war itself:

Some were afraid, some did it being afraid, but some were [saying] 'ah, we will get independence and we are doing on behalf of what we will get there', and some really did it just being frightened'. (Joanne)

It wasn't actually that people were loving them but they were afraid. So some were doing it, being happy. Some were doing because they were forced by the situation. (Ellen)

The ultimate dilemma of the conflicted self was eloquently expressed by Victoria:

During their presence we were happy, but inside we were scared.

These collisions of the personal and the political are at the heart of understanding women's participation in revolution, both in terms of their agency and consciousness. Joanne's journey through the minefield of political understanding gives us insight into the complexity of engaging with revolutionary politics. Her perception of politics was adversely affected by the arrest of her father for political involvement:

I can say I didn't see much problems because I was staying in town. I wasn't staying in the rural areas. When I was growing up I was staying with father there but I didn't know much. I can say I really got in these politics when I was married. Because all along I was staying in town, I didn't even mind about the war, about the people being taken. It was nothing to me because I had nothing to see which was really affecting me because I was young and protected. But I can just imagine when my father was arrested. I was about ten years old or so when he was arrested in Harare. My father was a policeman and he retired. After he retired, he was caught and went to Gweru to the prison .... It was said that time he was involved in politics. He wanted to go to where Mugabe went, to Mozambique. They were friends. He wanted to go that time. He didn't manage ... so the policemen heard about it and caught him.

Joanne's father was sentenced two years in prison, which angered her 'because we were young. We stayed alone with mother'. However, she was unaware of the politics of the situation as she was so young and so did not know 'why and how far it is bad, how far it is right'. The situation left her with a sense of anger towards politics, a reaction born out of the pain her father's involvement with nationalist politics caused her family. She said, 'I'm not satisfied in politics because I was brought up when my father was into politics. I got to hate that politics .... You know it was a big problem. The police were coming to our home every day so from there I had to hate the politics'. Joanne's feelings of anger did not clarify as political awareness and consciousness until she moved to Chiweshe after she got married:

> I can say my attitude changed when I came here. Because all along I was staying in town and here, when I came now, I started to talk with people connected to the war [about] things which I hadn't come across .... I can say that's when I realised what is meant by war, what is meant by what they are saying, these comrades, what really does it mean to me. I learned it meant the war. These soldiers meant they were on this side and these comrades were on this side. I had to learn it when I was here because I didn't know .... Other people telling me 'these are the comrades, you stay here. You are not allowed to say anything, you must stay like this. If you say something you are involved and you will be arrested'. So here you learn even if you see something you are not allowed to tell somebody from there 'why are you stealing my books there?'. You are not allowed. You just stay there and keep quiet. That's what the war meant.

Such an experiential understanding of politics resonates with a wider theme of the various narratives of war by the women in Chiweshe; their understanding of revolutionary war was a constant education in survival that required a keen awareness of where they stood at any time. It is this sense of consciousness, born of practical engagement with the everyday realities of guerrilla warfare, that illuminates these women's understanding of their battleground.[10] Their experiences of colonisation alongside their crises of war and poverty weave a rich tapestry of politics and participation. This deepens and challenges the more top-down readings of women's place in revolution found in the divisions of labour within public space by political and military strategy and rhetoric and theoretical notions of a collectively derived consciousness by women or peasants as sociological groups or agents. It is this understanding of political consciousness that guides the next two chapters in further mapping out the battleground of revolutionary war by women.

Summing up

This chapter has reconfigured women's participation in revolution in two significant ways. Firstly, it reassessed the forms of participation, the roles, taken up by women in the course of the war in Chiweshe. This reassessment challenges the notion of roles for women as necessarily revolutionary or positively transformative. This is reinforced by the analysis of the different and often contradictory motivations for participation expressed by the women I interviewed. This point of departure opens up a reassessment of women's political consciousness as the second source of re-configuring women's participation in revolu-

---

[10] The significance of different individual experiences and interpretations becomes evident when we consider the earlier case of Taurai, who cited her father's arrest as a primary motivation for joining the comrades and entering into politics.

1 & 2 Protected Villages, Chiweshe (National Archives of Zimbabwe)

tion. The exploration of women's differentiated political consciousness challenges us to consider more fundamentally the *context* of their participation in a revolutionary war. The 'consciousness of context' was suggested as a formative influence on women's revolutionary consciousness, impacting on the manner and understanding of their participation in revolution. The complexity of a civil war situation as viewed from a local perspective was a fundamental feature of the Chiweshe women's perceptions of the war and the politics that came to shape their lives. Their understandings of that context exhibit a strong theme of conflicted identities and relations.

In the next chapter, I turn to the PVs to closely explore the daily character of women's engagement with the war. These 'villages' provide the narrative framework for women's testimonies that reveals a rich vein of agency and consciousness, absent from many accounts of revolutionary wars. The considerations of 'living in war' will illuminate the formative influence of allegiances, injustices and struggles for survival in the course of revolution on women's participation and understanding of their participation in a revolutionary war. It concerns the stories of how women survived within a revolutionary context and the insights those stories hold for a fuller understanding of women's participation in a revolutionary struggle.

5

Living with & within Revolution

Challenges to Unity & Community

Overview

> The women, I can say, they were the ones who saw the war much different-
> ly from the men because they were staying here [in the Protected Villages].
> Whereas when you are staying in towns, there was not much pain there. What
> pain would you have? The [women] were more affected because they were the
> ones staying here, seeing every problem that comes there. (Joanne)

This chapter addresses the impetus for survival by women caught up in
revolutionary war. The underbelly of women's experiences is found in
their struggles for everyday survival and the strategies they devised to
mitigate the most adverse effects of living through war. The struggles
for survival along with the parameters of everyday social relations (with
the District Assistants (DAs), the guerrillas, and their community) are
key to understanding women's participation and consciousness in the
liberation war. The Protected Villages (PVs) transformed community
space and relations and created the militarised context wherein the
pervasive reach of state surveillance extended into the daily fabric of
women's lives. The DAs were the personification of the state and wom-
en's interactions with them were bound by the everyday mechanisms
of power practised through the control of time and space, harassment
through searches and sexual advances and arbitrary punishment and
brutality. Whilst supposedly protected from the 'terror' of the guerrillas,
women faced new threats in their everyday lives. Guerrilla surveillance
also adapted to the Keeps and turned the community against itself as
distrust and fear thrived in the culture of misinformation and the identification and punishment of sell outs. The unstable information networks
both created and tapped into personal grievances as neighbours sold
each other out in a bid to protect themselves from such accusations. The
wariness of life in the congested space of the Keeps provided the context
wherein social conflict was heightened, sometimes with deadly consequences. Women struggled to survive by adapting their routines and
continuing daily household and agricultural work that was essential to
the physical, moral and social survival of the families and communities

inside the Keeps. The management of everyday relations with the state, the revolutionaries and the local communities is shown to have been fraught with strategic and reactionary actions in a volatile and risk-laden environment. The resulting relational dynamics suggest a complex tapestry of self, relationship and community marked by self-policing, distrust, loneliness, despair, anger, social opprobrium and resistance. The pervasive reach of surveillance alongside the distrust provoked by unstable information networks revealed the strains amongst and within women that made unity or solidarity the exceptional rather than the usual experience of revolutionary war.

Four themes of survival in the PVs are explored in this chapter. The first relates to the living conditions and tactics of state surveillance within the PVs that defined the material context for the intensification of relations amongst women, between women and their families, and neighbours, and, finally, between women and the DAs. The second assesses the destructive effects of guerrilla surveillance on community life through the identification and punishment of sell outs. Along with state surveillance, the tactics of guerrilla surveillance created the unstable information and reporting flows that turned the communities in and on themselves. The third theme highlights the important part played by women in securing community survival through food provision and economic strategies to earn money. The fourth explores the human dilemmas of survival through the situation of women involved in sexual relationships with the DAs.

A note of explanation is required on the challenge of dealing with the issue of sexual relationships, consent, violence and risk that permeated this realm of relationships with the militarised representatives of the state and with the insurgent guerrillas roaming the countryside. Despite suggestions and accounts of sexual relations and incidents of sexual harassment between comrades and Chimbwidos, women were understandably reluctant to discuss this issue. I interpreted this in some cases to be a reluctance to admit perceived sexual transgressions of youth by women who were by now married and were respectable members of their communities. In other cases it was a strong assertion that comrades faced spiritual sanctions if sexually involved with young women while in the bush for purposes of fighting. In yet other cases it was simply too painful and embarrassing to be remembered and so women used euphemisms; the allusions to 'girlfriends', being 'treated' or 'beaten' by the guerrillas or the DAs are such examples. Some young people for example, took advantage of the freedom of chaos to get involved in relationships that would not usually have been permitted, while other women exchanged sexual favours for food and cash in desperation which they did not want to recall or recount. During the interviews I was respectful not to push social boundaries in asking women to be specific about their own experiences of rape, harassment or sexual activity during the war. This does not diminish the issue of sexual violence against women as a feature of the war but I am hesitant to impose a relatively recent political category of 'sexual violence' on the interview analysis that does not reflect how women talked about the issue or how they may have experienced it. There *was* violence but it was engrained in the everyday, which is precisely the power and the horror of it. The analysis here does not deny that the guerrillas had sex (forced or consensual) with the women and girls from the Keeps, nor does it deny that women were sexually abused by the guards. There are also quotes of women who talk of other women (and in some cases themselves) having sexual relations with the guerrillas and DAs. The prosaic, the everyday life of living in war where the normalisation of violence (including sexual violence and harassment) is but a part is mapped out in detail. I have taken the line that violence needs to be placed and understood in context while respecting witnesses'/participants' accounts, which is precisely what the framework of Gendered Localised Resistance allows.

'Seeing all this, we were left with no hope for change': Life in the Protected Villages

In their intention and effect, the PVs can be viewed as the apotheosis of state political violence in the liberation war. They marked the complete invasion of people's lives through surveillance so as to depoliticise the population, transform and disorientate 'normal' life and destroy community and social relations so as to render them ineffective for political mobilisation by the guerrillas. This policy of counterinsurgency effectively transformed the normality of rural life as evidenced through women's perceptions of social breakdown and heightened social conflict within the Keeps.

The trade-offs of protection: Living conditions in the Keeps
Feelings of instability and uncertainty marked the women's accounts of moving into the PVs. The overwhelming reaction was that the Keeps were to be a permanent fixture and that the people of Chiweshe were condemned to live there until they died. This fed a sense of fatalistic despair in the setting up of these false communities that were more akin to squatter camps than villages; they were intended for the purposes of military strategy rather than for the protection of the local people as the state propaganda claimed. The actual move into the PVs prompted limited actions of defiance and feelings of anger and hatred towards the colonial state and its agents. There was a sense of uncertainty and lack of information and consultation between the government and the people about the move; some people were told at meetings held by their village headmen that the lorries would come in three weeks' time to relocate them, only for it to happen five days later. The suddenness of the move compounded the difficulties of relocation, as it took weeks for families to actually construct shelter in the midst of the confusion, particularly at a time where crops were being harvested. Households were allocated small pegged spaces that were marked out in lines based often on the arbitrary measurement of the length of stride used by various DAs and officials. Neither toilets nor houses were provided, only open ground upon which goods and grain were dumped. Families constructed basic shelter using wooden poles and *dagga* (clay). Many resorted to tearing down their former homes to use the materials for rebuilding in the Keeps:

They [state officials] did not even tell us. They just took us and we had to stay in an open place where there were no houses built .... It was hard for us to leave our homes and go and stay in the open air where there were no houses. (Josephine)

It was a sight. I can still see it in my eyes. Nothing! No toilets, no houses, nothing! Things were just heaped everywhere, in the sand. How can you heap grain in the sand? This is what they had to do. They knew where their location was; just a peg here and a peg there, so they just leave your stuff there and that's it. (Fr Fidelis)

The loss and destruction involved in the move bred a sense of despair:

At that time we did not hope for any changes. We just thought that our life was going to be like that for ever ... Actually there was a state of panic because the Smith regime told us that we were no longer going to come back to our farms. As a result everyone was worried about it .... Even our nice houses which we had in our home areas were destroyed. Seeing all this we were left with no hope for change. (Agnes)

In the beginning, Hilda's family refused to build a hut, and when they did finally build it was only with a view to provide temporary shelter:

People from this area refused to build houses in the Keep at first, thinking that it would change. We were finally forced to go into the Keep .... We refused to build the new house with the intention that it [the policy] would change .... DAs came in lorries armed with guns and collected our goods and dumped them in Keeps. It was very difficult. All our goods and grains were thrown in the sandy areas so we lost both our goods and food ... [In the beginning, shelter] was only something like change-houses [temporary structures]. We then started cutting poles while others destroyed the old buildings [former homes] to take bricks for rebuilding.

Fr Fidelis recalled such resistance:

You know people resisted for a while. They refused to put up anything. You know they just put up the round poles and didn't put up anything else. They probably thought by so doing the government would change its mind. The government smiled. The rains would soon be coming.

In the end, people were forced to adapt. As Rosy said, 'During the first days it was so tough for the people but when they were used to it .... It became just as normal, just ordinary life .... There wasn't much freedom but as time went on, it is only that we got used to it so that you couldn't make any difference that time.'

The collective misery of living conditions in the PVs was expressed through the problems of overcrowding, lack of proper water and sanitation facilities and the effects of illnesses that arose from these conditions (Farasia; Mrs Moyo; Hilda; Veronica; Josephine; More Blessing; Juliet; Lorine; Florence; Joanne; Maggie; Polly; Trust). 'Prisoners', 'squatters' and 'cattle' are among the terms used by some to express their disgust (Mrs Moyo; Hilda; Stella). The space allocated to each family could not meet the basic needs of shelter and sanitation and was inadequate for family accommodation – separate sleeping quarters for older and younger or male and female household members was impossible.

The lack of toilets meant that, at night, many people used any available area to relieve themselves. This unhygienic situation was only slightly improved by the digging of pit latrines, which, given the space restrictions, were located adjacent to living and cooking areas. They also proved a draw for flies and mosquitoes and discharged a pungent odour that wafted through the entire Keep, particularly during the dry season:

> It was a terrible thing because I never experienced people living like that. Their houses were close together – a house and a toilet and a bedroom for the parents. There wasn't any space because they were built like compounds on the farms. And there were a lot of flies. When I came in the first time I couldn't eat because of the smell. Ah no, very bad. (Anna)

Sweeping of yards seemed a redundant exercise and bathing became a furtive task as water was scarce and privacy a risk and a luxury. Initially, women walked long distances outside of curfew hours to fetch water. Although standpipes were eventually installed outside the Keeps, one tap had to serve, on average, 2,000 people. Queuing for water became a time-consuming task and the amount that one could carry was limited. These conditions had implications for the health of the communities, particularly the very old and the very young. Women cited the prevalence of illnesses such as diarrhoea, scabies and malnutrition:

> You know we were living, eeeh! Crowded! We were crowded and we were not safe I can say from the health, as it is, the health, dirt, we were too many. You know when you are staying many, the sweeping and the control of the children, everything will be dirty. So it was very hard …. People died … especially this sickness diarrhoea …. Because eating and the toilets, it was not up to date. (Joanne)

The risks relating to childbirth also increased. For Chiweshe, the nearest hospital was at Howard, in the very south-west of the district, and getting there required access transport such as a scotch cart, car or bus. However, as travel was only allowed in daylight hours, the availability of such medical care was severely restricted. Veronica explained:

> During pregnancy, for example, one would need hospital attention but we sometimes found ourselves closed in the Keeps and some were not allowed to get out of the Keeps, even if their time of birth has arrived. Some had to give birth at home and sometimes this resulted in death …. Here in the rural areas there was no immediate hospital attention.

Although some women admitted to feeling protected from the crossfire positions of living in the open, in the same breath, they also spoke of the trade-off with the new risks within the PVs (Pardon; Hilda; Trust). For Agnes and Joanne, this was the increasing violence of the DAs inside the Keeps. Joanne said that a *quid pro quo* for such protection was remaining quiet and non-active: 'It was not allowed [to talk about the guerrillas] because you were told to stay there as protected people so you are not allowed to do anything'. Margaret also indicated how the new difficulties of surveillance became the price of protection:

> Life here was a bit better because we were now staying in Keeps. However, what I hated about staying in Keeps was to produce an identity card and a

stick with your national identity number. Without these two things you were
not allowed to go out of the Keep.

While Veronica had felt protected from the crossfire outside the Keeps,
she was also afraid of the increased vulnerability to state and guerrilla
violence. She said, '[W]e thought that in the Keeps we would be easily
killed because we were in one vulnerable place .... Because they [sol-
diers and guerrillas] were enemies, we thought they [guerrillas] would
kill us thinking that we supported soldiers'. This internal conflict of
protection and vulnerability was encapsulated by Veronica herself
when she says she felt safe 'from war, yes, but life itself, no'.

'They were punishing us for no reason':
The personal experiences of state surveillance
The new grievances, felt injustices and risks for women arose in part
from the culture of surveillance that was embedded in the geography of
the Keeps. In them, women were subject to the gaze of the state through
a structure that placed the living quarters of the DAs and soldiers in the
central fortress surrounded by the 'protected' people crowded together in very basic accommodation. Beyond this human shield were the
perimeter fences with outward-facing lights. Electricity was only available outside to power the perimeter lights and a public address system
eased communication and surveillance and was a propaganda tool
for government information. The themes of surveillance that emerged
strongly from women's testimonies were identity checks, searches
of water buckets, body searches, beatings and arbitrary punishments
(Trust; Alice; Florence; Ellen; Josephine; More Blessing; Juliet; Stella).
Water buckets were often checked by using guns and dirty sticks which
not only intimidated women but provoked and depressed them as it
served to undo the time spent queuing for water which was now unfit
for drinking. The DAs often left women queuing for long periods of time,
thus further shortening their time available for work in the fields.

    The control of movement and time structured the lives of women and
defined the limits of freedom. The use of curfews (usually between 6
p.m. and 6 a.m.), identity checks and the summary closures of the Keeps
if the DAs feared a strong guerrilla presence adversely affected the wom-
en's ability to plan and carry out routine chores:

> We were guarded by the DAs day and night. We were not allowed to leave the
> Keep. Our lives were so regulated. We were allocated time to go and tend our
> fields. Sometimes we were kept indoors until midday. When we were allowed
> to go outside that was the time people did everything, for example, fetching
> firewood and water. (Gladys)

> [There was] even a time for sleeping in the Keep. People were forced to sleep
> when they didn't like. You have to sleep by this time. You were not supposed
> to come out. If they only have a rumour that the comrades are nearby, people
> were not allowed to go out. (Ellen)

The indignities of incarceration were many. Mrs Moyo, who visited the
PVs with the Salvation Army, remembered elderly people wearing their
identity numbers because they could not remember them: 'When they
went out they used to have some tickets or numbers. Some of these people

were old people. They couldn't remember the numbers. You know, you can't remember what number you are as an old person so sometimes you could find them wearing these numbers'. Everyone had to have a *situpa* (national identity card) registered in the Keep. There was also a system of identification using wooden sticks with the national identity numbers carved on them. These sticks had to be given to the DA on the way out and retrieved on the way back in. In this way, time and mobility could be controlled and punishment meted out to those who returned late from the fields and failed to observe the curfew. Other indignities include the loss of privacy as fathers and daughters, mothers and sons, were forced into one room; the lines to leave the open gate; the lines to reach the solitary tap; the dirty sticks used by DAs to 'check' the water upon return; the rough handling of women to 'search' for food; the 'punishments' meted out to belittle and discourage; and the emasculation of the men, who were left standing unable to intervene and to protect.

Joanne, for example, talked angrily of the body searches that women were subjected to by the male DAs:

> It was not really a good thing. Because if you have a baby you have to move that baby off and say what is there. They thought you can put something and put the baby there. They really did that because they knew you can carry something[1] .... They [DAs] were not concerned about that [how women felt]. They were really saying, 'we are doing our job'. Then they would just do it without managing whether you like it or not ... [Women] were worried. It's not good because if you must be searched you must be searched by another woman not by a man ... even at the border they do like that, a woman and a woman, not a man and a woman. In those days they were [not] doing that.

Generational respect for women could not be assumed; old or young, women were simply not treated well. In the words of More Blessing, 'They just give as they want. They don't say 'Ah, this is the woman, and this is the *ambuya* and this is the old woman, better to do this and the *ambuya* will be better'. No, just the same'. She also highlighted the more arbitrary forms of 'punishment' that seemed to depend on the type of DA one encountered at the gate, saying that:

> They give the women a difficult time. I don't think it is a good idea that time. It was hard for the women specially. You know the woman used to carry water, you know in time to cook food for the children. Sometimes she is late to go to the fields to do some work there and then she thinks it is better to stay here a little bit .... Then the DA come and say 'what are you doing here this time?' Nothing to say, just hitting you, no reason, just hitting you .... Ah, it is too bad. Sometimes they are hitting people who don't do anything. If you need to come inside so they punish you to dig the hole where you go down and you can't see the people. It is punishment, so it is too bad. If you are late outside, maybe they think you go outside to feed the *gandangas*, so we must punish you to dig something or to do some hard work and sometimes hitting you with the gun.

---

[1] Women usually carried their babies on their backs, securing them with a *kitenga* (a wrap or shawl) One of the strategies for sneaking food to the comrades was to hide parcels of maize underneath the baby when women were going to the fields. These strategies are discussed further in Chapter 6.

The provocation and humiliation of women by the DAs was not only restricted to physical violence:

> Sometimes when you were coming in the Keep the soldiers would ignore you. Maybe they were writing letters to their girlfriends and you would wait maybe for two or more hours before they attended to you. Sometimes we were carrying heavy goods and they did not even bother about it. Actually, they were punishing us for no reason. (Phyllis)

> You know there was time to go out, time to come in. If you come late you would be punished. You would be sent to wash the clothes for the DA, clean all the pots, clean all the houses as a threat of punishment, and even the yard. (Ellen)

> The DAs also abused their powers in passing false information to Rhodesian army soldiers (Judith).

Susan attributed the DAs' excess violence to boredom:

> In the first days they were not rough but when they got fed up with their job they were ill-treating the people. For example, if someone comes late by even a minute he/she was punished. The punishment was that of weeding the mountain for the whole of the day'.

Rosy said that '[i]t was just being boastful of their job. Maybe it is because they had guns'. Women were expected and forced to report the comrades and were questioned about their work in the fields. Alice pointed to the policing of conversations in the Keep that was to deter any talk of the comrades: '[The DAs] surveyed the area [of the Keep] by going right round it ... They didn't want anyone to talk about comrades'.

All of this meant that within the 'protected' villages there was no one to protect people from the 'protectors':

> There was no alternative. People had no one to complain to. They were expected to obey and to do what they were told to do. (Gladys)

> The soldiers were very rude. They used to beat us all the time. They were blaming us for feeding the comrades .... There was no way we could protect ourselves. (Phyllis)

In immediate terms, the women of Chiweshe relied upon their own limited resources to survive and reported brutal DAs to the comrades:

> Some [DAs] were rude and threatened people with death. Some guards had to be punished for being overzealous. I know of one guard who died after punishment by lead piping in Harare. (Veronica)

> It seems the DAs who were at Nyachuru were more cruel than those who were here [Bare] because you know the people would go out and they would meet those guerrillas and they could give reports about the behaviour of the DAs. And they [the guerrillas] would come into the Keep even during the night. (Rosy)

Bad fences and bad neighbours: The rise of social conflict
The intensity of social life resulting from the living conditions and sur-

veillance of the PVs had serious implications for the ability of the new communities to be cohesive:

> Being together in that way, it was too much. It was too much because we had too many .... Even the communication. Being together ... you don't love each other really because there is much talking and because you are crowded. Whereas when one stays there and one there [apart from each other] when you meet you are happy. When you are just meeting any time it doesn't really make you feel. (Joanne)

Morality also became a byword for policing women's behaviour and creating social conflict; gossip and accusations tended to centre on witchcraft and prostitution and were often initiated by other women. The consequences were not simply social opprobrium but also the 'political' implications of such accusations being viewed by the comrades as actions of selling out to the other side:

> [Living together in the Keep] caused tension and friction amongst people. Some were accused of witchcraft, creating ill feeling as well as concocting false stories and rumours about each other. In the end some people ended up as enemies in the Keep because they were living close to each other. (Gladys)

Witchcraft accusations placed the burden of proof on women and pitted them against the power of the traditional spirit mediums who decided whether one was a witch or not. Tendai told me that 'Once they [comrades] heard that you were a witchdoctor they would kill you. Also they first had to prove whether it was true. They did this through asking those who were possessed by ancestral spirits'. Women were also subject to charges of immoral behaviour. The war and the Keeps claimed some were the progenitors of contemporary social problems including baby dumping, elopement and HIV/AIDS (Margaret; Veronica; Fr. Fidelis). The integrity of 'traditional' life was seen by Polly and Agnes to have been undermined in the Keeps:

> Some people's behaviour changed for the worse because we were overcrowded. Some were just staying together without formal marriage. (Polly)

> Our children's behaviour changed because of different culture which was found in the Keep. They lost their sense of identity. (Agnes)

Veronica claimed that this was because '[m]oral values were lost. People just wanted too much money and did bad things for it'. Examples throughout the interviews included women having sexual relationships with the guards and selling out people to the soldiers for money. There was also a proliferation of basic social conflicts within the overcrowded Keeps:

> 'There was no understanding of closeness because people end up fighting because of the children going to next door and tak[ing] the neighbour's property or even chickens going to someone's house and eat[ing] the food. People would fight because of that .... And this toilet was being used by several people. It was therefore very difficult to control people on how to use the toilet. (Polly)

> Life was hard. We did not like life in the Keep. Also staying close to one

another in the Keep brought a lot of conflicts amongst ourselves. Some people did not like to see other people's children playing in their yards and it was very difficult to control young people. As a result, conflict resulted over the issue of children. (Agnes)

Sometimes the other ones are fighting because some other one say, 'Oh, I left my food there, who is taking my food? Are you taking my food?' and then the people start fighting. (More Blessing)

Generational tensions were also a feature of social conflicts as older and younger relatives felt the limits and possibilities of the new communities:

They [parents] were not happy these young people were being taken from schools or even when they met the comrades in the bush therefore there was no way a parent could refuse the fact. (Polly)

However, maternal love also meant that women were simply glad to have their children with them, even if the Keeps were unhealthy and dangerous places. Trust said she 'was not very happy' about having her children in the Keeps 'but they were close to me. That mattered most'. Veronica said '[i]t was good for me because I could take care of them.'

Household tensions and marital strife arose in some cases from the loss of male authority and the effects of mainly male migrant labour patterns. The demoralisation of sexual harassment, desperation and starvation were not only community phenomena but also were reflected in deep personal crisis. This demoralisation was faced by women and men alike. Men had to stand by and feel paralysed in the face of their loss of authority and ability to protect their family from the suffering of war (Kesby 1996:573-4). More Blessing saw this helplessness when women were harassed by DAs, saying that 'Ah, even the man, if he want to try to defend the women .... The DA, that time is doing that he wants and no-one says 'no, please don't do that to her' .... They were afraid.'

Fr Fidelis gave an account of the men he met in the Keeps:

It was demoralising because you didn't feel a man in the sense the way the soldiers behaved .... You were belittled in front of your wife, in front of your children and then when you go back home you just go and sit there. So just to quench your thirst, to forget about everything, you go drinking .... You went in after 11 o'clock and you couldn't talk to anyone, people were drunk. I couldn't talk sense to anybody. They were drunk. They said 'We are drinking because life doesn't mean anything any more'. For example, several times I went in during the summer period. There had just been a battle four or five days before. So once there was a battle out there the Keeps were locked for three, four, five days. That meant the cattle were outside the Keeps and so cattle out of hunger break out of their pens, go into the fields and destroy the crops. A lot of these elders and chiefs [said] 'It's all death anyway. You are telling us you are not allowed by law. We want to go and look after the cattle. These cattle are destroying our crops; those cattle are going to die because after eating so much they will drink water and die. So we will lose the crops and the cattle so we may as well die in one or two shots if we try to go out there and are mistaken for something. That situation may be controlled but what if they are going to kill us of starvation. With no crops or no cattle, the next thing we will be dead' .... It became difficult because I feel, morally, once you have been used you feel so demoralised, so objected, that you no longer have the self-respect and you get drunk, etc.'

He also attributed the rise in domestic violence to this emasculation of men in the Keeps:

because if you know your wife is being taken by someone you want to kill him. The guy has no power, the children are living day to day. There is no morality, there is no work, you just live there. When you rub shoulders hard with each other your rivalry increases and there is no communication except for violence. That's all that is there.

Marital and family relations also faced the strains of migrant labour, an invention of the colonial regime. The women's testimonies revealed feelings of loneliness and abandonment that were sometimes offset by a desire to keep their men (husbands and sons) away from the risks of war. For Joanne, like other women, migrant labour was a way of saving their men from the violence of war and the prospects of state harassment or guerrilla recruitment:

[In the city] when you are staying with your husband it is much easier than when you are staying without your husband because any problems you can work together. It wasn't easy being here in the Keeps .... Because when the war came the men, many young men, were working so women who were here were many because their husbands stayed out. So they didn't even want to come because in the Keeps there was a big problem when they come home .... The soldiers there at the gates, they will ask you 'Where do you work? Your RIC number?' If you don't know you are in the soup .... He didn't even come home! He didn't even come. We were going there because when those who are working come here they were very much troubled. They didn't want to come.

Migrant labour was also an economic necessity for a wage-earner to buy food for the families in the Keep when self-sufficient farming proved impossible. Ellen's husband worked as a teacher in town while she worked as a community development worker with the Ministry of Internal Affairs in Chiweshe and stayed with his family. 'There was no alternative because I wanted to work ... because of life, because of money,' she said.

Therefore, the crucible of the war in the rural areas was not simply about the state and revolutionary forces, it was also about the impact of the disintegration of community life. The most potent example of this is the issue of selling out when trusting your neighbour was to place your life and livelihood in the firing line.

'There was no trust anymore': Guerrilla surveillance and sell outs

Guerrilla surveillance was primarily conducted through the identification and punishment of sell outs. The women's accounts suggest that selling out and fear of being sold out became endemic to the context of daily survival and deeply affected their relations with the guerrillas, the DAs and with family, friends and neighbours. This issue is key to

understanding the fractured dynamics of secrecy, uncertainty and distrust that underpinned the rise of social conflicts; it is in the question
of 'selling out' that we witness guerrilla war as a war of each against all
within the Keeps.

Who were the sell outs? There are contradictions in the terms used,
depending on who is naming the 'sell out'. This elasticity of definition
is found in Tendai's distinction between 'selling out' to the soldiers and
'reporting' to the comrades:

> These people who were selling out the comrades were being given money by
> the soldiers. But if one goes to report to the comrades that he had seen the sol-
> diers he was not given anything because they were saying they were freedom
> fighters, fighting to free everyone from the bondage of oppression.

For Josephine it was straightforward: 'Those who were not sell outs
would report to the comrades'. Dorothy, however, cautioned that it was
not always so apparent: 'There were some people who were supporting
both sides, the comrades and the soldiers'. Emily also said '[i]t was very
difficult to tell [who was a sell out] except when he or she did it openly'.
The unstable flows of information and reporting made the task of identifying a sell out virtually impossible or at the very least subject to errors
of judgement.

Three categories of sell out emerged through the women's stories.
The first category was made up of local informants for the state who
were recruited through violence and financial inducement to gather
intelligence concerning supplies to the guerrillas. Phyllis said that such
informants were nicknamed *kabibiyas* (someone who cannot keep a
secret) and were the main target of guerrilla surveillance. The second
was those identified by the *Mujibhas* and *Chimbwidos*, who were the
eyes and ears of the guerrillas within the community. This category
included 'tit for tat' killings where a suspected sell out was accused of
having sold out one the comrades' supporters to the Rhodesian soldiers.
However, the youth also abused this power and avenged personal grievances by lying about suspected sell outs. The final category was made up
of those sell outs identified by their neighbours (not necessarily *Chimbwidos* or *Mujibhas*, who were formally tied to the guerrillas) who were
often motivated by jealousy or vengeance. This category of selling out
was the most dangerous as it often resulted in the killing of innocent
people by the soldiers or the comrades. The sources of jealousy included
money, status and adultery. These are the parameters of the volatile context of accusation and counter-accusation that were part of everyday
social relations inside the Keeps. Such extensive motivations to deny
your neighbour, within a fragmented community struggling to survive,
exacerbated feelings of distrust and tendencies to withdraw.

Many of the women feared being sold out by neighbours to the soldiers and DAs for supporting the comrades:

> Sometimes there would be people saying that we know the comrades. At one
> point my husband was beaten and they were saying he was giving them food
> from the shop. (Margaret)

> If people gave food to the comrades, others would report them to the soldiers.
> (Pardon)

People who sold out others to the soldiers often became targets themselves and faced brutal consequences for their actions:

> They [sell outs] were making arrangements there and telling them [soldiers]
> what's happening here and what's happening outside .... I really know one
> man down there. He was cut on the mouth by the comrades as a sell out. He's
> the one I really know. (Joanne)

Polly recalled a sell out who was killed by the comrades for reporting
some people who had been feeding a wounded guerrilla in the bush. He
was a paid informant. The destructive impact of the information flows
can be seen in Emily's case:

> I know of a sell out who was killed when he sold out some Mujibhas that they
> were giving food to the comrades. This sell out had reported my brother to the
> soldiers that he was giving food to the comrades. After the report my brother
> was killed by the soldiers. After he was killed the comrades came to kill the
> sell out also.

Ellen, Anna and Rosy recounted the way in which comrades were used
by local people to settle scores or vent grudges and personal jealousies
against neighbours. All highlighted the fact that comrades became
aware of this and attempted to curb this by grilling and punishing their
informants:

> Some of them [alleged sell outs] were innocent because if somebody has got
> hatred he began to say anything so if the type of comrade doesn't reason, he
> is just an innocent victim. But you know some [guerrillas] said you have to be
> really sure because you will be the one to kill. (Ellen)

> And the unfortunate thing is that some people were sell outs. They thought
> these boys were there to solve their personal problems and some of these boys
> got into it. They came at times when somebody, say we were discussing yes-
> terday, someone would say Mrs so-and-so is a witch. They would be gathered
> at her village and then they would maybe sing *Chimurenga* songs where they
> would hit that person to bits .... Now, they later discovered that some people
> were not telling the truth so what they did is when I reported that so-and-so
> made such a mistake I would be made to kill that person myself. Because they
> would say you are the one who has been made sad so you kill that person
> yourself. That is when the people stopped reporting. (Rosy)

> It created a very bad situation after the war, but in those days people didn't
> like people who were better off in their life than themselves. So they could
> tell the guerrillas that these were sell outs. That one is selling us, that one
> is selling you, which is not true. At first, guerrillas were just acting without
> thinking, without asking the person. But as time went on they were now talk-
> ing to the person concerned, finding the truth. Then they could punish him
> if there was a mistake. If they were given wrong information they would go
> back to the one who has given them the wrong information and treated her
> or him. (Anna)

Such scenarios were countered by incidents of neighbours warning
families who had been rumoured to be sell outs in order to protect them
and urge them to leave before an inevitable visit by the comrades or the
soldiers took place:

We had only one meeting when the comrades called the people. There, they threatened all the traitors. There were about 25 comrades. They called everybody from all over to gather at the headman's house. They told us that they had come to protect our lives. They disliked traitors. They also told us that they had already heard there were three traitors in our area but everyone denounced this .... After the meeting [midnight] they pretended to have gone yet they were still in the areas waiting to hear whether there were some traitors.[2] (Hilda)

The violent consequences of these unstable networks of information-gathering, reporting, distrust and surveillance came home forcibly to women in Chiweshe. For those accused, the possibilities were bleak and punishment brutal. The fact that women had to leave the Keeps to tend their fields during the day merely created another space of risk for them. Both public and private killings marked the treatment of sell outs by the comrades. Before the PVs were established, guerrilla surveillance activities involved direct threats, gathering information through *Mujibhas* and *Chimbwidos* and public executions that included the display of bodies to deter other informants from lying.[3] Suspected sell outs received night-time visits, as neighbours withdrew, relieved for that night it would not be them. The verification of accusations was not always rigorous, particularly given the confinement of the Keeps and the guerrillas' dependence on the youth to bring them supplies and information. As a result there were negative perceptions of both *Chimbwidos* and *Mujibhas* because of the power they wielded in their role as intelligence-gatherers:

If it was proved that the person was a sell out, they would kill him in front of the people using their guns .... It was the duty of the *Mujibhas* and *Chimbwidos* to prove why they were saying someone was a sell out. If they were to lie and later be found out ... they would be killed themselves .... In some cases some *Mujibhas* and *Chimbwidos* were able to lie and get away with it. As long as they were able to convince the comrades that it was true .... The comrades believed them since they were their investigators .... People did not like the idea of lying about other people being sell outs when in actual fact, they were not. People were actually afraid. They could not criticise it. Actually, they had to sing whilst the innocent person was being killed .... The comrades thought that killing sell outs in front of the people was going to stop others from being sell outs. (Susan)

Before they were relocated to the Keeps, people had been summoned to *pungwes* where public accusation and punishment would be administered in kangaroo court-style proceedings. Dorothy was 19 when she witnessed such a scene in 1976:

We became more aware of [war] when Mr ... who was my neighbour was

---

[2] My later investigations placed this night as 2 February 1973, the night before Anna was visited by the guerrillas and charged, along with her husband, with being a sell out. In fact, Hilda was the one who had warned Anna that she was one of the named sell outs targeted by the guerrillas at the meeting. Anna's story is told on pp. 107-10.

[3] These tactics were also used by the state. The CCJP (CIIR and CCJP (Rhodesia) 1975) reported on the public display of bodies of 'terrorists' to deter locals from helping the guerrillas.

killed by the comrades because he was a sell out .... Because when the comrades asked him to give them some clothes and food since he had some shops, he went to report them to the police station. And when the comrades became aware of this, they wrote to him warning him that they were going to kill him. From what people were saying and the death of the sell out, war was just terrifying. When the sell out was killed we were also there. We were being asked to sing. It was at the *pungwe*.

Florence painted a similar picture:

They wanted to find out who were the sell outs. They would ask from the masses who the sell outs will be. People were forced to say who the sell outs were. If they refuse they were beaten until they mention them. During these *pungwes* people were singing and also if the sell out was mentioned he would be beaten or killed.

The brutality of the public executions evoked a sense of the collective terror and silence:

The comrades could kill people, those who were sell outs. Some had their lips cut off and some were killed and people were not allowed to bury them and they would be eaten by dogs. (Margaret)

People were beaten and killed by soldiers and guerrillas.[4] Some had lips cut, leaving teeth exposed, especially those *Mujibhas* who belonged to the soldiers. Some would be tortured to death by hot plastics. (Veronica)

Those who were selling out the comrades to the soldiers were killed by the comrades. However, sometimes they would just cut your lips and leave like that to suffer the pain. The process of killing was very painful. Most of the times they were not using guns just to shoot you and die. They would start by cutting your ears, arms, legs, and after that they would stone you until you die. (Tendai)

The PVs transformed some of these features of guerrilla surveillance; the reliance on the youth for information seems to have increased because of decreasing contact between the guerrillas and individuals or families. More deceptive strategies were deployed to lure the suspected sell outs to the fields where the comrades would confront them; outside the Keeps, they were fair game. Dorothy says that the comrades:

had their own tricks and they were also helped by mountains .... They could come during the night and collect the sell out. They could also just wait for you in the bush if you have a car and when you pass through that place they just catch you, burn the car, and kill you. First of all they had to collect information of where you work, what time you leave work, where do you stay, etc.

Phyllis said:

The comrades would send the *Chimbwidos* and *Mujibhas* to call those who

4 Veronica reminds us that the inhumanity of torture and brutal death was not the sole preserve of the guerrillas. People from Chiweshe were detained at Chombira or Bindura and beaten and tortured by soldiers and Special Branch operatives. Chombira was the central security complex inside Chiweshe and was located near Nzvimbo (CIIR and CCJP (Rhodesia) 1975).

had sold them. When they were sent they would lie to the sell out that in your fields there are cattle eating your crops. The sell out would hurry to the field where he would meet the comrades. When they met him they would take him for trial. They would cut an ear off, then a leg and so forth until he dies.

Sarah, who would have been no more than 11 or 12 at the time, remembered a sell out that was caught in this way and, as a *Chimbwido*, she witnessed her terrible end at the hands of the guerrillas:

> The sell outs can go outside to their fields. So the comrades will know the sell out, this is his field or her field so that they can go there. They can take her to the base then they can treat her with a stick ... it happened when the sell outs were caught. And sometimes they can kill the sell out .... They just use banging. Or they say 'can you dig your grave?' Then they put him in that grave [when he was alive] .... They shoot or they just chop .... I was afraid at that time. It was my first time to see it.

The effects of such violence created personal traumas reinforced the atomised individualism of secrecy and distrust that marked the community dynamics in the Keeps. Sarah remembered her suffering following the incident above, saying 'Ah, the only thing I was thinking was to go back to my family. But at the time when I sleep I used to see violent pictures in my face. Other times I would end up crying when I was asleep'. The killings and intimidation alienated some women, such as Joanne and Ellen, who may have wanted change but not in this way. Joanne's grandfather was threatened by the comrades and to this day feels angry and holds a grudge. Such coercion affected Joanne's belief in the revolutionaries. 'You know you didn't know you were going to be independent when you were treated like that,' she said.

The violence of the killings caused Ellen to turn away from politics. When asked if she had any interest in politics during the war, she replied:

> Ah, not so much .... Because I am not so good in politics .... At that time! You know when we stayed in the Reserves, I had experienced people being murdered. You know when you say people who say out what they think. Some were killed ... by the comrades and some were burnt .... [Violence] turned me away.

Ellen judges that the killings actually intensified grief and conflict in the community by 'created hatred'.

In such a confused and high-risk environment, talking out was not encouraged and secrecy became a tactical decision of survival; it meant absorbing the horror and surviving. No criticism could be made openly as soldiers or comrades might retaliate. There was an impulse to 'not talk', yet there was a reliance on hearsay to learn about what was going on; the compulsion to listen and be aware is juxtaposed with the compulsion to report and the threat of being accused of reporting. As is the case with similar surveillance situations, such pressures bred distrust and hatred as neighbours turned against each other and sought to protect themselves in this web of reporting, vengeance and punishment. The lack of freedom and sense of surveillance was felt in respect of both the DAs and the guerrillas:

They [the comrades] accused us of being on both sides since others were traitors .... Sell outs would report to the soldiers that these people had been collaborating with the comrades, or they say the *gandangas* wanted to kill us because of Mr so-and-so. Also, if the comrades came and heard that soldiers had been at the same house they would accuse them of being traitors. (Hilda)

'I blamed the local people. It was only that they were jealous of my life':
A case study of guerrilla intimidation and selling out
The multiple dimensions of selling out were revealed in Anna's story. She was a schoolteacher and along with her husband, a headmaster, was subject to accusations of state collaboration. Anna was a card-carrying member of the former NDP and made regular contributions to ZANU and to local comrades. She continued such contributions when she moved from Chiweshe after the attack on her home. She insisted that this support was out of duty not out of fear, and resolutely blames particular neighbours, and not the comrades, for the attack on her home. On 3 February 1973, Anna was visited by a group of guerrillas at her home in the school grounds in the north of Chiweshe:

It was very late when I met the comrades [in Chiweshe]. I saw, face to face, the first comrades, in 1973, February 3. I had heard of them before that. I had heard some women reporting to me of their meetings they were holding. I had some information from friends warning me about the comrades, that they were talking about coming to my house. I told these friends 'Let them come. I am ready any time' .... I heard someone warning me before that 'the comrades would like to talk to you', and she said 'You must be ready' and I said 'Ready for what?', and she said 'Last night when we had some meetings, some comrades were talking about your husband', and I said 'What were they talking about?' The woman said 'Don't say it to anybody' and I said 'Ah no, I'm not that young to just go around saying things to other people' and she said 'They were saying you are a sell out and we would like to talk to her' .... It was on a Thursday and she told me this at a prayer group. The next day was Friday, that is when they came during the night, Thursday. I had already my supper. The children had gone to bed something like past seven because in those days as soon as you had your supper you had to go to bed because we were all afraid. So I heard a knock. I thought it was [my husband]. He had gone for beer drinking. I opened and I was surprised to see a boy with a gun. As soon as I opened the door the boy came in but I could see that there were other boys outside ....'

They were 18 [years] and above but they were very short and tough. Then when he came he asked for [my husband]. He was standing at the door and I said 'He has gone for beer drinking', and he said 'We would like the school radio'. I said 'I am not the deputy head who has the keys for the office. I can't even give you the radio .... I'm just an ordinary teacher'. The other one came in and said 'Kick her! She can't answer us like that'. Then this one [the first one] said 'Ah no, we didn't come here to kick her, we want to know what we want' and this one went on 'We would like your records so we can play them outside'. And I said 'Well, you can have them, they are my records. You can take them'. He was standing, and said to me 'Sit down!' Then I sat on the chair and he said 'Where did you get all these things?' We were in the sitting room by then. And I said 'I bought them'. He said 'Why is it you have all this? You have a refrigerator. All your children sleep on beds'. They never went into the bedroom of my children!'[5]

[He continued] 'You have a nice house. We have been to your house. Why is it that you have all this? You are a sell out with your husband. You are getting all this from the whites'. And I said 'No, we are not getting all this from this from the whites', because I knew and I was very strong and bold. I wasn't afraid and I said 'No, the thing is we have been working for quite a long time, so do you think we would work and not buy furniture for the house?' He said 'No, you can't. Your husband has five new suits here in this house'. I said 'Five new suits?' and he said 'Yes'. Then I got the suits. I am the one who went into town and those new suits were on account. They were five, of course, new ones. They were told [by a woman neighbour]. Then I brought in the invoice. I showed them. These five suits are all on account and the refrigerator was on account. We had finished it and the stove was on account. We had finished, and all the beds. And he [the comrade] called the others and said 'Come here, all we have been given is false, now we can't be talking of things that are not like that'. Then he said 'Well, we want all the clothes. We want to take all the clothes, we have no clothes'. So they took all the five suits and four trousers, three jackets, two jerseys and all the shirts he had and even the vests, socks, pair of shoes. They took all this into a very big bag which I had bought, a new one, and put all this in that, and they took one of my t-shirts. And I say 'Ah no, that's not a man's t-shirt. You can't take that'. Then they said 'There are also girls where we are; we are going to give this to some of the girls'. After taking all this they took a new blanket from the bed. Then, what else did they take, ... records, and they said 'We would like your husband to come and we would like to ask him where he got all this'. That was another one. The other one said 'Ah no, we came here for the man. We did not want to talk to this woman. We wanted [her husband]. We will wait for him'. They collected all this, went out a few metres away from the house and they sat there. Then all the others were alert to watch. Then one came and said 'We want the food that you have prepared for your husband'. I gave them the food. And we had tins of jam, we had peanut butter in the refrigerator. He opened the refrigerator and collected all the food which was there.

I wasn't afraid because I was just thinking 'Thank heavens, if the children wake up they will cry. Then they will cry, these boys will beat them'. No one woke up. They were all asleep and I wasn't afraid until they left. That's where my conscience now was really back and I was thinking 'What was all this?' I was feeling as I was seeing TV when they left. That's when I started shaking and I said 'I just hope [my husband] doesn't come. It's better because I think they are just new' .... If they met him I'm quite sure they would have killed him .... Then after 20 minutes I couldn't hear any foot noise. I was thinking if he just arrives we are going to just leave the house and go somewhere. Then after an hour and a half that's when I heard footsteps. It was something to 11. I knew here was [my husband]. I looked through the windows and he came through the front door. It wasn't closed anyway. He opened the door and came in and saw all the papers down and some of the records were on the floor,

---

[5]   Someone had told the comrades about the beds. From the next exchanges it transpired that they had also been to her home a few miles away to check out their house there. Anna and her husband had built and furnished a house a few miles away from the school where they had a smallholding.

some of the clothes were on the floor. I was sitting on the chair [....] When he came home he cried when he came in, finding all the things in disorder. He couldn't see that I was in the house. He cried 'Oh, all my family, all the people have been killed, what am I going to say!' Then I heard and I said 'Shut up, you are happy, you would have been killed. They have been looking for you. I told you that day that some people in the village are saying the comrades would come here and then you said it wasn't true. Now they have been hunting for you. If you shout I think they are just near'. He kept quiet and he sat down. He was crying the whole night.

Then something like half past three I woke up, I took a bag. I collected all my children's clothes in the bag. I took only two dresses. He had no shirt. He had only that one he was wearing and the jacket and trousers and the pair of shoes. That was all he had. I collected all my children's clothes, no blankets. I had a big bag and I put all the clothes there. I had five children. I had some money which I had in my bag. I took the money. I put on my tennis shoes and a blue jersey. I still remember .... I woke all the children up, washed them, gave them good clothes. The first boy who was doing Grade Seven said 'Mam, where are we going? What happened?' I said 'You need not ask me. We would like to go to town. Everybody is going to town today. If you want to come back we'll come back'. So he was very happy, putting on new clothes and shoes. He asked me for socks. Then by half past four I was ready. Then I told [my husband] 'Wake up, you have nothing to put on. We are going to town'. 'Where did you get the money?' he said. Then I said 'I have got some money with me'. 'Where are the office keys?' he said. Then I said 'You are thinking of the office keys. You don't care about your life. Leave them and we will put the keys here. That one [who had sold them out] will come and collect the keys from this house'. At first he thought I was joking. But by something to five, because the bus was leaving at five o'clock, I was out with my children and I said 'If you want to be killed, I am leaving you. I am going to Harare to my brother's house with all these children then I can hear from you'. I walked about ten metres from the house. That is when he closed all the doors, then followed and we boarded the bus to Harare.

On the night of the visit, there were other teachers in their houses who would have heard what happened, but everyone stayed indoors:

They heard it but they didn't come out. They heard it ... That day we were three houses they attacked. They attacked [village A] and they attacked [village B] and a few days after this happening they came here and killed the husband of that woman we talked to .... The husband was killed. They just came and had a bundle of sticks. They beat him to death.

Anna claimed it was the deputy headmaster who, in an act of jealousy, had reported her husband to the guerrillas:

I know he did it. The other thing was they [local people] were thinking that all the things that we had, we were given by the whites ... the deputy and the local people because we had beds, refrigerator, we had stoves, good furniture and here this house here had some furniture and some blankets and dresses which I was keeping here because I couldn't take everything to [the school where I worked].

Anna showed acceptance in her attempts to move beyond the feelings of anger she felt at that time. In rebuilding her life in Chiweshe after the war she re-engaged with the family of the man who had sold her and her family out:

> The wife [of the deputy head] was so good to me and we were friends ... We always meet at our [prayer] meetings. Ah no, and I don't think of doing that [feeling bitter]. I can't revenge because I just take it that it was my turn to have that. If it was somebody's turn I should not have seen this. That's how I take it.

Family food security

New routines and new risks

Food shortages were also a feature of the new communities in the Keeps. As people were separated from their land agricultural production fell. The women's struggles for food security provide a microcosm for the daily engagement with the surveillance culture of the Keeps and illuminates those struggles that are often ignored as 'personal' (and by implication non-political) and therefore secondary experiences of revolutionary war. The mapping out of these struggles excavates the vital role of women in ensuring the basic survival of the families and communities inside the Keeps and places these daily struggles at the centre of women's experiences of revolutionary warfare. The general context of close surveillance and the squalid and impoverished environment of the Keeps had a direct impact on the women's capacity to feed their families. Farming was, and continues to be, the staple source of income for rural women and is the locus of their sense of food and economic security. It is also an indicator of social security and status within the local community. 'If you are not a good farmer you do not get money and the children won't go to school and it's very painful to the mother even though the father is affected as well, it is more painful for the mother,' Susan said. This strong sense of maternal responsibility was a pervasive theme in women's accounts of their survival strategies during the war.

The centralisation of people into PVs transformed the agricultural routine for women. In the context of migrant labour and guerrilla recruitment, women now carried fuller responsibility for planting, weeding and harvesting their crops as well as tending cattle. State and guerrilla surveillance meant that doing ordinary chores involved running the gauntlet of intimidation, questioning and arbitrary punishment in the Keeps and in the fields. In addition to food shortages, poor cultivation, time restrictions and harassment by the DAs, the women had to cook and eat in sub-standard conditions. Basic survival became a challenge, as water and food were two essentials that could not be taken for granted. In parts of Chiweshe, firewood for cooking was difficult to find and involved long treks to the boundaries with the commercial farms. Dirty drinking water, often sullied by the DAs at the gate, added to the constant sense of struggle and effort that now accompanied women's attempts to run a household in the midst of war and dislocation in a place that was no longer home. They now had to organise childcare, household tasks and agricultural tasks around a new set of obstacles and threats.

The structure and control of the Keeps prevented people from growing and harvesting food as they had done before; therefore, there was in very real terms less food for everyone:

Sometimes we could not find food. (Florence)

We had very little food to eat. (Josephine)

It was not very nice. Life was hard because we had not enough water and also food itself was a problem. (Margaret)

Shops and grinding mills inside the Keeps were treated with suspicion by the guards. Women could not purchase too many supplies at one time, nor did they have much choice as shopkeepers found it difficult to hold large stocks. Also, women could not always afford to buy goods. Using the mills to grind maize required cash or trading part of the maize, but if they ground or held large quantities of maize in their homes, the women would be suspected of feeding the guerrillas. The shops and mills were sometimes closed without warning if a strong guerrilla presence was suspected in the area.

Crop damage was frequently cited by women as a cause of food shortages. The crops were at risk from baboons, which are time-honoured crop raiders. For those living close to rocky areas there was always the task of banging saucepans and buckets to create noise to scare off these local food bandits. However, once people were in the Keeps there was no possibility of being in the fields and protecting their harvests in this way. The breakouts of hungry cattle from the kraal when they had been penned in for too long was also a major threat to crop production. When the Keeps were closed for days at a time, this threat mounted:

[The crops] were just left out and when the Keeps were not opened, and you know when the cows were hungry they would break the kraals and just break into the fields. And you were not allowed out even if the Keeps were closed for two days. It would be two days of this kind of thing. (Rosy)

The 'protectors' were implicated in the difficulty to cultivate. Phyllis and Stella suggested that the DAs deliberately let cattle loose to destroy crops and harass the people in the Keeps:

The soldiers did not stop the cattle from grazing our crops. As a result we had very little yield year after year and we could not afford to sell the crops. (Stella)

Life was hard because of the way the soldiers were treating us .... During [some] days we weren't allowed to go to our fields. The soldiers would take our cattle from the kraals to our fields and they would graze our crops. As a result, some of us, we could not get anything from the field by the end. This was very painful, to imagine the power wasted in growing crops which you will never harvest. (Phyllis)

The treatment was harsh by those at the gate .... [They] accused us of collaborating with guerrillas if we arrived late at the gate. When late from the fields, they would claim we were cooking for the guerrillas. They would close all of us inside the Keep whilst cattle and baboons destroyed our fields. This meant hunger for us. (Veronica)

Harassment by DAs extended to taking food from people when they came from Harare on the buses. Such personalised state interventions heightened a sense of insecurity around food as women would have paid to travel to town and spent scarce cash to buy food, only to 'lose' it at the gate on their return (Florence). Mrs Moyo remembered that visitors to the Keeps could not bring or take food. The DAs also policed the cooking of food within the Keeps and were suspicious of large quantities, which could be shared with the comrades:

> You know because that time, the people were starving because even if you got lots of people, the soldier doesn't want you to make two buckets of maize, of mealie meal, only to give you a little bit of [offal] and then is always coming to check the mealie meal in here .... Sometimes the children eating porridge on the morning only, no sadza in the afternoon, and then we would see sadza in the evening for supper. Ah, the people were starving. (More Blessing)

Time restrictions and distance to the fields affected women's capacity to feed their families. The time available for cultivation was tied to a curfew, which meant the Keep was usually only open from 6 a.m. to 5 p.m. Women were under pressure to make the most of their time outside the Keeps. This involved balancing time spent on various tasks such as queuing for water at the lone standpipe; walking long distances to find firewood; trekking to the fields with little time left for actual cultivation; and coping with the sudden reorganisation of time and tasks when the Keeps were summarily closed. In these ways insecurity surrounded time and the management of necessary activities:

> Life was hard. Everything which we were doing was tied to time. We could go to the fields and work for a limited time and we had very little food to eat. (Josephine)

> Cultivation of land was now limited and also fields were very far from the Keeps and sometimes we were prohibited from going there. (Veronica)

Alice, for example, had only an hour in her fields by the time she got there, after completing her other chores and taking into account the time she would need to be get back to the Keep. 'Sometimes the Keeps could be closed early in the morning so that no one could go out or we could be given a specified time to do all that we wanted and then come back,' she said. Polly said she and other women walked five kilometres or more to reach their fields.

These restrictions of time and distance were exacerbated by the prohibition on taking food to the fields. Women often carried young children with them to the fields as they did not want to leave them roaming around the Keep. Babies would also need to be breast-feed and so were strapped to their mothers' backs and carried to and from the fields. As a result, they 'had to work on empty stomachs or hide the food somewhere' (Veronica). This inevitable resulted in severe hunger and malnutrition:

> The big problem they had was you know when going out in the morning and coming back in the evening, with little kids, with no food. So most of these young kids suffered kwashiorkor. Most of them suffered it, even elder people

were affected. They stayed there with nothing to eat, drinking water only. Then they would come back in the evening. That is when they would have their supper. You know some of them had to walk very far to their fields so going and coming back was so difficult. (Ellen)

Women were exhausted by the long trek to the fields and the hours worked without food. They were forced to work in the fields in the heat of the day, which was not the traditional way of working. In normal circumstances, women would return home at this time to cook food and wait for the sun to lose some of its power before resuming physically demanding outdoor work.

In the fields they also had to deal with a new food bandits – the comrades, who would demand ready-ground or cooked maize.[6] Providing food for the guerrillas had a severe impact upon tight household budgets and supplies. Any food given to the guerrillas meant less food for a woman and her family. There was also the additional expense of satisfying the guerillas' insistence on expensive *nyama* (meat) rather than the readily available *muriwo* (rape vegetable) to eat with the sadza. Though there was a spiritual rationale for this in terms of taboos set out by the spirit mediums to protect the guerrillas in their capacity as fighters, it obviously had cost implications for the women.[7]

In response to all these difficulties, women sought to find alternative ways of gaining access to the scarce resources of food, durable goods and cash to replace or supplement family incomes from farming.

Strategies for economic survival and enhanced food security
In place of, or in addition to, their meagre harvests, women depended on securing an income to supplement or ensure family subsistence. Some women depended on husbands and sons working in Harare to send or bring part of their wages at the end of each month. Within the Keeps others struggled to find economic opportunities that would provide cash or allow the barter of goods, labour and services. Cash was essential if women wanted to buy food from others in time of failed or poor harvests, purchase seed and fertiliser for next year's harvest, buy household items such as salt, oil, sugar, soap and tea, pay for transport to town and pay school fees and for the children's uniform.[8] The paradox, however, was that a maize surplus was the main route to acquiring the cash needed to pay for other food and household essentials. Agnes and Hilda described how food shortages were worsened by the breakdown of markets, whereby selling and buying food depended on informal local relations involving barter and money:

'Life in the Keep was terrible. We had no food to feed our families .... We

6   The fuller details of food provision to the guerrillas are outlined in Chapter 6.
7   Tendai explains this taboo as follows: 'It is true some vegetables were not allowed to be eaten during the war because they were believed that they would weaken the bones of the comrades. The ZANU-PF comrades had several things which they considered as taboos. This is because they worked together with the people who were possessed by spiritual mediums who were warning them and guiding them in what to do and what not to do.'
8   Some women needed to travel to meet with other family members and sometimes to pursue an errant husband for some of his wages.

depended on buying maize from other people. Ourselves, we hardly harvested anything because where our fields were was outside the Keep .... We had difficulties also in getting to buy food since we were not selling any products to the GMB [Grain Marketing Board]. (Agnes)

It was hard in the fact that although we could get food from our fields, we were financially poor. We could not sell our crops to the GMB. (Hilda)

Josephine's husband had a drinking problem, which affected the family's ability to provide for itself. During the war he was out of work and Josephine took responsibility for eking out an income from the fields and brewing beer to support the family:

It is difficult but the thing to do is you, as mother, take control .... We could not harvest enough crops to sell. As a result we had problems in feeding our families. However, we had to use the maize which was rotten to brew beer. We would sell the beer. The money which we got from beer we would use for buying food for our children.

However, housekeeping money was a source of tension as her husband controlled the income from her beer-brewing and gave her very little. In Stella's family, mother and daughters co-operated to secure sufficient household income to cover household essentials and school fees; brewing beer was one strategy, along with farming and the income earned by her daughters through work on the commercial farms. Some women used their sewing and knitting skills to earn an income or trade for food. Eva, for example, grew up in Chiweshe and lived there until 1975, when she was 21. Then she got married and moved to Bulawayo with her husband who worked with the railways. Of her situation, she said:

Sometimes he gave me [money] but sometimes he did not. It was hard because I could sometimes live without having any meals because I did not have the money .... He could not give me the money because he was getting very low wages .... He was using the money for buying beer.

She earned a little money by sewing 'small dresses' and used the money to buy vegetables for the family. Tendai knitted jerseys to support herself and her family, saying that she 'was only able to knit. After knitting these jerseys I had to sell them. That was the only thing I was able to do. I was 12 years old when I started knitting .... I was actually sending the jerseys to the [commercial] farms for selling'. However, the money she earned in this way was not necessarily hers to spend. 'Most of the money I was giving it to [my husband] because he was demanding it,' she told me.

Group and household savings were other sources of income drawn upon to cope with the crisis of poverty. Women's clubs provided money-making opportunities for some women. One strategy was to set up savings clubs so that women could afford to buy household utensils. Another was to make clothes in sewing groups for use by the family or for sale to neighbours for cash or maize:

We benefited through learning new ideas and we ended up having a lot of knowledge. We were also giving money to one another every month and we could buy plates and pots. (Polly)

Susan relied on personal savings rather than group savings schemes to see out the war. She and her husband worked in Harare for eight years until 1973 but used up their savings over the course of the war. External interventions by welfare organisations (for example, churches and Red Cross clinics) also supported the women's efforts to provide for their families. The Salvation Army ran pre-school groups in some of the Keeps that provided supplementary feeding to young children to combat malnutrition. Such groups enabled mothers to go to the fields and tend their crops.

For some girls and young women, marriage was an economic and social strategy in a context of limited opportunity; it was also an option that was socially acceptable. Such rationalising was not limited to wartime situations but may have been heightened by levels of impoverishment and insecurity (physical, emotional and social) that accompanied the war. Add to this matrix, the lack of money or interest to educate girls and the range of choices became very limited. Doreen's mother died when she was young and her father struggled to support her and her siblings. Having finished school at Standard Six she got married in 1968 at the age of 16:

> I was disappointed and I thought all disadvantages and problems which I and my sister were facing was because we did not have our mother. And the only answer to my problem was to get married .... I swore when I got married I was going to send my children to school because I did not want them to be like me .... And when I got married I wanted to go back to school. But this caused a lot of conflict in the home. My husband did not want me to go back. He said if I went back it means I would be more educated than him and I would leave him.

Marriage was also a chance for girls and young women to escape tense family situations and secure independence and respect. Like Doreen, Joanne's education was also cut short and she sought to escape life with her divorced mother and stepfather:

> I went home to stay with my mother and was just staying there going to the fields and I thought 'Ah, it is better for me to find a husband' because so far I have no chance to do anything so I found a husband .... I thought it would be better [to get married] because the way he [stepfather] was treating me was not very fair. When he comes [home] he starts quarrelling .... I thought it was better for me to move and leave him with his home and his wife.

Dorothy got married in 1972 at the age of 15. Her parents had separated when she was young and she and her two siblings lived with their alcoholic grandmother:

> At that time I found my life to be very hard. This is because my parents had separated and it was only my mother who had to buy us some clothes and send me to school. My father did not even look after me .... What I remember most is that my grandmother was a drunkard and she used not come home. Since I was the eldest I had to look after my younger ones. I could do all the household and field work .... I had to get married because my life was tough .... I hoped that when I have a husband I was going to live a happy life. When I grew up life was very hard for me so I thought when I was going to

get married things were going to change. But unfortunately my husband was poor. As a result my parents took me from my husband. We did not divorce as such. When my parents took me it was like they were demanding *lobola* [bride price] but my husband never came to take me back. It was not good. Even though I loved my husband I could not go back to him because they were demanding for *lobola*.

Mary felt that losing out on her education impoverished her choices for the future and defined her life during the war. She vented her anger toward her father for having failed to handle and distribute resources in their polygamous household in a way that would have allowed her to go to school. Mary's mother was the second wife and was divorced by her husband when Mary was still a young girl; she rarely saw her mother again as in line with traditional practice she remained in her father's household:

When I left school whilst others were still going to school I was very disappointed and troubled why my father just decided to drop paying fees for me …. I was still young but when I grew up I did not like her [the third wife] because father did not afford to take me to school because of having too many women. He could not even afford to buy clothes and blankets for me …. We were growing vegetables, doing domestic jobs and pounding mealie meal and also ploughing with the cattle. I was also herding cattle … These times I thought of my mother because if she was there I was not going to work like a slave.

The daily struggles of personal and household survival are difficult to separate out from the effects of war. In Chiweshe, women engaged in a variety of strategies to gain access to key resources of food and money that were central to surviving day to day in a very precarious context of deprivation and the constant threat of injury, loss or death. While some collective strategies have been given here as examples, the overwhelming experience of these women was of localised, individualised survival strategies. Their struggle was often against poverty and the effects of poverty – the lack of food and money, a poor diet and social isolation. Poverty in Chiweshe was exacerbated by the war, but some of the women interviewed also cited it as a persistent feature of the colonial and independence periods. Poverty does not require war to have a debilitating impact on the lives of women or to be the progenitor of survival strategies developed to cope with its worst effects. However, what these women's survival strategies reveal is that the battle against poverty was placed in a context of precarious risk during the liberation struggle. This profile of food insecurity also begs the question of government intentions; to what extent were the Keeps deliberately about impoverishing the people such that struggle for subsistence would directly impact on their ability to give food to the guerrillas? Whether this was a stated intention cannot be claimed with certainty; however, in effect, basic subsistence as a way of life was the situation women faced.

Dilemmas of survival:
The case of involvement with the DAs

The impoverished and insecure setting of life in the PVs placed women in vulnerable situations; staying alive involved difficult choices. Some survival strategies pushed the boundaries of social and moral acceptability within the Keeps' communities. The dilemma of women engaged in relations with the DAs as a deliberate strategy to access scarce resources is one example of this. For many women involved in such relationships, the main motivation appears to have been economic. The DAs received salaries and also had access to goods not otherwise available in the Keeps. Good relations could also ensure a woman would not be harassed as she went about her daily chores. Trust and Hilda understood the economic rationale but imply that women behaved badly:

> Some women were misbehaving, taking advantage of the war. Young girls too were involved with the DAs for sacks of money. The situation was chaotic and we wondered if this was ever to end. (Trust)

> In the Keeps many women had become prostitutes of the DAs ... [back then] they didn't have money. When the DAs showed them money, they changed their behaviour .... Some of the women who became prostitutes never changed from that way of life. (Hilda)

The negative moral agency of women tended to be assumed even by those who claimed to understand an economic motive; the implication seemed to be that women were being greedy rather than desperate. Gladys said that '[t]here were problems. Some women started going out with the DAs. Some were made pregnant .... They were not forced. They were attracted by money which the DAs were willing to give them in exchange for their bodies', while Joanne commented that '[t]here can be bad circumstances but you have to make them up yourself, you can't make them up that way. Is it good? It's not really good, that way, having sex with anybody there so as for you to make a profit or benefit from there'.

For Tendai, a *Chimbwido*, the affairs were a symptom of the power wielded by the DAs in the Keeps. She told me that 'the DAs were forcing us to fall in love with them. They would, for example, take girls to the bush and give them punishment of cutting wood and they would end up having swollen hands. As a result you end up forced to fall in love with them'. Rosy, however, felt that the women had the chance to reject such harassment:

> 'Most of [the DAs] were just after women .... Well some [women] were interested in it. They responded but for those that were not interested they could just leave it .... When getting out of the Keep and a DA approaches you, you refuse to agree to what he wants. When you are getting out when he is on duty then you could face a problem'.

Others attributed these relationships to the climate of general moral decline within the Keep communities. Veronica was very strict in her criticism and at the time had supported social sanctions to alienate the women involved. Her view was that 'only those who were loose [had trouble with the DAs because they] saw these women's immorality at the gates when they left and came in to the Keeps .... We saw them as immoral outcasts because some of them left their families completely'. Dorothy claimed that the '[w]omen were easily carried away. They could be seduced by the soldiers'. Polly's line between poverty and immorality was very clear: 'It's because they were loose. Poorness does not kill'.

However, a number of the women interpreted these affairs as coming from a combination of economic survival, moral breakdown and harassment, rather than one factor in isolation. Agnes cited all three factors and suggested a wider context of immorality that involved affairs not only with the DAs but with other women's husbands:

> Even some married women were behaving in an awkward way. Women tended to be loose. This is because we were no longer getting enough food in the Keeps .... [In the Keeps] women were more than men. There were some women who were divorced and some women who had their husbands died .... It caused a lot of problems because these women who did not have husbands started going out with other women's husbands. In other words, all women started to become loose, even those who were married were falling in love with other women's husbands in revenge to their husband's actions .... It was because women could not afford to feed their families. Hence they thought falling in love with these husbands could help them financially. This was the major and only cause .... Some soldiers were harassing women and forced them to fall. Those women who were not strong, end up falling in love with the soldiers because of fear.

For Joanne, the affairs involved a combination of moral breakdown and economic survival:

> I think it was a time when ... women were not really used to meeting many people and so they came in here [the Keeps], they started ... learning many things; things which are not really very good. They started seeing the DAs, making affairs and some had to make money with the DAs, saying 'we are looking after the children'.

For More Blessing, it was a combination of economic survival and the result of harassment from the DAs:

> 'You know, the DA was doing to the woman, sometimes the man [husband] was here [from Harare] and then the DA, he can come and say, 'Oh, I love you' that time. If you said 'No, I don't love', you will see when you are going out. He just mark you and say 'Why did you say you don't love me, tell me, what is different, me and your husband, I love you'. He just force you, if you don't want, he just force you to do so, to love.

She herself had faced harassment from a DA who tried to force her to have sex with him. 'He said "Oh, I love you" and I said "Oh no, I am too young'. He had to leave me alone.' Unlike many of her contemporaries however, More Blessing was more pragmatic and less judgmental in her assessment of the situation:

Ah, that time, I don't think those other women looked very bad, they were just living. They have nothing to do. If you just say 'Oh you, what are you doing'. They say 'Oh leave me, what do you want of me. If you want, you do'. Nobody say 'No, don't do it' .... [Women were doing it] because of money, I think because of money. Because the DA give lots of food that time. Especially the women want the food, beef, beans, everything, just giving you for free, but sex first.

Fr Fidelis witnessed these 'difficult choices' in the course of his investigations with CCJP:

It was really a pathetic situation which history would never bring forth – a young woman who was attractive and all these men who have a gun and do what they like; to young women who were left with no means of income and all these men were receiving good money. They are coming up to you, you have to make a choice and these were difficult choices.

Whatever the causal factors, the women involved in these relationships were held publicly and privately accountable for their choices; they faced punishment from the guerrillas as sell outs; the social opprobrium of gossip and isolation of this strategy of economic survival was not without extreme risk. The risks included the contraction of sexually transmitted diseases, identification as sell outs, physical harm, social ostracism, loss of marriage prospects and single motherhood:

The DAs forced them into love .... Some women had children with the DAs .... Some women died .... They would contract sexually transmitted diseases because of prostitution in the Keeps .... Some women were beaten by their husbands. Those unmarried just stayed [they were not harmed] .... They [single mothers] faced problems in upkeeping those children because they had no fathers. (Judith)

Some had children with the DAs. Some even had to break their marriages. A husband at work, the woman here doing such things; when he comes home he is disappointed about that so he breaks the marriage there. (Joanne)

People would ridicule the wife because she was being unfaithful to the husband. (Pardon)

The loss of an accepted role as married woman and mother is a strong social cost in rural areas where age, marriage, and children afford women status and respect. The loss of such respectability was the price women paid for their relationships with the DAs, irrespective of whether they had been forced to submit to such relations. These threats of course have to be weighed against the perceived advantages of access to food and money, protection from physical harm by other DAs and the relative power over other women in the Keeps.

The risks these women faced reinforced the daily reality of negotiating relations. They faced harassment from the DAs and had to trade that against the possibility of being sold out to the comrades as traitors. Having a voice and being believed was not something women could rely upon to escape physical harm. Silence too, was often interpreted as guilt. 'If girls were being forced to fall in love with the DAs they would report that they were forced. But if they kept it secret then the comrades would assume that you were interested; that's when you would be punished,' said Tendai. Public knowledge of the affairs was a danger to the women involved as they would now become a target of the comrades as accused sell outs. They would even avoid going to the fields for fear of meeting the comrades:

> When they go out they would walk carefully and even to avoid going out to see those comrades there .... They were afraid of being beaten .... They were afraid so they had to avoid going out and staying here inside. (Joanne)

> They made sure that they never went out of the Keeps and met the comrades. They knew they would be punished. (Gladys)

And if they did venture out:

> Some were threatened! Beaten up by nearly everybody, threatened .... They said, 'You are doing wrong things. You need to know things that are right so you need to be beaten'. (Joanne)

Florence recounted one particular incident:

> A DA who was going out with one of the women was killed in the Keep. The DA got married to a daughter of a policeman and he was told that he was going to be killed together with his wife and father-in-law. But later it was him and his wife who were killed .... They [comrades] captured them. They surrounded their home and then went away with them.

Gladys heard about a similar incident at Chinehashe:

> They were in love with the DAs. The comrades went into their Keep and told the women to follow them. When they got to the place where the comrades had their base the woman in question and the man she was having an affair with were all killed.

Agnes, a widowed mother, was concerned about the fate of her daughters in such a tense situation:

> There were some women who were actually beaten by comrades because they were considered as sell outs because of going out with the DAs. The people who were in the Keeps were reporting them to the comrades .... Most of the women who were going out with the DAs were being beaten by the comrades.... [and] the soldiers were beating those who were refusing to fall in love with them. The comrades started complaining if girls were delaying in marriage. They were saying because they were going out with the DAs therefore they did not want to get married. My daughter was actually beaten by the soldiers and my daughter was told to get married before she fell in love with the DAs.

This incident also highlights the fact that marriage for young women was not only an escape from poverty but also an escape from the vulnerability of illicit sexual relations. For Tendai, it was a simple matter of avoiding involvement with the DAs:

> It was fair for the comrades to prevent girls from falling in love with the DAs because if they were not doing that those girls were going to get married to the DAs and later on meet the comrades who knew them. And when the comrades would get to know the girl was married to a DA they would kill her. In fact

a certain girl I went to school with got married to a DA and she went to stay in Masvingo and when she met the comrades who knew her she was killed. Therefore it was better to prevent the situation before it got worse.

However, Rosy who had two ex-husbands who were policemen, disapproved of the negative reactions to these relationships and argued that love does not always respect the dictates of war:

> I would say it wasn't fair for these people to beat up people because it wasn't the people's fault. It is all natural for people to fall in love. Those DAs are people, the policemen are people .... The people had said that all those that are in love with civil servants, when the war is over they are going to be murdered.

In this scenario of private relations between women and the state military we find a mix of social approbation, moral outrage, political treason, witchcraft and economic rationalisation. These are all explanations of a phenomenon that defies categorisation as private/public or woman as prostitute/camp follower. Rather, such women may be simultaneously a mother, a wife, a guerrilla supporter, a state collaborator, an economic agent, a victim and a survivor. The implications of everyday social relations in the context of a guerrilla war became more dangerous and violent. These dilemmas of survival remind us how difficult it is to have a moral viewpoint, a right or a wrong, in evaluating women's actions in war. They signify the limitations and risks in the room for manoeuvre that women had had to survive and illuminate the volatility and uncertainty of community attitudes, solidarity and trust that affected their experience of, and participation in, revolution.

Summing up

The community dynamics and personal dislocations experienced by the women in Chiweshe in trying to survive through a revolutionary war led them to establish the room for manoeuvre in their daily lives. This is exemplified by women who negotiated a variety of relations, responded to varying demands and were active agents in daily survival of the self, family and community. Their accounts of their struggles for survival have uncovered a plethora of actions that can appropriately be termed 'everyday resistance' in withstanding the pressures applied by the DAs, guerrillas and neighbours. The difficulties of separating survival and everyday resistance were apparent in the daily lives women forged through their engagement with a context of revolutionary war. This terrain of daily survival adds an important counterbalance to the context of revolutionary participation outlined in Chapter 4. It illuminates the 'consciousness of context' as embedded not only in an anti-colonial struggle but also in these women's struggles for survival; the context of the revolutionary struggle is also a context of their struggle to survive. The development of such consciousness is grounded in the volatile context of deprivation, distrust, surveillance and fear. It is accentuated by new injustices, risks and expectations that came from the challenges of simply staying alive in the course of the revolution.

Accordingly, women's participation in revolution needs to be extended from revolutionary roles and labour to take account of this necessary participation, dictated simply by the fact of living where they did, when they did. This is not to assume passivity; on the contrary, mapping out daily life in the PVs revealed the furrowing agency – the minute acts of everyday survival – that illuminates our understanding of women's lives in the context of a guerrilla war. The concrete manifestations of the revolution are found in the practices of power and surveillance as experienced by the Chiweshe women in their relations with the DAs, guerrillas, families and neighbours. The impetus for survival and the social dynamics this unleashed demonstrate the necessity of individuated agency and consciousness by women in their engagement with a revolutionary war. This atomisation of women in their daily lives challenges more romantic notions of community solidarity in the course of revolution. These interactions mark the nexus of surviving and enacting a revolution. They indicate the complexity of consciousness and agency that undermine the possibilities of a singular revolutionary practice, consciousness or subjectivity. The wider effects of the interactions of these survival strategies with revolutionary resistance are explored in the next chapter.

6

The Front Line Runs Through Every Woman | Resistance & Survival by Women in Revolutionary War

Overview

The undercurrent of women's position as being 'caught in the middle' finds its fullest articulation in this chapter. The previous chapter highlighted how important women were to the survival their households and communities throughout the war; it also highlighted the impact revolutionary resistance had on these efforts to live through war. The struggles for survival affected resistance by causing women to become both disaffected with the guerrillas and further angered by the colonial state. The illustration of these tensions culminates in this chapter when I address the Chiweshe women's participation in revolution as food providers to the guerrillas. The interpretation of resistance from these women's testimonies extends revolutionary resistance beyond particular militarised roles to include forms of everyday resistance in the context of the social relations of war; they were enacting local resistance in their dealings with the DAs, the guerrillas and their neighbours as well as enacting revolutionary resistance by feeding the guerrillas. The survival and revolutionary dimensions of food provision reflect how revolutionary resistance and the struggles for survival by women in a revolutionary war, interacted, supported and conflicted or contradicted each other. The dilemmas of food provision demonstrate how localised resistance in practice gave rise to a host of resistances that cannot readily be demarcated as revolutionary versus everyday resistance or political versus non-political agency. These resistances included self-interested, compliant, resistant and predatory behaviour. The argument is that everyday resistance was part of the war and that it involved risk-taking behaviour as well as risk-avoidance. Everyday resistance was not separate from revolutionary resistance and was not always readily distinguished from the struggle to simply survive the war.

Family food provision was the *sine qua non* for food provision to the guerrillas, whereby the latter tapped into the daily routines and tasks of women to ensure their survival and the success of the war. One cannot talk of political participation by women merely in terms of fixed revolutionary identities, the ways in which the functions of daily life were inscribed by war, and in turn affected the conduct of war, also have to be taken on board. That women in Chiweshe took precisely the same risks to feed their families as to feed the guerrillas underscores the unwritten and depoliticised dimension of their experiences of revolution. These struggles for economic survival and food security in themselves define the women's lives as revolutionary. The negotiation of these aspects of food effected, and was affected by, the crisis of community that defined life in the Keeps. This battleground was not simply geographical or physical, it was also a sentient terrain of personal identities. In Chiweshe, the women all had different faces for the state, the guerrillas, their neighbours and not least for themselves – the picture they wished to project of themselves and the way they later understood their part in the liberation struggle. The embedded nature of the front line of revolutionary war is seen in how women positioned themselves in the conduct of daily life and relations, and the conduct of these risk-laden relations lies at the heart of localised resistance as an interpretation and explanation of women's experiences of revolutionary guerrilla war.

The front line of food provision is explored here through three themes. The first addresses the modalities of the food supply networks of the guerrillas in Chiweshe and the ways in which women contributed to their operation, underscoring the vital importance of women's participation to the military effectiveness of the guerrilla war. It also addresses the unstable dynamics of the supply networks which suggest a failure in Chiweshe to consolidate and maintain organised and collective lines of supply.

The second theme explores the redrawn battleground for women in Chiweshe that takes account of food provision both to the guerrillas and to the family in defining the battleground of revolutionary war as a coterminous and conflicted terrain. This opens up the redefinition of revolution and participation as conflicted and involving the constant re-positioning of self in relation to others.

The third theme addresses this redefinition through the exploration of risk and the women's attempts to renegotiate the middle ground between state forces and agents, revolutionary forces and local family and community relations. The complexity of women's everyday relations defined the middle ground as a place of constant repositioning and representation that was infused with risk; measuring it, sensing it, falling into it were all considerations and consequences of their attempts to find relative day-to-day security while living through a revolutionary guerrilla war.

The build-up and breakdown of food supply networks

The case of food provision reveals the maelstrom of fear, risk, uncertainty and courage that underpinned women's agency in effecting resistance and survival. Feeding the guerrillas was the most typical self-identification of revolutionary resistance amongst the women in Chiweshe. As highlighted in Chapter 4, the melange of motivations driving such participation included voluntarism, coercion, fear, uncertainty and commitment to fighting for an independent Zimbabwe. The women's participation in the war was also influenced by the destabilising community dynamics of the PVs. These aspects of participation and community interlock in the emerging narrative of food provision by women in Chiweshe and signal the fundamental instability in the food supply networks of revolutionary support, and a crisis of survival for women struggling to feed their families and communities.

The functioning of food supply networks in Chiweshe placed women at the heart of guerrilla strategy; what army could survive on an empty stomach? The closer the guerrillas got to their strategic targets – commercial farms, military outposts and urban commerce – the more important the availability of regular provisions to maintain the roving bands of fighters became. In terms of making contact, the guerrillas had various points of entry into the community, particularly during the pre-Operation Overload days, when *pungwes* or home visits were common. This signals an individualised and informal type of networking that co-existed with the war committee structures or acted in place of such committees in situations where formal organising was difficult or not expedient. Hilda, as the wife of a village headman, found her home was a frequent port of call for the guerrillas:

> They could come in the night and knocked at the door so that we could give them food. In the first place they appeared only three. Others came later.... They only stated what they wanted, like food .... They expected to be given chicken, goats, and maize cobs. [They didn't talk politics] unless it was a meeting.

Other women recalled washing and ironing clothes for the comrades at this time, as well as providing warm water for bathing. Veronica cooked for the comrades before moving to the Keeps and recounted the seeming regularity of requests for food as well as the role of threats in securing such supplies from local people:

> It was done randomly but on a daily basis.... They came, many of them, when we were harvesting in the fields and asked my father if he knew what was meant by '*vakomana*' [the boys]. My father said no and they told us what they were and wanted food.... We did a lot of cooking for them. Some women were beaten by them until we were taken to the Keeps for safety.

Stella's experience was also one of relatively organised contact, but through the offices of the village headmen rather than by direct contact:

> The headman was the only one who was aware that the comrades were around. He would nominate a few women to cook food for the comrades. The majority were not aware.... The headman instructed people to collect food from house to house.

Many women faced the fear of visits from either comrades or soldiers and the terror of one side finding out the other side had visited.

The sense of organised supply networks, formal and informal, continued into the Keeps (post-1974) where contact was more difficult. Women faced more threats from the soldiers as they were now incarcerated under guard. Despite this, Phyllis said the expectations of supply from the guerrillas were unabated. 'Everyone was expected to help as long as they were able to bring the food out of the Keep,' she recalled. At the very least, in the Keeps women had to give food to the *Mujibhas* and *Chimbwidos*, who were then responsible for getting it out of the Keeps without being detected. They were also key actors in the purchase of provisions for the guerrillas from local stores and from Harare. Money was often of little use to the guerrillas unless the women bought the supplies of food, clothing, soap and cigarettes. According to Judith, this task involved strategic awareness. She told me that '[i]f one was sent to buy food for the comrades, they could get into the shop one by one, after a certain period of time. This made it difficult for the soldiers to know that the food was for the comrades'. For Veronica, the shops were the source of last resort when the restrictions of the Keep became too much. 'There were many Keeps. If all were closed, people would rob shops of food in order to feed guerrillas,' she said. Building up such networks also involved gendered and generational divisions and perceptions of revolutionary labour.

Gendered and generational divisions of labour
The leadership of the local war committees oversaw the formal development of these networks. Inside and outside of these war committees, the supply networks were grown upon individual visits to people's homes in the pre-Keep period; the mobilisation of *Chimbwidos* and *Mujibhas* to carry requests from and deliver food to the guerrillas; and, amongst the women, the setting in place of a generational division of labour. The war committees were largely the preserve of men, who would delegate tasks to 'mothers' and *Chimbwidos* in the acquisition of cooking and food. Although women were seldom part of these committees, the *modus operandi* of the latter was based upon women's work; their willingness and capability to grow crops, harvest, buy supplies and cook sadza. Polly said women sometimes acted as secretaries or treasurers on the committees, but that few were directly involved in the decision-making:

> The committee comprises of the chairman, secretary, treasurer and the committee. The chairman leads the people and the meeting. The secretary writes the minutes of the meeting and the treasurer looks after the money which people contributed towards the food for the freedom fighters. The committees were there to see whether people's plans and goals were being met.... There were many [war committees] and a committee could be changed depending on its performance.... [Members] were voted into positions by the masses if they trusted that they would do a good job in the struggle.... Some people sacrificed their life because they wanted to liberate the country, hence they did not bother about the negative consequences of being involved in the war.

Veronica seemed to suggest that women were not quite up to responsible positions because they lacked the stamina to perform duties of leadership, although women's workloads inside the PVs could also explain this fact:

> We set up committees made up mostly of young people. [Membership] was changed time and again.... Few women were given responsible positions because they would not manage the tiresome schedules associated with such positions as Chairperson.

Such self-deprecating views were also voiced by Joanne and Hilda:

> Women can be given some positions, but you know women they are used to just talk things, many things, whereas men can stay with something for years and these women they can't manage to keep it. She will just stop it. (Joanne)

> Only men were very active. Women could not keep a secret. They could easily reveal secret information. If women were angered by their husband they could easily reveal secret they had kept in their hearts.... [However] the coming of the comrades made it possible for both men and women to attend meetings. [Women changed] because they had heard all the promises that troubles would come to an end after independence. (Hilda)

The women's accounts of the setting-up of the chains of supply reflected elements of gender and generational assumptions of power in the communities. Young men seemed to have been the main vehicles of the new authority gained through the war. Judith remembered seeing the comrades for the first time in the mountains near Chipiri in 1972, but she said they did not talk to her, that '[t]hey talked to men only.... Men were responsible for everything, especially if comrades wanted money. Also if they wanted food, they told the men who in turn told the women'. She also highlighted a generational dimension to participation when she said the comrades 'could see and talk to young boys and girls. The youths would tell the elders'. Emily remembered a gendered and generational division whereby women and young boys played a greater role than elders. 'Women worked a lot. Older men were just seated but boys also did a lot in food movement,' she stated.

In southern Chiweshe, where state security forces exerted greater control, cooking food for the guerrillas was more difficult and so commodities were often given instead. Veronica, a young girl at the time of the war, recalled that beer and cigarettes were the main focus of supply and that the network was run by young men. This seems quite different to the north of Chiweshe, where leadership positions involved older, married men. Food provision tasks were thus experienced differently by the women around Chiweshe.

Socio-economic differences also informed the types of contributions women made to the networks. Veronica, for example, recalled that 'Women like me who had men working were asked for money to buy cigarettes and that our husbands should send money to the guerrillas. We were asked to go to meetings'. Anna, as a schoolteacher, was keenly aware of the importance of salaried people to the comrades as a source of financial support. 'It was compulsory [to attend meetings] but they knew that teachers couldn't come because of the government. They knew that if teachers were sacked away from work by the government, they were not going to have support because this is the working group,' she said. The tension of this relatively better-off socio-economic position was contradictory, as persons working for the government were also subject to being targeted as sell outs by the local community and by the guerrillas.

There was also a generational division of labour amongst women in the work of the supply networks. Mothers (older, married women) and *ambuyas* were charged with overseeing and conducting the cooking of food, while *Chimbwidos* mainly delivered food to the guerrilla base camps and to carried requests from the guerrillas back to the villages. Unlike their older, married counterparts, these young girls were also part of the guerrilla intelligence-gathering network. They sought information on the movements of soldiers and identified potential sell outs within the local community.

The rationale of a generational division of labour amongst women and girls in the provision of food rested on the physical demands of different tasks. Hilda recalled that '[some] girls would fetch water and firewood while others carried food to the comrades because they would move faster than old people'. These young women and girls 'could command people to carry food out of the Keeps. They would give people tricks of how to get out with the food.... The *Chimbwidos* were also listened to. Sometimes they would carry the food outside the Keep"' (Florence). However, within the tasks of the younger women as *Chimbwidos*, there was a crosscutting gendered division of revolutionary labour with their young male counterparts, the *Mujibhas*. This was commonly expressed as '[t]he *Mujibhas* were the ones who informed the comrades about the whereabouts of the soldiers and the *Chimbwidos* were the ones who cooked for the comrades' (Farasia). Tendai and Sarah emphasised the elements of food provision and intelligence-gathering that defined their activities:

> We were so many because [for] every boy and girl it was a must that he or she must be a *Mujibha* and a *Chimbwido*. The duty was to report to the comrades; to report if there were some girls who were in love with the soldiers or people who were sell outs. (Tendai)

> Myself I was a youth, a *Chimbwido*. If they [comrades] see a person, they try to contact her, since it was a scout for them to get food. So they used to talk to the people to tell them 'Can you give us food? So, if you don't give us food, we cannot fight for Zimbabwe'. (Sarah)

The *Chimbwidos* however, were in an ambivalent situation of power in their dealings with the guerrillas, the DAs and the local community. On one hand, they were a vulnerable part of the supply network in terms of acquiring food for the guerrillas and being largely responsible for its delivery. On the other hand, they were also the voice of the guerrillas in that they were the main points of contact outside the Keeps and often the source of information to label sell outs. This gave them a power and status that sometimes went beyond their usual generational position of subservience in the rural community structure. Older women were fearful of this reversal of generational status and power because of the threats the *Chimbwidos* wielded:

> They were always saying they would report us if we do not give them what the comrades had asked for. (Phyllis)

> If they decided that somebody was going to die, he would die that day. (Pardon)

Nor were *Chimbwidos* trusted, for fear that they were exercising a double power relationship with soldiers and guerrillas, acting as local informants by both:

> They were not good people because they would support the comrades and

soldiers... because they were liars, they were sell outs.... They were there to keep in touch with the community and then communicate that information to the comrades or the soldiers. (Josephine)

These perceptions of the *Chimbwidos'* power were rendered more complicated as the comrades were also subject to the power of the youth who could disclose their movements to the soldiers. Emily said that the comrades treated the *Chimbwidos* well because 'they were afraid of being sold out to soldiers'. Phyllis stated that 'they had power because they were able to protect the comrades from the soldiers by hiding them'. In the midst of these power struggles, however, Tecla saw the *Chimbwidos* as powerless:

They did not have a lot of power. Some people did not listen to them but some did. In our area there were very few *Mujibhas* and *Chimbwidos* because they were scared of the results of the war.

Chimbwidos were also a challenge to parental authority and created conflict within the family. Josephine, as a mother, and Lorine, as a daughter, reflected the clash of tension around such participation. Josephine worried that girls were not suitable for such tasks and did not appreciate young adults going against their parents' wishes:

Girls were refusing to listen to their mothers even when they were told not to participate in such things. They were refusing to listen. Parents just thought it was for boys because they could not imagine girls being able to travel or run for a long distance.

Lorine went against her parents to conduct such tasks:

Our parents would not allow us but sometimes we cooked for the boys.... The boys used to come to our place and so we would cook for them.

This web of power relations can be read as being 'caught in the middle'. Young girls were expected to work for the comrades but were also under constant surveillance and suffered harassment from the DAs and soldiers. For Emelda, risks for a *Chimbwido* included being used by the soldiers as bait for the comrades:

They were beating us all the time, forcing us to tell them where the comrades were. Once you mention where the comrades were they could ask you to lead them to the place where the comrades and this could result in your death if the comrades fired.

By contrast, Stella says the youth faced threats by the comrades if tasks were not performed:

They [*Chimbwidos*] were brave, but the bravery they had was through fear, because if they were going to be weak the comrades promised to beat or kill them.

The threat of violence from both sides, as well as parental worry and anger, meant that young girls had to react and think quickly to avoid punishment. They also had to cope with negative gendered perceptions such as those suggested by Juliet when she said that '*Chimbwidos* were sometimes seen as loose but were considered very brave'. These contradictions suggest that a romantic reading of *Chimbwidos* as exercising new-found generational power through taking up revolutionary roles has to be tempered by the persistence of gendered expectations of the tasks being performed and also by their relatively subordinate position to male youth. Their double-edged experiences of power as contacts for the guerrillas also have to be taken into account. Any gains in status or resources have to be offset by the greater dangers and fears they faced, as well as the hostility of some reactions within their own community to their war-related activities.

Under the wire: Strategies of provision

The innovation and courage of women were nowhere more evident than in the strategies devised to take food outside the Keeps to the guerrillas. These strategies of provision often revolved around 'routine' tasks so as not to arouse suspicion. These included carrying of children, fetching water and firewood, taking manure to the fields, shelling groundnuts and washing clothes at the standpipe or the river. Women took advantage of the appearances and requirements of their domestic tasks to disguise food delivery. One of the strategies was for women to hide parcels of maize underneath their babies on their backs when they went to the fields (Sarah; Josephine). Despite the restrictions on carrying any food to the fields, mothers would plead allowances for their small children and then give the food to the comrades (Gladys). Another strategy was to play the role of mother-to-be:

> Taking food out to the guerrillas was complicated and risky, but they did it wisely. For instance, *Chimbwidos* would wear maternity [clothes], put food inside them and soldiers took them [for] pregnant women. (Emily)

Maize parcels smuggled out of the camp by being disguised as sanitary towels and placed in underwear. As cited earlier, women also bought provisions at local stores under the guise of procuring household supplies. Carrying fertiliser to vegetable plots provided another decoy, as food could be stored underneath manure in a bucket or scotch cart:

> Some [women] cooked when they are going out to the garden. They put the food in a tin and then put manure. So as if you were going to the garden. So if you ever get there, if you find someone who doesn't say 'Ah, let me see what is there', he can say 'Just go', you've got an advantage. The food is there; take off the manure and the food is down there. (Joanne)

Concealing food inside carts' tyres was another way of getting through the inspections at the gate: 'We were very clever. We could open a scotch cart tyre and put some mealie meal inside [it]. And we would pretend as if we were going to carry some firewood with the scotch cart,' said Phyllis. Those with cars used similar tactics to get the vehicles out the Keep with supplies on board. Various strategies for literally getting food over and under the fence of the Keep were devised, and all generations played their part:

> People could dig ... and put the food under the fence since they were being inspected by the gate. Sometimes the comrades could come and get their food over the fence. They were organising a time to meet them. (Josephine)

Some would throw it over the fence and then they could collect it on their way to the fields. (Rosy)

Small boys, they can put roasted maize in plastic, then make a ball. They kick it outside so the comrades have food. (Sarah)

All these tasks of daring were not without fear or risk as women faced a number of threats in performing the role of food provider. The related risk involved in integrating food delivery to the guerrillas into women's daily routines of agricultural and household tasks is assessed later.

The myth of collective resistance

Whilst war committees and a generational division of labour give a semblance of organised networks, the women's experiences reflect the breakdown of such networks or, more precisely, the failure to build and consolidate organised lines of supply in Chiweshe. Many testimonies reflected a distinct informality and instability within the food supply networks. Few women seem to have worked through the war committees, and even when they did, there is little sense of a stable supply system being in place. This may be because the strict surveillance culture of the Keeps militated against formal organisation since people were so closely watched and fearful of talking to anyone about supporting the guerrillas. Contrary to an organised supply system therefore, a more persistent informal pattern of individual contact with the guerrillas emerges, namely, pre-Keep (when visited at home) and Keep (when visited in the fields outside the Keep).

Ellen, as a Community Development worker during the war, witnessed women's clubs in Guruve (a district north-west of Chiweshe) organising food and clothes for the guerrillas. However, her experience of the PVs in Chiweshe was that the levels of jealousy, distrust and self-surveillance due to fear of the women who were having affairs with the DAs militated against collective and overt organisation of such supplies in the women's clubs that were being attempted in the PVs. Margaret also challenged the prevalence of collective organisation around food, saying that 'We could not organise together. We did it individually'. Stella's experience of receiving requests through the village headman also highlighted the secrecy surrounding the giving of food and conduct of cooking duties with the guerrillas. The apparently centralised focus of such supply strategies masked a concern with secrecy which emphasised instability in the supply networks in Chiweshe. The sometimes fearful quality of relations between mothers and *Chimbwidos*, indicates the potential for fear and distrust to undermine the image of women across generations co-operating to supply food to the comrades.

In making contact it seems as if both local women and the incoming guerrillas used secrecy as protection. The comrades visited Agnes's neighbours but they did not talk to her about it:

They [neighbours] didn't say anything to me, but it is possible that they were probably told not to say anything to me by the comrades'.

Florence recounted a meeting with the comrades in the pre-1974 context:

They asked for sadza and we cooked the sadza and carried it to the bush because they were not supposed to come indoors. The following morning I woke up at four o'clock and I boiled the water for them to bath. I carried the water into the bush. After that I cooked the food for them. They did not want many people to take the food to their base. They were afraid of being reported to the soldiers.

Such secrecy of movement was also confirmed by Tecla:

We did not see them often because they had to go to different parts of the country. However, there were different groups. They normally used to come after two weeks in different groups. They told us they were coming from Mozambique but we didn't see which direction they were coming from. They made all efforts to make sure that people could not see where they were coming from.

Local people were also keen to disguise their contact. Hilda gave me an example, saying, 'We saw people visiting the mountain. They said they were going to see a prophet. They didn't want to publicise the fact that they were going to see the comrades'. This climate of ignorance and silence was further reinforced by the unreliability of arrangements for food provision. Victoria did not know how or if other women on the farm compound where she lived were supplying the guerrillas. This uncertainty prevailed in the fact that guerrillas often did not observe pre-arranged dates for collecting food:

They were telling me that they were going to come on a particular day and I was supposed to prepare the food and meat, but unfortunately they never kept to their promises. They were not coming on the dates they had given me, but they would come sometime later after the date which they had set. (Victoria)

Women were afraid of being sold out by their neighbours if the comrades visited their home or if they were seen carrying food to the guerrillas. For example, Hilda, as the wife of a village head, was feeding groups of 15-25 comrades before the Keeps. She often took this task on alone, as she did not trust the neighbours sufficiently to seek their help and feared they would report her to the soldiers. She did not tell her neighbours if the comrades had visited during the night and did not talk about them:

We feared to ask for help from the neighbours. We thought they could report to the soldiers so we did everything on our own. It was only after the comrades had called for and told everybody to bring food to the headman's place that we received local help in cooking for the comrades.

The prevalence of fear, secrecy and uncertainty in food provision for the guerrillas arose in part from the nature of the guerrillas' visits – individual house visits under cover of darkness – and the fear of talking about these visits with neighbours. Although mentioned above as the beginnings of food supply networks, it would seem that over the course of the war these visits came to define the individualised, secretive and random approach to food supply which prevented overt and collective organisation:

My first experience of the war was when the boys came during the night, knocking at our door. But they didn't want anything, they wanted food only. So we just prepared the food for them. (Ellen)

They were actually coming to our house and calling us for *pungwe*, and even when we were in the fields they were also coming to ask us for food. (Margaret)

I did not see them [other women] because they [comrades] were coming to individual houses and it was very difficult to know what was happening since people were not allowed to gossip about them. (Victoria)

These experiences reinforce the serendipity of food supplies and challenge the enduring idea of a regimented, co-ordinated and organised system of supply as central to the conduct and success of a guerrilla war. The disorganisation and unreliability of the supply networks contributed to and stemmed from the atomised communications and contacts with the comrades that discouraged people from talking to each other. The arbitrariness of requests and supply was also reflected in Veronica's account:

Guerrillas randomly asked for food in large numbers and one would have to ask for food from a neighbour if he or she did not have enough to supply the large numbers.

The failure to consolidate effective supply routes was also partly tied to the issue of location. The availability of rough terrain to provide cover made the north of Chiweshe more accessible for the guerrillas whereas the open land of the south was more dangerous to cross. Home visits also stopped once people were moved to the Keeps and the counter-insurgency measures began to take effect. In this ebb and flow that marked the battle for the control of people's resources and movement, women and where they were became of strategic importance to the guerrillas in making contact with the key players of food provision.

Women were particularly vulnerable to requests as the more likely places to meet the comrades coincided with the conduct of their daily chores – tilling the fields, herding cattle, gathering firewood and washing clothes at the river. Women came into contact with the comrades more often than men because they were out of the Keeps while 'men usually stayed indoors' (Veronica). With people now locked up for hours and days at a time, the guerrillas shifted tactics. The fields where women worked became the focus of political contact. Guerrillas met women here to request and collect food, to gather information on soldiers and DAs, and to confront sell outs:

Since they [women] were in the Keeps so it was not easy to see comrades now.... People, they were invited by the comrades when they were in their fields. They can tell them there is a rally in the mountain base where they are going to meet the people. (Sarah)

Anytime they wanted to say something we used to be called to our fields for meetings. We did these in the afternoon when going to our fields. We sang loudly and danced so soldiers would hear us, for the guerrillas said we had to do this for we had signed for death by starting the war.... Some fell ill because of fear. [Most people went to the meetings] because some could go to look for firewood, fetch water and herd cattle. All these attended meetings too. (Veronica)

Maybe others managed to [get food out of the Keep] but most of us were unable.... The comrades would only meet those women whose fields were far away and they would seek food from them. As we were in the Keeps we could not provide them with any food as we were not allowed to take food with us out of the keep, but water only. (Agnes)

Fetching firewood also became a negotiated strategy:

The comrades made contact with the people when they were in the Keeps. They used to meet the people when they were going to the field or to fetch some firewood.... The people took the food secretly to the comrades. (Stella)

It was only those fetching firewood who could see them and be told that they needed food. (Pardon)

The problem was of firewood because they could fetch firewood from the fields and that is where the comrades could be. And sometimes they could meet them, but there were some naughty ones who wanted to make love to the women, so that was one of the main problems we faced. And at times the water system would break down and so when they went to fetch water from outside, getting into the Keeps, oh, they would be harassed at the gate. It was just to make them suffer, there wasn't any apparent reason. They just wanted to make them suffer'. (Rosy)

Time-consuming tasks such as washing and ironing became more difficult in the Keeps as clothes and water could not be taken from the Keep without alerting suspicion at the gate. Moreover, women could easily be seen to be washing lots of clothes, which would lead to them being questioned. This was also true of the cooking of large quantities of maize. Going to the fields became fraught with risk and worry as women dealt with the triumvirate of suspicion from the DAs, the guerillas' requests and the need for neighbours' silence so as to avoid being implicated with either side. Such constraints further weakened supply networks that were in operation before the move to the Keeps. They also signify the shaping influence of location on possibilities and forms of resistance and struggles for survival by women. What these insights on location reflect is that women in the conduct of daily tasks were imbricated in a pervasive battleground of revolutionary war.

The battleground of localised resistance: Struggles of resistance and survival

The performance of the revolutionary role of 'food provider' was effective to the extent that it drew upon and hid behind the assumed domesticity of women's work in the Keeps. As the breakdown of food provision tasks and strategies of delivery suggests, the Chiweshe women's daily routines – a set of agricultural and household tasks which gave women mobility and anonymity in the generalised routines of the Keep life – were of military importance precisely because they centred on food provision. For this reason family food provision is the *sine qua non* of guerrilla food provision. The latter would not be possible without the fundamental necessity of the former, which meant women had to be allowed to move and work if communities were to stay alive. Therefore, the explanation and understanding of women and food provision in the context of guerrilla war involves assessing both guerrilla and family food provision as the collapse of public/private, military/non-military space where women's struggle to feed the guerrillas becomes coterminous with family food security. There was also a tension in the often contradictory demands, as giving more food to the guerrillas directly affected their ability to feed their families. Carrying food in this context was an act loaded with many meanings, including compliance, resistance, powerlessness and sacrifice. The interlocking nature of threats to family food security *and* guerrilla food provision suggests these women faced similar risks regardless of who the food was for. This struggle for food epitomises the collapsed boundaries of revolutionary participation such as political/non-political, combatant/non-combatant, battlefront/home front, military/civilian, supporter/collaborator, citizen/traitor, participant/non-participant, public/private, food provider to guerrillas/food provider to family and, finally, mother/revolutionary.

The volatility of everyday relations was embedded in this battleground, and for women it involved the daily negotiations of social relations and personal risk. The breakdown of community mapped out in the previous chapter illustrates the limited room for manoeuvre within the Keeps, where women fought to navigate a mid-line course between the state and ZANU. However, identifying a 'them' and an 'us' in any guerrilla war is not an easy task. During the liberation war, the concrete experiences of these relationships at the local level included war committees, village headmen, DAs, girlfriends of DAs, churches, mothers of guerrillas, women's clubs and Muzorewa's Auxiliaries.[1] This pitting of families, villages and communities against each other reflected the tense dynamics in Chiweshe, where both DAs and guerrillas had been recruited. Mrs Moyo of the Salvation Army described this in the following scenario:

> I think our [church] leaders during that time did what they could because I remember sometimes when the stories would be told, mostly the blame was placed on the other side, not on the government, and yet sometimes the blame would have been the soldiers.... Our problem was, with us Africans, other ones would go on the other side. So my two [brothers] are fighting each other. Which one will I support? Again, our problem was if anybody came with a gun, it doesn't matter if it is this side or the other side, what can I do?

Counterinsurgency actions also confused the battlelines as they frequently involved soldiers disguising themselves as guerrillas, which posed further confusion and risk for women in their interactions with the revolutionary forces. Such actions were the hallmark of the dreaded Selous Scouts, the Rhodesian counterinsurgency force that specialised in undercover operations to entrap people when they gave support or failed to report to the police or soldiers:

> We weren't actually afraid but we were surprised. You never know who they

---

[1]   These were pro-government militia ostensibly led by Bishop Abel Muzorewa of the UANC.

were actually because on the other side some soldiers can pretend to be 'boys' too. (Ellen)

Family relations and friendships also became strained as women feared being sold out or having to sell out to save themselves and their families. They worried about husbands and sons who were away in town, about their children who were forced to live in the Keeps and their friends who might be at risk from rumour or attack. The ambiguities of food provision and politics thus indicate a terrain of participation where domestic (family food security) and political (guerrilla food provision) strategies merged and operated in an environment that was beset with risk and was shaped by the negotiation of these key relationships by women with the state (DAs and soldiers), revolutionary forces (ZANLA guerrillas in the main) and other families in the PVs. The dominant attitude, even for those who actively supported the guerrillas, was the struggle of survival over revolution.

The implications of placing women on the front line were manifold. Agricultural and domestic tasks in the fields such as collecting fire-wood, planting or weeding were now conducted in a battlefield where guerrillas or soldiers could intrude at any time. The performance of these tasks was closely scrutinised by both guerrillas and soldiers, the former aiming to secure supplies from women and the latter working to prevent it. The women were easy prey for the comrades as they had the task of providing food for their families and would have to tend their plots whatever the risks:

> They really knew you were coming. They asked us [for food] but we told them 'we have nothing to do'. Where did you get it? How can you reach there with the food? (Joanne)

The pressures to supply the guerrillas, face suspicions by the DAs of such supply, and also feed one's own family conflated the challenges of daily survival. As Stella recounted, 'The women were not happy. They could not get money for supporting their children because when they go out to sell their crops and vegetables to the farms [commercial farm compounds] they were blamed and beaten that they had gone to give the comrades sadza.' Women also faced beatings from the soldiers if they were caught. The physical risk of supplying the comrades was thus fraught with the tension of being caught by the soldiers and punished or seen by the comrades as not doing enough for the struggle and being accused of being a state collaborator.

Of this, Veronica said:

> Some just got caught on their way to the guerrillas, through suspicion by soldiers and sometimes these would have been sold out by traitors within the Keeps who supported the soldiers.... [Those who were caught were] sent to Bindura, Harare, and Chombira and beaten and also killed.

Veronica also described the indifference shown by guerrillas for the risks people faced by feeding them:

> They did not bother. They told us this would make us more clever. 'We just need food only', they said.

Paradoxically, the very performance of daily chores provided the best disguise for revolutionary activity:

> When we were staying in the Keeps, the girls just pretend to go to the river to do washing yet they were taking food to the comrades. (Emily)

The fields were no longer simply a place of family crop cultivation where the food and income of the family was secured. The fields now became a strategic part of the guerrilla war. Washing and cooking as indicated earlier became dangerous tasks as women faced the risk of intimidation by soldiers accusing them of supporting the guerrillas:

> It was dangerous if the soldiers caught you doing the washing or cooking. They could beat, arrest, or kill you. (Florence)

> We were doing the cooking, the washing of their clothes and we were also carrying the food to the bushes which was the terrible point where one could get shot by the soldiers if seen. (Phyllis)

The daily chores of women now involved negotiating their encounters with the guerrillas, the DAs and the fearful distrust of neighbours such that the most mundane of tasks became major undertakings of strategy, patience and risk. Women struggled to gain access to sufficient supplies of foodstuffs such as mealie meal to feed groups of comrades. Some resorted to asking neighbours for help even though this risked exposure to the risk of being identified to the soldiers as a traitor. Sarah and Joanne reflected the near paranoid effects of this fear:

> When they [comrades] are having meetings, I think when the people go there to the base. Other people know that these people they are going to the base. They are going to tell the soldiers, 'these people, watch them, they are going with food to the comrades'. So when those people who were carrying food to the comrades, when they are going outside... the soldiers were going to search them. (Sarah)

> It was very difficult, being taken, going to Chipiri [guerrilla base camp], staying there for the whole day and coming back. So you would be frightened. You just walk and you just think 'someone is seeing me while I was there' and actually there is no one. (Joanne)

The common experience of women facing these insecurities of daily life in guerrilla war was of 'being caught in the middle'. The tense coexistence of fear, support, hatred, compliance and resistance points to a terrain of participation for women which involved risk, avoidance and survival in a context of daily struggle. This battle for the hearts and minds of the people defines the captive nature of the PV communities; each side (the state and the revolutionary forces) sought to define the other in various ways, and local women had to become adept at reading the signs and giving the right answers. The middle ground was epitomised for Trust by the fact that '[s]oldiers accused us of supporting guerrillas and the guerrillas too made the same accusations'. Maggie and Tendai also experienced this tension:

> I heard that people were going outside and meeting the comrades and singing there and giving them food outside the Keep. And the soldiers were coming

in the Keeps asking people 'why do you go outside and give sadza to the comrades?' And some they were killed by the soldiers and some they were killed by the comrades. (Maggie)

The soldiers were always beating us and asking us to tell them where the comrades were. Sometimes if you feel pain and decide to tell them where the comrades were they would go. But if they failed to find them they would come back and beat you again so that in the end you would die as a result of that beating. And most of the times they would take you with their trucks to the place where you will be saying where the comrades were. If they find the comrades you would also be in trouble with the comrades. (Tendai)

Occupying this middle ground both created and exacerbated the conditions for the fragmented community dynamics discussed in the previous chapter. The pervasive sense of insecurity bred fatalism and despair:

I thought we were going to die because others were dying.... I was afraid that the soldiers or the guerrillas were going to kill me. (Monica)

We were undecided whether they [guerrillas or soldiers] were good or bad before we attained independence. We thought both of them were up to no good at all. (Veronica)

It was very difficult to foresee independence coming. We were only dreaming about death. Because when the two opposition groups started fighting for example from 6 p.m. to 6 a.m. [curfew time] you could not run away because there was nowhere to go. And we just thought we were going to be killed. You could visualise yourself being buried. We just felt there was no future. Our life had come to an end. (Dorothy)

Traversing this battleground was a complex, risk-laden prospect. No map could guide women through the maze and survival became a matter of strategic awareness and skilful management of everyday relations.

The front line runs through every woman

Strategies of negotiating the middle ground
There was more to the strategies of women than simply the tactics of survival or resistance in providing food for the guerrillas as well as their families. The practical business of participation or non-participation can be described as tactics, but the combination of these as strategies involved short- and long-term considerations in the weighing up of personal, familial and political risk. The stress of reconciling the demands of disparate identities and consciousness reflected the middle ground of being caught up in a revolutionary guerrilla war and defined the front line as running through every woman.

The front line involved two types of positionality or negotiation that were defined by practical and psychological struggles. The psychological struggles involved the individual consciousness of a woman caught up in the inward struggle to reconcile conflicting demands and identities. The case of women as food provider to the guerrillas *and* to her family and community is just one example of these struggles of identity.[2] Furthermore, both these dimensions were intimately connected in practice. Much of the negotiation revolved around practical dilemmas, for example, avoiding going to the fields so as not to meet the comrades, struggling to do a task on your own rather than ask a neighbour for help thus exposing yourself to too many questions, or delaying fetching water to avoid harassment by a particular DA.

The room for manoeuvre was constantly shifting in the volatile context of war and the fundamental distrust of everyday relations. Many claims were made on a woman's identity in a web of felt allegiances and expectations. The negotiation of daily life by women in the PVs reveals a sentient dimension of revolutionary war that speaks of the deeply personal and psychological battles that women had to fight to make sense of their lives. Those women who were ideologically committed as well as those who sought to avoid involvement faced the psychological elements of negotiation. However you felt about the revolution, were you going to risk your children, trust your neighbour, sell out your friend? The issue became one of how to or whether to show allegiance when there is no trust.

Surviving this battleground involved negotiating social relations every day in the performance of chores, duties and expectations. This necessitated a juggling of roles or positions which included mother, farmer, collaborator, daughter, food provider, etc. There was in effect multiple positioning with respect to the state, ZANU and with respect to local community and family relations. The experience of multiple positionality arose from the need to satisfy different constituencies and assert different relations with these constituencies. It is this negotiation of subjectivity that is invoked in Gendered Localised Resistance. The agency and consciousness of improvisation underpins the strategies of survival and resistance devised by women in response to the war and constitute the subtext of women's experiences of revolutionary war in Chiweshe. This subtext reveals that there is no separation of politics with a big 'P' and politics with a small 'p' for women as they negotiate their daily lives; rather than the personal becoming political, it is the political that becomes personal. The mobility of this terrain is defined by women's narratives of individuated consciousness, conflicting forms of participation and day-to-day engagement in a fraught context of alle-

---

2   The analysis of food provision used here is a segment of women's lives which captures only part of the daily terrain traversed by women during war. Household dynamics and struggles which prevailed outside of these extenuating circumstances of war also remained a feature of the terrain. Some of these were outlined in Chapter 5 and included domestic violence, drinking problems, struggles over access to and control over household income and resources. In terms of relations there were the supportive and undermining interventions of extended family. Altercations with mothers-in-law over children were cited by some women as a cause of marital distress during this time. Migrant labour while a necessary source of income also created loneliness and tension as women worried about getting money from their husbands and also in some cases worried if husbands had girlfriends in town and were spending money on them. The fuller extent of this daily terrain in the form of simultaneous struggles which co-existed with and shaped those struggles that can be seen as arising directly from the context of guerrilla war are not fully treated here. However, they are flagged as a reminder of the continuities of life that cut across the experience of war as an aberration of 'normal' life.

giances and relationships. These inward and outward psychological and practical struggles for women in the midst of revolutionary war highlight the individuated workings of identity and positionality that are at the heart of Gendered Localised Resistance. Furthermore, they denote the indeterminate elements of subjectivity that defy ready categorisation of act or intention.

'No-woman's land': Profiles of the middle ground of guerrilla war
The following profiles are 'snapshots' that capture the varied dangers and psychological dynamics of the middle ground between women and the DAs and the guerrillas.

Dorothy: Dorothy's sister was a casualty of crossfire. Both were *Chimbwidos*. As with other statements cited here, the negotiating with both soldiers and guerrillas was revealed to have been fraught with risk:

> At one point, my sister was arrested and stayed under custody for two weeks.... She met the soldiers when she was going to base camp to give sadza to the comrades. On her way the soldiers started firing at her but the comrades could not fire back because she was in between. If they had fired back she should have died. So the comrades had to run away. My sister went to surrender herself to the commander of the soldiers. When she was taken to detention they asked her where she had been going and she told them the truth. She said she was asked to bring sadza so she did not have any choice since she was scared of both sides.... She was detained and beaten, [but] not like the other girls and boys who were arrested together with her. These other people are still suffering from backbones because of the way they were beaten. They were also tortured using electricity.

Tecla: Tecla was forced to participate in burning tractors owned by local commercial farmers and used by Keep occupants to collect firewood from outside the Keep. Women often had to walk five or six miles to find firewood for collection:

> At one point myself I was taken by the comrades when they found me collecting some firewood. They forced me to burn some tractors.... I faced a lot of trouble. I was arrested by the soldiers. But I had to tell them the truth.... They [the comrades] asked us to burn the tractors because they said we were supporting the whites since we were fetching the firewood using their tractors. To them it meant we were not scared of the soldiers but that they were our friends. To them, burning the tractors was going to create enmity between us and the soldiers. Since we were scared that the comrades would kill us, we had to fetch some firewood and we set fire to the tractors.... I was scared but I had to help them because the comrades told us to be strong and help them.... They were going to kill us. They also kept some sticks for beating us.... But when we were coming back to the Keep that's when we faced lot of trouble. When we got to the Keep the gates were closed and we were supposed to be killed by the soldiers. But we told them what had happened. After having explained to them it became clear to the soldiers that it was not a planned action. The soldiers agreed amongst themselves that if we had refused to burn the tractors we were going to be killed. That's how we were forgiven.

Tecla faced the threat of beating by the comrades if she did not comply with this act of political resistance as defined by the comrades. She also faced the threat of reprisal by state agents if she was found to be involved in sabotage. Luckily, in this situation the individual soldiers involved decided not to punish the women. One implication of this act was to deprive women of a means of collecting firewood from far away. (Firewood was a scarce resource particularly in the southern part of Chiweshe which was relatively flat and bare.) Looking for firewood within walking distance of the Keeps meant running the risk of meeting guerrillas and having to deal with the possibility of being unable to cook if sufficient fuel could not be found. This is an example of the middle ground where political and non-political, domestic and war spaces became entangled. Tecla's experience also demonstrates how the politics of war determined the politics of the pot in terms of household survival.

Tendai: Tendai, a *Chimbwido*, thought of becoming a comrade so that she could escape the middle ground by being definitely on one side. She was frightened by the threats and felt confused by the barrage of information and politics coming from all sides in the war:

> We did receive political education but we did not store the information into out minds when the war was over because we thought that was the end of the education when we obtained our independence.... They [comrades] taught us but we do not remember anything anymore. We forgot about it soon after the war was over. Also, it was very difficult for us to keep in mind what the ZANU-PF guerrillas were teaching us because soon after they had taught us something the soldiers would also come and teach us something, as well as the Sithole, Muzorewa [Muzorewa's Auxiliaries] and Nkomo guerrillas. As a result we found it very difficult to keep all that information in mind.

> We were being told about the war. We were warned that there were different freedom fighters from different leaders. And these freedom fighters had different guns and also different songs. Therefore we were supposed to be able to tell which group belonged to Mugabe. The comrades were teaching us their songs. We were supposed to follow the ZANU-PF freedom fighters. Also, their slogans were different so we could tell which ones belong to the ZANU-PF party.... They were telling us that if they [Muzorewa's Auxiliaries] come we must give them food because we are powerless. We could not refuse because they would kill us since they had guns. But we were supposed to bear in mind that they do not belong to our party.

> I thought life was going to be a little bit easier because being an ordinary person was very difficult those days. The comrades would give you a list of rules which you were supposed to follow and the soldiers would come and do the same thing, and as a result we ended up confused, not knowing who to follow because of having so many preachers. I therefore considered it better to join the comrades and be settled, knowing that I support one side. If the soldiers come I would just fight with them.

In any event, her ambitions of fuller participation were thwarted by familial responsibilities; the two roles that could not easily be combined. Tendai married a *Mujibha* in 1977.

Judith: Judith lost her husband in the war, and in the middle ground. He worked for the government telecommunications company repairing telephone lines and was killed by the comrades while he was working on the lines north of Chiweshe. Judith had contributed much to the comrades but lost all interest in the war and politics thereafter, especially as she had four children to look after single-handedly:

> They were shot while in a lorry and unfortunately my husband died in that incident. Others sustained injuries. It only happened that he was unfortunate. They [guerrillas] thought by repairing telephone wires, the wire would be used to inform soldiers about comrades. I suffered severely. I became ill because the children were very ill such that I could not manage to bring them up alone.... I was very bitter about them nine comrades but I could do nothing. I only lost interest in them. I had no interest in them. My children were doing Grade Five and Seven while the other one was not going to school. I only became happy when the war ended.

Strategies of engagement

There was a need for strategic awareness if one was to successfully negotiate the risks of being 'caught in the middle' and forge a route to surviving the war. Women had to incorporate into their daily routines an awareness of military strategies and how these might endanger them and their families. The awareness of war imbued every aspect of women's lives such as washing, cooking, farming and talking with neighbours. Daily tasks were politicised and in themselves became military strategies of avoiding detection. Agnes and Hilda, for example, used to sweep their yards clean and straighten out the tall grass around them to disguise the fact that guerrillas had visited during the night. For Hilda, this middle ground, in the time before the Keeps, became a simple matter of day/night, non-curfew/curfew time-spaces predicated on would visit and what they would want:

> [The comrades visited my place] almost every day because it was the house of the headman.... It was very dangerous. There were two things; either they could meet and fight here, which would result in us being killed, or some people would betray us so that we could get punished by the soldiers.... Comrades could only come during the night and soldiers in the morning because they avoided each other. We could give then give the comrades food and early in the morning we could sweep the yard to rub off their footmarks and remove the remains of the cigarettes. We could also raise some grass in the direction where the comrades would have taken.... We responded to the soldiers during the day, but at night we responded to the comrades, giving them food.

Agnes used her widowed status to negotiate the middle ground and deflect attention from her home:

> The boys only came to my place once, in the evening. I was worried, especially since at that time my husband had just passed away. I was sad and full of fear and I didn't know what next to do. There were two of them that I saw outside, so I did not see them properly. In fact, the boys didn't want to come to my place because I was a widow and any male shoes or footsteps that the soldiers would see in my yard would result in me being beaten up by the soldiers.... It was because I was a widow and the presence of the comrades would

mean that I would be susceptible to harassment, and in addition it would bring back the bad memories of my late husband.

Negotiating the middle ground involved strategies of flight, avoidance and day-to-day innovations in the procurement and provision of supplies. One negotiating or coping strategy was simply to absorb the risk. Josephine, for example, continued to feed the guerrillas despite the threat of punishment if discovered:

> Life was very hard for us in the Keep. However, we did our best to help the comrades. We could cook sadza and try our best and to get out of the Keep with the food. Those who were clever were managing to carry the food out, past the inspection.

Another coping strategy was to be defiantly supportive of each side as you encountered them. It was one adopted by Veronica as she went about her daily tasks:

> We were taking sides and not showing it. We were pretending to favour both.... It was difficult but better to be neutral and therefore if one took sides this meant death.... There was harassment by both guerrillas and soldiers when we left the Keeps to look for water or firewood.

A variation of this for Florence was to deny to each that you were supporting the other:

> It was hard and you end up confused, not knowing which side to support. However, in the end we had to help the comrades. If the soldiers found out that you were feeding the comrades they would kill you or take you to jail and if the soldiers were seen at your home always the comrades would question you and even beat you.... They [people] just had to be strong and if you go to the soldiers you would tell them that you were not supporting the comrades. Similarly, to the comrades you would say the opposite.

The last in the bag of tools was the strategy of saying nothing. The ability to keep secrets was the ability to stay alive. Talking politics in public was to engage in risk-seeking behaviour. Women avoided talking too much to each other, even in the relative privacy of the daily walk to the fields when the gates of the PVs were opened. Silence and secrecy were better tactics. Hilda, for example, did not talk about politics in the Keeps 'because one could not know what type of person he was talking to. Others were sell outs so they had to be avoided. [Survival] was a matter of avoiding too much talking. It was difficult but there was no other alternative'. Judith said that '[w]e had no time. The DAs would beat us.... [On their way to the fields] We did a little talk but it was not political. If we would get caught we were going to be beaten by the DAs. Soldiers were also patrolling the place'. Trust recalled that '[p]eople did not show their political affiliations openly but I knew only a few who were very active. A few people [talked] only when they were discussing in small groups'.

The fear of talking extended to collective gatherings such as women's clubs organised by community workers to distract women from the war and teach them domestic skills and various crafts. According to Ellen, a community development worker at the time, little was said about the

war because of their fear of the DAs, and of their girlfriends who might
be present and subsequently sell them out:

> Ah, during that time it was difficult for us to discuss anything really in the
> Keep, of war, because you know people were afraid of these DAs. You know
> there were some of the women who were girlfriends of these DAs so it was
> difficult for anyone to say it out. They could only do clubs.

Judith said she survived the war in the Keeps 'by avoiding too many
friends who could involve you in politics and end up being beaten to
death'. For Joanne too, learning to keep quiet was an important aspect of
living through the war:

> Other people telling me 'these are the comrades, you stay here. You are not
> allowed to say anything, you must stay like this. If you say something you are
> involved and you will be arrested'. So here you learn. Even if you see some-
> thing you are not allowed to tell somebody from there 'Why are you stealing
> my books there?' You are not allowed. You just stay there and keep quiet.
> That's what the war meant.... I can say here in Chiweshe you had no chance
> [to talk politics] until you go out in the fields. You can meet the comrades and
> talk there and finish there. When you come here and even if you are asked
> 'Did you see the comrades?', you say 'No'. You were not allowed to talk about
> it. You were not allowed.... You would talk but you would only talk there,
> not including even a little bit about politics because the DAs were walking
> around the Keep.

Joanne made sure to talk to both soldiers and comrades when outside,
treating both separately and equally to ensure she did not implicate
herself:

> It was 1974, September, that is when we came here [in to the Keeps]. It was
> very hard for us now to stay out because the soldiers came, the comrades
> came, and you didn't know what to do. The comrades talked to you, they want
> theirs. The soldiers came, they want theirs. You didn't know what to do....
> The comrades were there, soldiers were there. Once you walk there you meet
> the soldiers; you walk there, you meet the comrades! So when we were here
> [Keep] it was far better.... We would talk about what is going on, seeing the
> comrades there, talking to them, even talking to the soldiers; talking to each
> other [saying] 'I've seen the comrades there' and you [another] 'I've seen the
> soldiers there, they've gone that way'.... The balance is there because when
> you see the soldiers you just talk to them and finish with them there. You
> won't even tell somebody. If you meet the comrades, you talk what they want
> there and talk to them and finish it there. You were not allowed to carry what
> is there and with it even tell somebody. It was your own secret.

The battleground of revolutionary war for the women in Chiweshe has
been revealed as intimately constructed and embedded in women's
daily routines, tasks and location. This is nowhere more obvious and
politically potent than in the area of food supply as the oxygen of guerrilla war. Food provision is an exemplary case in point of localised
resistance that brings together the struggles for survival and the revolutionary context of political support for the liberation struggle. Women's
management and negotiation of this middle ground of revolutionary war
is a testament to survival within and through war.

Both survival and resistance are dimensions of participating in a revolutionary war and become intermeshed to produce a web of agency and intentions that involves survival, everyday resistance and revolutionary resistance. The narratives of these women reveal the personalised trajectories that inflect the relative strength of each of these aspects in any given situation of daily life. Whilst we can separate these intentions and actions to some extent, we must acknowledge that they are part of a dynamic entanglement of subjectivity and agency that is lived by each woman in her engagement with the everyday context of living through a revolutionary war. These personal testimonies have provided an account of these interactions of overt revolutionary resistance and the everyday struggles of survival and resistance that define the battleground constructed through and around women. They reveal that beyond the fixed identities of revolutionary resistance (fighters and food providers) there exists a discourse of localised resistance that illuminates a host of resistances and strategies for survival. Rather than a demarcation of revolutionary versus everyday resistance, or political versus non-political activity, we find instead a host of resistances that include compliance, self-interest, everyday resistance, avoidance, deception, predatory behaviour toward equals, defiance and courage. These represent the complex battleground of revolutionary war for women.

The excavation of this host of resistances and strategies for survival involves the understanding of subjectivity in the ways women responded to the various and contradictory expectations and pressures placed upon them. A discursive rendering of the 'local' emerges to define women's immediate experiences of revolution; the war penetrated all aspects of their lives and their lives penetrated the war. This Daedelian maze of agency represents the interactions of agonistic and disciplinary power outlined in Chapter 2. Resistance in such a scenario is bound and unbound; bound by the desire of resistance and change in face of the oppressive effects of the PVs, and unbound by the daily struggles for survival enacted through a host of responsibilities, fears and desires that were caught up in the social relations of a community at war. The responses to war went very deep and involved the constant reinvention of allegiances and identities to forestall the worst effects of war on themselves and on their families. In the theoretical terms of Gendered Localised Resistance, I expressed these as multiple positioning, intersubjectivity, positionality and investing in and thwarting subject positions. These strategies are potentially both contradictory and complementary in producing possibilities of action in a context of social relations. They involve the taking up, refusing and transforming of many subject positions on a daily basis. Food provision exemplifies this through the dilemmas of women as mothers, protectors, *Chimbwidos*, farmers, wives, lovers, neighbours, sell outs, prostitutes, survivors and revolutionary activists. These identities sometimes reinforced yet often contradicted each other. They are embedded in a context of resistance and survival as parameters of revolutionary participation. These identities were in a constant state of negotiation, both in terms of the material context of incarceration and poverty and the political impact of everyday social relations. The strategies of the women of Chiweshe reflect the dislocations of self, family and community that accompanied revolutionary and counter-revolutionary aspects of guerrilla warfare. It is this dynamic negotiation of identity in a context of ever-present risk and differing sets of social relations that represent an alternative map of women's participation in revolution.

Conclusion | Women's Agency & Voice in War Reconsidered

Looking Back

Feminist arguments

This study of women in Chiweshe illuminates our understanding of women's participation in revolutionary wars. My engagement with revolutionary resistance was grounded in the explanatory theses of peasant/guerrilla relations arising from the liberation war in Zimbabwe and in the bittersweet narrative of women's participation and the transformation of gender relations through revolution that has emerged from feminist writings. I highlighted the limitations of these approaches by providing a full and critical account of women's participation in, and experiences of, revolutionary struggle. My critique called for a gender analysis that explored the lives of women in revolution and the difference between them. In the specific context of the liberation war, I challenged the meta-narrative of revolutionary resistance as romantic nationalism through the differentiation of peasant consciousness and the problematisation of women's experiences that were noticeably absent or not fully explored in their own right.

The importance of context in understanding the complexity of women's consciousness and agency contributes to feminist analysis and understanding. Women's revolutionary consciousness is revealed in this study as a differentiated series of political and personal understandings of oppression and change. This moves us beyond the restrictive explanations of women as victims or heroines of war or occupying public or private space in terms of war-related activities. The assumed causal relationship between the roles women take up in war and revolutionary political consciousness is substantially weakened by the differences found between and within women who performed such roles in the liberation war in Zimbabwe. The variegated profile of participation challenges the enduring nature of guerrilla-defined roles, particularly in the area of food provision. Different and conflicted expectations form the picture of participation that emerges from these women's voices. The profiles of participation also challenge any notion of a collective consciousness for women or an authentic, shared voice for women. The

147

relational categories of gender are extended beyond 'men' to guerrillas, soldiers, families and communities; they also involve relations amongst women.

The women of Chiweshe do not readily fit the romantic iconography of the revolutionary woman, fighter and mother. Sometimes referred to as those 'left behind', these women were in fact the front line of a guerrilla war that came to their homes, villages and fields. They are the assumed 'peasants' of many revolutions and best exemplify the contradictions of public and private space in guerrilla war that challenge fixed revolutionary identities and consciousness. Placing women's voices at the centre of an alternative narrative of revolution reveals that 'woman in revolution' is neither valorised mother nor male-spun warrior, but is a woman for herself, speaking of herself. The focus on Chiweshe thus yields an understanding of war as viewed from below, from the daily lives of women caught up in a war that has come to their homes and their community. *Pace* the interpretive optimism of a feminist narrative of empowerment or the solidarity narrative of peasant consciousness, it is the particularisation of everyday resistance that is more resonant with women's voices as an explanatory framework for their resistance and their survival. The profusion of accounts and experiences of war belie the search for one representative story of women and revolutionary wars.

Peasant historiography
This study of Chiweshe extends the 'curve' of main studies of the Zimbabwean war; Ranger (1985) in Makoni District, Lan (1985) in Dande and Kriger (1992) in the Mutoko district. In building my analysis, the contradictory and disputed roles and consciousness woven through women's perceptions of revolution posed a provocative counterpoint to the context of revolution found in the existing historiography of the liberation war; both Ranger and Lan's benign context of mutually reinforcing peasant-guerrilla relations, and Kriger's context of overwhelming guerrilla coercion, provide only partial images of the full extent of the local battleground of revolutionary war. Not all revolutionary political consciousness is inevitably cohesive, collective and continuous, as understood by Ranger and Lan. Neither, I contend, is the radicalism of revolution rooted only in collectively derived pre-existing conflicts inside rural communities, as Kriger suggests. Rather, it is the interaction of these elements in an individuated consciousness that emerges from the Chiweshe women's testimonies. Such consciousness is not necessarily linear, collective or radical but involves elements of resistance and survival in the daily engagement with war.

The varied expressions of political consciousness also challenge a purely instrumental rationalisation of differentiated consciousness which can be read from Kriger. Certainly, outside of a few remembered promises made specifically to women by the guerrillas, there is little indication of a group consciousness or political agenda for women, either by the guerrillas or perceived by women themselves. The radicalism of internal conflicts is not to be found here in the form of a gender agenda. However, what is evident is the power of personal motivations for involvement. The treatment of gender as a site of conflict and differentiation within rural communities in revolutionary war moves beyond the exclusivity of a self-styled agenda for women and reveals the power and shaping influence of personal motivations for differentiated accounts of involvement.

The fiction of unity as key to mobilisation masks the struggles of survival which fractured communities. To some extent, Kriger's coercion thesis is upheld in the rule through fear by the guerrillas to motivate unity and support. The effects in Chiweshe can similarly be seen to have divided rather than united the Keep communities. However, I caution against the overstatement of a purely coercive explanation of fragmented communities. The evidence and experiences of the women included here indicate a wider set of relational forces underpinning fractious community dynamics. Kriger's guerrilla coercion is counterbalanced by the spectre of state counterinsurgency coercion; the women of Chiweshe were as likely to blame the soldiers and guerrillas for their misfortunes as they were their neighbours. Relationships with the DAs, which were predicated on a mix of protection, fear and surveillance, contributed to the atomisation of society in the way that the surveillance and interventions of the guerrillas sometimes did. The relationships between neighbours are also important in understanding the wider ramifications of relational dynamics with the soldiers and the guerrillas. The levels of distrust and uncertainty within communities prompted retreat, silence and secrecy at an individual level.

Rethinking agency, consciousness and resistance
The ethnographic analysis illustrates that women's participation in revolution is more complex than explanations of revolutionary roles or group mobilisation would suggest. It maps out the practices and consciousness of Gendered Localised Resistance and reflects the complexity and risk involved in women's participation and identities in revolutionary struggle. The multiple subject positions adopted by women in the localised experiences of war refute the idea of a radicalised revolutionary subject and the expected and assumed opportunities for the transformation of gender relations. This shifts the viewpoint away from the centrality of guerrilla mobilisation toward community relational dynamics as the context of consciousness, resistance and survival in revolution.

Gendered Localised Resistance reinterprets revolutionary resistance to understand survival, resistance and change as witnessed and experienced by women participating in a revolutionary war. At the heart of this approach, gender identities are argued to be embedded in the fluid workings of subjectivity as women engaged with the context of a revolutionary war. They are seen to be contested through such engagement as the women sought to manage a series of responsibilities and tasks in their social relations with DAs, guerrillas and their community. The strategies of local resistance that mark such explanations tell us much about the modalities and consciousness of being caught up in revolution. We learn that revolutionary consciousness is not a blank sheet. The women in this study are aware of and able to articulate the pre-existing conflicts, revolutionary ideology and the new conflicts and grievances that arose directly and indirectly from the war that shaped their agency and consciousness in revolution. The outcome is a strategic consciousness of negotiating a host of allegiances, old and new, to ensure survival within the context of revolutionary war. Far from being in need of politicisation, the sensitivity of these women to their political context was a striking feature of their daily negotiations for survival and resistance in the course of revolution. For the women of Chiweshe there was no non-political, non-war space, no opt out. Rather, there was the constant negotiation of a web of relations and emotions to survive. It was very difficult for them to avoid being implicated in the webs of information gathering, reporting, talking and punishment. The challenge was to negotiate the positions they could take up, reject and transform on a daily basis. This indicates a battleground widened, deepened and made more complex by the struggles for daily survival. It is nothing less than a context where the political was personal and one had to tread carefully and strategically.

The explanatory power of women's own stories of revolution provides rich insights into the differentiated, personalised and negotiated nature of their participation in revolution. The power of these testimonies is that they illuminate the lives of women lived between revolutionary resistance and survival; these are the narratives of self, relationship and community that emerge from the dislocations caused by revolutionary and counter-insurgency aspects of guerrilla war. The women's experiences, interpretations and understandings of revolutionary war are shown to be differentiated in the ways they participated, in the way they viewed the war and perceived their participation and struggles in the war, in the strategies they developed to survive the worst effects of war, and in the motivations and attitudes they adopted in supporting the guerrillas. We thus become aware of the labyrinthine agency of being during war; the will to survive, the will to avoid involvement, the pain of loss, the political convictions of necessity and the stoicism of acceptance all came together, conflicted and co-existed in everyday war-time life. This illuminates a host of resistances beyond the confines of the fixed identities of overt revolutionary resistance. It also outlines survival as part of the political landscape. Women's revolutionary actions of food provision affected (often adversely) their own survival. The many subject positions taken up by women and the mixed motivations they express for supporting the guerrillas underpins the 'incoherent identities' that forge Gendered Localised Resistance.

This consciousness of context produced a repertoire of war-related actions that defy simple categorisations of revolutionary resistance or self-seeking survival. There was a constant maze of decisions, circumstances, thoughts and actions that responded to the middle ground of guerrilla and counterinsurgency warfare. The battleground was not a remote one but came into the intimacy of women's lives, shattering illusions of community or trust. Survival in a revolutionary context meant that the political became personal in the calculus and chance of everyday decisions. Survival, local resistance and revolutionary resistance intermeshed and impacted on each other. Their bid to survive, even if directed against others, is a measure of the attempts of these women to subvert constraints as much to accept them. Considerations of survival sometimes yielded a withdrawal from supporting the guerrillas; such considerations also induced support if one feared being labelled a sell out. The women faced similar dilemmas with state agents: not wanting to support them but afraid of the consequences, when called upon, if they did not. A revolutionary consciousness is certainly present in the life experiences of women and was buttressed in some instances by contact with the political parties and the guerrillas. It was also strengthened in some instances by the anger against the suffering inflicted by the colonial state. However, these accounts are also peppered with instances in which faith was lost in the revolution because of the behaviour, pressures and expectations of the guerrillas. These multifarious workings of the conflicted participation of women in revolutionary war through strategies of constant positioning typify their experiences of localised resistance.

The precarious outcomes of operating in such a shifting site of struggle raises questions about the way in which women's involvement in revolutionary struggles is understood and lamented for lack of long-term transformative effects for gender relations and the status of women in post-revolutionary societies. This alternative perspective of women's participation in revolution challenges the misplaced question of failed revolutionary outcomes for women; the question is not why do revolutions fail women but why do we continue to expect that revolutions should serve women well? In a localised context, it is not surprising that women, even in war, do not gain liberation because in the local sense it is more plausible that there are more continuities than discontinuities. In order to understand women and their situation we have to jettison the heroic and tragic notion of resistance.

Gendered Localised Resistance suggests a number of challenges to the optimistic expectations of revolutionary participation for women by depicting the complexity and instability of life from within a revolutionary war. It challenges the notion of women as a distinct group mobilised with a sense of common purpose as women. It also challenges the prevalence and durability of transformative revolutionary roles for women, and in so doing undermines the categorical assumptions about identities in war. At the centre of their war experience women were not only food providers to the guerrillas but, with the same degree of risk, also undertook the responsibilities of feeding their families and communities. Gendered Localised Resistance also challenges the unity and extent of revolutionary consciousness held by women. This it does by highlighting the multiple sites of struggle, only some of which are conventionally treated as political, and identifies the pressures on women to adopt, defend and negotiate identities tied up with specific social relations and responsibilities. This lack of politicisation of the Chiweshe women's struggles (in themselves and in their signification of wider nationalist agendas) underpins the sense in which any expectations of revolutionary transformation would have been misplaced. The cumulative outcome of these challenges is to redraw the revolutionary battleground of women as an improvised and conflicted public and private space that forges a consciousness of context within revolution.[1]

---

[1] One implication of this analysis is to suggest that men's identities must also be re-examined and challenged in that same context. If fixed identities tied to role-playing have masked women's agency and experiences of war and over-simplified the realities, then men too are

Looking forward: The struggles continue

Zimbabwe today: Resilience, resistance and survival
Although the war of liberation may have opened up spaces of participation in a promised future of an independent Zimbabwe, it did not always enable women to reach such personal, local or national transformations:

> They just oppressed us. It is only those women who are learned who have a better life, but those women who suffered during the war did not receive anything from the government. Government did not give help to us. They only gave us blankets, beans, and those *kapenta* [small dried fish] soon after independence.... Those blankets and beans were just a way of trying to silence us for the hardest times which were ahead of us. Today things are tough. (Phyllis)

The women's struggles displayed a continuity of survival strategies that underlay the struggles of poverty, rights, security and governance beyond and outside of the liberation war. It is worth noting some of the trends post-independence that women identified during their interviews; these included struggles to cope with, and respond to, frequent drought, the lack of maize and the adverse effects of structural adjustment through their declining access to health and education. The issue of war compensation was also very prominent in the interviews. This was particularly so for the war veterans who were given inadequate demobilisation packages which were quickly spent. The destitution of many veterans bred much contempt and anger towards the rhetoric of revolution and by 1993 had become an issue the government could no longer ignore.[2] It is haunting to revisit the interviews and see how prescient these dynamics were for the farm invasions, the corruption of the term 'war veterans', the rise of the youth militia in the rural areas and the resurgence of political education in the form of patriotic history.

Given these developments, and the deterioration of life and liveli-

---

1 (ctnd) constrained by roles and stereotypes of masculinity and war and differ among themselves in terms of roles, experiences and identities in war. The wider implications of Gendered Localised Resistance as an approach to making visible the complex lives of women in war thus invite further investigations of other gender identities in that context. A critical exploration of men's experiences of war is similarly needed if we are to improve our understanding and responses to gender, violence and war.

2   This perspective is not shared by Kriger (2003b) who outlines political constructions of 'veterans' to include being viewed as victims of neglect by Government in the early years of independence when in fact support packages were provided. However, as she states herself, the identification of who is a legitimate veteran was contested – both symbolically in terms of patriotism, and materially in terms what you did during the war and where. For the women in Chiweshe, they were as likely to angry about the lost cattle, crops and food to the guerrillas as they were to the colonial regime and many felt aggrieved at the lack of compensation for losses and suffering during the war. And for the women who returned from the camps in Mozambique (as fighters, cooks, teachers or porters) and entered politics their experiences and legitimacy as veterans was as likely to be dismissed by their male 'comrades'. I also met ex-combatant men who were destitute and disabled with no support and too few political connections to ensure that they and their families got something.

hoods in post-independence Zimbabwe, women are as likely to be awkwardly situated in the current struggles, local/national, political/social/economic as they were throughout the liberation war. Yet there is little said or written about where women are today in Zimbabwe in the ongoing crisis and in the responses of resistance, survival and resolution to it.[3] The nature and evolution of the ZANU-PF Women's League captures the centralised control of women as a constituency of supporters whose role has been cynically observed to don *kitengas* emblazoned with the 'great leader's' face and sing and cheer as the welcoming party at airports and form a ululating chorus at political rallies. The League remains a force within ZANU-PF, evidence that women can simultaneously participate in ongoing oppression and seek to cope with the impacts of crisis. These women are not completely outside the exercise and abuse of power and the accelerated capture of the state by a military-political elite; leading women and structures of Zimbabwean women's interests are implicated in the misrule, the political violence and the corruption. Women too have been the targets and victims of crisis in cities, villages and schools through Zimbabwe. They have also been part of the drive for organised opposition and participation in the MDC and civil society organisations. We need to better understand this participation and recognise it so that deals being brokered and consultations and negotiations for a new, more peaceful and prosperous Zimbabwe can learn from women's erasure from the scripts of the liberation war and the post-independence ruling apparatus.

Achieving the liberation of women by liberating the state may always remain a myth, and the struggles of rural women may remain a site of resistance and challenge to a reinvented post-independent government. Three particular instances capture this echoing of war into post-war experiences and legacies for women and their communities:

Operation Murambatsvina in 2005[4]: In May 2005, the government launched a clean-up operation of high-density urban areas across Zimbabwe. Operation *Murambatsvina* ('Clean out Filth'), or Operation Restore Order, as it was officially known, destroyed illegal flimsy structures built as homes by the dwellers, targeted vendors, money changers and the informal workers. Within a space of weeks, 52 sites had been targeted, including Harare, Bulawayo, Chinhoyi, Gweru, Marondera, Rusape and Victoria Falls. The poorest and most vulnerable were disowned and displaced. A fact-finding mission by the UN Special Envoy, Anna Kajumulo Tibaijuka, concluded that around 700,000 people lost homes, livelihoods or both. Roughly 2.4 million people were affected indirectly, by the cutting off of access to vital health care and education services, to give but one example. The government enforced colonial-era bye-laws as a cover for the actions that many observers saw as punishment for support for opposition politics and the MDC as well as a means of forcing people back to the rural areas to reduce pressure on urban

3   A notable exception is Irene Staunton's (2010) collection of women's stories of contemporary Zimbabwe entitled *Damage: The Personal Costs of Political Change in Zimbabwe*. It is fitting that this too echoes the past in terms of her earlier collection, *Mothers of the Revolution: The War Experiences of Thirty Zimbabwean Women* (1991).
4   For more on this see United Nations (2005), ICG (2005), Bracking (2005) and Potts (2006).

services. In its damning conclusion, the UN report found that 'Operation Restore Order turned out to be a disastrous venture based on a set of colonial-era laws and policies that were used as a tool of segregation and social exclusion' (2005:7-8).

This operation echoes Operation Overload, which established the Protected Villages during the counter-insurgency in the 1970s and saw thousands of people herded into open spaces and their crops and possessions dumped in the filth. The dispossessed and displaced of *Operation Murambatsvina* find cause with the dehumanisation of whole communities who were targeted and branded as 'suspect' by the Rhodesian Front government.

The Green Bombers: The youth militia of ZANU-PF are trained and organised as the eyes, ears and fists of the ruling party around the country. In 2003 some of those who had been trained were interviewed by a writer for *The Guardian* newspaper:

> 'They teach political orientation and history of the liberation struggle,' a young man who went to one camp said. 'They do teach some skills, like carpentry, but we did lots of military training and physical exercise. We learned songs. In military training we learned methods to interrogate and beat people.'[5]

This description harks back to the children and youth who went to Mozambique (some voluntary, some forced) to train as guerrillas in the camps. It echoes also the boys and girls of the villages who were the conduits for food and information – the *Mujibhas* and *Chimbwidos* – whose stories are part of the landscape of the liberation war described herein. The new 'patriotic history' now defining the teaching of the youth milita echoes the political education drilled into people at *pungwes* and the tests of loyalty to the guerrillas. Today, the Green Bombers' threats of violence and the identification of sell outs all resonate. Like their predecessors, the youth militia are caught up in their own web of resistance and survival.

The Front Line of Political Violence in Chiweshe: On the evening of 5 May 2008, when the official results of the March 2008 elections were finally posted, 200 ZANU-PF militia headed for the village of Chaona in the rugged north-east of Chiweshe:

> By daybreak ten people lay dead and the injured bore the hallmarks of a new kind of political violence [...] women were stripped and beaten so viciously that whole sections of flesh fell away from their buttocks. Apart from forcing people to drink Paraquat, a deadly herbicide, the militia and soldiers inflicted serious injuries by dipping their knobkerries and sticks into the chemical before beating their victims. This caused the serious wounds not to heal and many of those beaten died months later in agony.... The militia used genital mutilation [of men] in their attacks.[6]

[5]   *The Guardian* (2003) 'Living in Fear of Mugabe's Green Bombers' by Andrew Meldrum, 19 February. See http://www.guardian.co.uk/world/2003/feb/19/zimbabwe.andrewmeldrum (accessed 2 March 2011).
[6]   *The Zimbabwean*, 'Fresh Violence Rocks Chiweshe', article written by SW Radio Africa, 26 October 2009.

In April 2009, the militias returned to Chaona and targeted the schools and teachers; 50 homes of suspected MDC supporters were burned down and 80 teachers fled from schools as the youth militias carried out public beatings. The MDC MP from a neighbouring district told reporters that '[t]he militias now operate with impunity, arrogance and blatant violence'.[7]

As Zimbabweans reflected on 30 years of independence on 18 April 2010 and Robert Mugabe marked the official celebrations at Rufaro stadium (the scene of jubilation in 1980), villagers in Chiweshe were again targeted by the Green Bombers for being suspected supporters of the MDC. The tensions related to ensuring public support for the ZANU-PF position for the new Constitution is currently being drafted as part of the Global Political Agreement:

> The ZANU-PF party is allegedly using the infamous Green Bombers in the name of youth officers to identify MDC supporters and new faces in the areas, interrogating them before torturing them at the their base.[8]

Chaona was a hotbed of guerrilla activity during the war and one of the strongest areas engagement with civilians all through the 1970s of the Protected Villages. It was where Anna (see Chapter 5) faced down her visit from the guerrillas when she was named as a sell out by jealous colleagues and where she and women in the Keeps navigated the middle ground for six years. It was a ZANU-PF stronghold in the first decade of independence. Everyday relations, fear, survival, and resistance are, it seems, the lot of not only the *Chimurenga* generation but also a post-war generation who struggle and still await the prospects and dividends of peace and independence.

Women's agency and voice in contemporary wars and international interventions

For women in contemporary wars, the struggles of resistance and survival as outlined in Chiweshe are their daily reality. Our failure to fully understand and respond to them and locate them in the wider structures of war, government, society and economy blight our prospects for enduring peace and the lasting transformation of violent conflict. In Liberia, where the situation is ostensibly post-conflict the legacy and lessons of war endure. Writing of experiences of women in that war, Mats Utas (2005) describes an ethnography of social tactics, or what he terms 'tactic agency', to understand the strategies, roles and options that young women in the bloody civil war adopted to survive and gain access to resources, whether from rebel forces or from humanitarian agencies. 'Victimhood', he suggests, is one such form of 'tactic agency'. This theme of negotiated roles is reinforced by Myriam Denov and Christine Gevais (2007), writing of girls and young women with the Revolutionary United Front in Sierra Leone. Their argument is that in spite of very real gendered vulnerabilities and insecurities, including sexual and physical violence and forced marriage, the girls exercised capacities to negotiate the insecurity to ensure survival and, in some cases, empowerment.

---

[7]   Ibid.

[8]   *The Zimbabwean*, 'Villagers Beaten for Wearing Red', article by Itai Mabasa and Tony Saxon, 19 April 2010.

These capacities included volunteering and training to become a soldier, committing acts of violence to improve standing with commanders and marrying a powerful commander in what were 'modes of acquiescence and resistance'. These accounts of Liberia and Sierra Leone echo the terrain of war mapped out by women in Chiweshe.

In the Democratic Republic of Congo (DRC), rape as a weapon of war, particularly in the eastern part of the country, has led to the unwelcome notoriety for the country, and media and political pressure for international actions. The chronic and widespread nature of violence has made it impossible to define civilian and military spaces and actors. In addition to the official armed forces and UN peacekeepers, there are many armed militias with regional influences on the ground. The government forces remain weak and undisciplined, despite many international programmes and resources for security sector reform and military cooperation. Soldiers are poorly paid, and sometimes not at all, and include ex-militia members who have been absorbed into the national army. The UN mission has also been much criticised as it pursues an impossible mandate to enforce the disarmament of militias in the east *and* protect civilians from attack. As a result, insecurity reigns as civilians in remote areas are left to cope as best they can and run the gauntlet of potential attack, abduction or rape as they forage for food, plant crops or go to markets.

There is consensus on the need for a new security agenda in Africa for feminist research and women. The need for greater feminist research on militarism in Africa and both its historical and contemporary structures and trends drives the requirement for such an agenda. So too does the acknowledgement that women's security is not only threatened by war and violent conflict but also by post-war peace and the pre-war build-up of tensions, identities and assumptions about who and where women are (Mama and Okazawa-Rey 2008). A special issue of the *Feminist Review* (2008) demonstrated that such a research agenda is emerging in Africa and embraces themes as diverse as security sector reform, democratic election processes, gender-based violence, rape as a weapon of war, transitional justice institutions and the role of global economic structure and actors in driving conflict and violence in Africa. Sokari Ekine (2008), for example, sets out a global-local perspective from the Niger Delta of what security might mean to women who have developed strategies of resistance and survival in responding to the militarisation of their communities, particularly the effects of state violence. Within this situation, the global economic structures of oil, energy and the interests of various international governments play their part. The African Union (AU) having declared 2010 the Year of Peace and Security and 2010–2020 the African Women's Decade may provide impetus for greater action as well as research on women, peace and security in Africa.

On the other side of the world, Afghanistan and Iraq reflect new threats and new tactics in the global 'war on terror' in forms of fighting, technology, terrorism and counterinsurgency. Nevertheless, there are similarities between the daily negotiations of Afghan villagers as they decide how to respond to American and British troops under NATO and their dealings with the Taliban-associated insurgents infiltrating and emerging from their own communities and the representatives of a weak and emerging national army and police. Afghan women worry about how to feed their families and keep them safe and how to negotiate the front line of war in their homes, markets, villages and fields. In Iraq we see continuities with the Gendered Localised Resistance from Zimbabwe of the 1970s. Nadje Al-Ali and Nicola Pratt (2009), in *What Kind of Liberation? Women and the Occupation of Iraq*, testify to the lives of women under occupation and how international intervention brought new risks and vulnerabilities to their daily lives; many were widowed, impoverished, subject to violence and killed. Women have also become an ideological battleground as international claims to protect their rights are used to provide grist to the war mill and insurgents use morality codes as guises for violence and social control. These contemporary analyses highlight new areas of interest and concern for understanding women's agency in war but also testify to the enduring continuities of themes that have historical origins and resonance.

If we fast forward to the early months of 2011 we arrive at a new front line for women's engagement in revolution, when protest movements erupted in Tunisia, Egypt and Libya. In Cairo's Tahrir Square two young women bore witness to a new generation of women who participate in emerging struggles for political liberation and change:

> The women played an important role that night. Because we were outnumbered, we had to secure all the exits in the square. The exits between each end of the square would take up to ten minutes to reach, so the women would go and alert others about where the danger was coming from and make sure that the people who were battling swapped positions with others so that they could rest before going out into the battle again. The women were also taking care of the wounded in makeshift clinics in the square. Some women were on the front line throwing rocks with the men. I was on the front line documenting the battle with my camera. It was like nothing that I have ever seen or experienced before. (Gigi Ibrahim, age 25)

> I was one of many women, young and old, there. We were as active as the men. Some acted as nurses and looked after the wounded during the battles; others were simply helping with distributing water. But there were a great number of women that were on the front line hurling stones at the police and pro-Mubarak thugs. The duties in the square were divided. We were very organised. Something changed in the dynamic between men and women in Tahrir. When the men saw that women were fighting in the front line that changed their perception of us and we were all united. We were all Egyptians now.[9] (Salma el Tarzi, age 33)

In terms of international responses to women, peace and security and the momentum of Security Council Resolution 1325, many agencies, including the ICRC, the UN, the specialist international conflict NGO International Alert, and the European Commission and EU member states have commissioned background work to inform political decision-making and aid strategies.[10] National Action Plans have been developed, including in Liberia, Uganda and the member states of the EU, to imple-

---

[9]   These testimonies are taken from the Al Jazeera website and were collated as part of its feature on 'Women of the Revolution'. See http://english.aljazeera.net/indepth/featur es/2011/02/2011217134411934738.html. (Accessed 2 March 2011).

ment 1325. The role of women fighters and the years of displacement and violence have also haunted communities and shaped international attention on sexual and gender-based violence and support to survivors while also seeking to reshape classic post-conflict programmes in disarmament, demobilisation, and reintegration (DDR) as well security sector reform (SSR), transitional justice and economic rehabilitation. The success of these programmes, however, depends on the quality of engagement and understanding of how people and communities have emerged from war and what they have experienced.

The research agenda of feminist international relations as a critical and interdisciplinary project of global politics needs to engage more fully with these developments and reflect upon them. The front line continues to thread itself through the lives of women in locations of war and chronic violence around the world. There is consensus among feminist scholars and activists that there is a dearth of studies on women's experiences of war and post-war situations, including those in Africa. As a result there is a lack of substantive engagement about gender in contemporary peace and security debates despite political gains such as UN Security Council Resolution 1325 on women, peace and security in 2000.

Academics need to engage in fieldwork at the front line of transforming commitment into action that is marked by institutions (multi-lateral, governmental, regional, non-governmental, networks) and interventions (diplomacy, development, aid, peacekeeping, military intervention, human rights, humanitarian assistance, advocacy alliances and networks, peace-building and state-building). This requires a type of ethnographic approach that is advanced in this study of Chiweshe. There is currently a lack of field studies to interrogate, investigate and test how well policy is being translated into practice and how the past and the local are being engaged in that process. New field research linked to these very real areas of practice on women, peace and security can help us avoid the pitfalls of prescriptive programmes that are airlifted from one conflict zone to the next as UN peace operations and their associated regime of development and security interventions in post-conflict peacebuilding and statebuilding are established in areas as diverse as Timor-Leste, the DRC and Afghanistan.

Engaged ethnographic research can help shape more appropriate programmes based on an understanding of the context and gendered realities of male and female youth. The same is true for programmes targeted at victims and survivors of sexual violence, where agency needs to be reclaimed in terms of the viewpoint and experiences of those who have been subject to such attacks and how they live, survive and reintegrate in war and post-war situations, identifying what resources can be built upon and worked with to help that process. This depth and detail of engagement and learning is essential if the greater participation and protection of women in and after war, as well as a genuine gender perspective on war, peacekeeping, peacemaking and peacebuilding are to become new facts on the ground.

[10] Relevant examples of such work include E. Rehn and E. Johnson Sirleaf (2002); United Nations (2002); ICRC (2001); Council of the European Union (15671/1/08); International Alert (2002); Amnesty International (2008); and I. Specht (2006).

APPENDICES

1 Select Chronology of War

1923   Southern Rhodesia becomes a self-governing British colony.

1957   The Southern Rhodesia African National Congress (SRANC) is founded, with Joshua Nkomo as President, James Robert Chikerema as Vice President; this involves the coming together of the Bulawayo-based ANC and the Salisbury-based African National Youth League.

1959   February – The SRANC is banned; Nkomo goes into exile.

1960   January – The National Democratic Party (NDP) is founded. Michael Mawema is elected president but gives way to Nkomo in October. Robert Mugabe is given a leading position in the party.

1961   December – The NDP is banned and the Zimbabwe African People's Union (ZAPU) is founded, with Nkomo as President.

1962   September, – ZAPU is banned and the struggle goes underground; in December, the Rhodesia Front (RF) comes to power.

1963   August – ZAPU splits and the Zimbabwe African National Union (ZANU) is founded, with Ndabaningi Sithole as President, Leopold Takawira as Vice President and Robert Mugabe as Secretary-General.

1964   August – ZANU and ZAPU are banned and their leaders detained.

1965   On 11 November a Universal Declaration of Independence (UDI) is announced by the RF government, now led by Ian Smith; independence is not recognised by Britain nor by the international community and a policy of economic sanctions towards Rhodesia ensues.

1966   The Battle of Sinoia in April marks the beginning of the guerrilla war as ZANLA undertake their first significant military engagement with government troops.

1968   The UN imposes sanctions on Rhodesia.

1971   Talks take place between Ian Smith and the British Foreign Secretary, Sir Alec Douglas-Home, to agree Anglo-Rhodesian Settlement Proposals for a transition to African rule. These, however, include the deferment of majority rule. In protest, the ANC (African National Council) is founded by Bishop Abel Muzorewa in December.

1972   May – The Pearce Commission is formed to canvas African opinion on the settlement proposals and reports that there is overwhelming rejection of the proposals. In December, the military campaign begins its intensive phase in the north-east of the country. An attack is launched on a white settler farm near Centenary on the boundary of Chiweshe Tribal Trust Land (TTL).

1974   Leadership conflicts in ZANU see Robert Mugabe selected as leader in place of Sithole. With the end of colonial rule in Mozambique and the support of FRELIMO, the war in Zimbabwe intensifies.

1975   March – ZANU's leader in exile, Herbert Chitepo, is assassinated in Zambia; in April, Mugabe and Tekere go to Mozambique to oversee the military campaign.

1976   October – ZANU and ZAPU form a Popular Front but the military wings, ZANLA (Zimbabwe African National Liberation Army) and ZIPRA (Zimbabwe People's Revolutionary Army) continue their military campaigns separately, despite the brief existence of a joint force called ZIPA (Zimbabwe People's Army); ZANU/ZANLA continue operations out of Mozambique and ZAPU/ZIPRA operate from Zambia.

1978   A militia known as the Auxiliaries come into being in the TTLs; it is connected with Muzorewa's United African National Council (UNAC). In March, an Internal Settlement Agreement is negotiated between the Smith government and Muzorewa's UANC. It allows for a transitional government, with Smith remaining as Prime Minister. Power-sharing includes the allocation of Ministries to African candidates. This takes place in the context of an intensification of the war in the rural areas.

1979   New Constitution for Zimbabwe-Rhodesia. Elections held in April see UANC winning 51 of the 72 seats and Muzorewa becoming Prime Minister in June. However, these elections are not recognised internationally and the search for a negotiated settlement continues, with brokering by the United States and Britain.

        On 10 September, the Lancaster House talks get underway in London, chaired by Lord Carrington, the British Foreign Secretary, and attended by all parties to the conflict. Agreement is reached in December, allowing for a reversion to British rule for an interim period to oversee the ceasefire, the disarmament processes and the holding of fresh elections.

1980   February – Elections are held at the end of the months; Mugabe breaks the Popular Front and both ZANU and ZAPU fight the elections independently; ZANU sweep to power, having gained 57 of the 80 seats. On 18 April independence is officially declared.

APPENDICES

2 Biographical Profiles

Name	Age	Education	Class	Marital Status	Household Structure	
Agnes	60 (27-37)	Standard Three	3 / 4	W / W	Female-headed: 6 children – 5 girls; 1 boy	Female-headed: 1 daughter at home
Alice	33 (10-20)	Grade Six	4	S / M	Nuclear: with her parents until 1978; then with husband	Nuclear: with husband and 5 children
Anna	56 (33-43)	Standard Six, plus 2 years of teacher-training	1 / 1a / 3	M / W	Nuclear: husband; 5 children – 3 girls, 2 boys	Female-headed: alone with male labourer and house girl
Doreen	41 (18-28)	Standard Six	4 / 5	M / D / M	Nuclear: husband and daughter until 1975; then with second husband	Nuclear: with husband and children of second marriage
Dorothy	36 (13-23)	Grade Six; Dressmaking	5	M / D	Nuclear: with parents until 1975; with husband and 1 son for 3 years; lived with parents in townships (Concession and Glendale)	Female-headed: lives alone in co-operative housing tied to work place; son with her parents
Ellen	45 (22-32)	Standard 6; Community training	1 / 1a / 3	M	Nuclear: with husband in school housing; Extended: with husband's family, as he worked away	Extended: mother-in-law, husband, 5 children – 4 girls, 1 boy; 1 girl working away; husband no longer works
Joanne	37 (14-24)	Form Two	3 / 1a / 3	S / M	Grew up in polygamous household; lived with husband's extended family – he worked away	Female-headed: lives with 5 children, 2 boys, 3 girls; husband works away
Josephine	late 40s (e) (24-34 (e))	Standard Three	4 / 5 / 6	M	Female-headed: with children, husband worked away	Nuclear: lives with husband and 8 children – 7 girls, 1 boy
Judith	47 (24-34)	Standard Three	1a / 3/4	W	Female-headed: 4 children – 3 boys, 1 girl; husband worked away	Female-headed: 1 boy, 1 girl at home

Name	Age	Education	Class	Marital Status	Household Structure	
Juliet	42 (19-29)	Standard Three	4 / 5	S / M	Nuclear: with parents and 5 siblings; married in 1978 and moved to Harare with husband	Nuclear: lives with husband and 9 children – 5 girls and 4 boys, in Harare
Lorine	39 (16-26)	Grade Seven	4 / 5	S / M	Extended: with her husband's family in Chiweshe Nuclear: with her husband in Harare	Nuclear: lives with husband and 6 children – 4, girls, 2 boys, in Harare
Lucia	34 (11-21)	Form Four to O-levels; Nursing	3 / 1 / 1a	S / M	Nuclear: with parents and 6 siblings	Nuclear: lives with husband and 1 son, in Harare
Mary	37 (14-24)	Grade Six	4 / 5	S / S	Polygamous household: her mother was third wife – divorced; then female-headed, living with grandmother	Nuclear: lives with husband and 4 children, in Harare
Maggie	40 (17-27)	Standard Six, Dressmaking		M / D		Female-headed: lives alone in co-operative housing attached to workplace; 4 children – 3 boys and 1 girl live with their father
Margaret	41 (18-28)	Standard Two	5 / 4	S / M	Nuclear: with husband in farm shop	Nuclear: lives with husband and 6 children – 4 girls, 2 boys
Mercy	36 (13-23)	Form Four	1a / 3 / 1	S / M	Female-headed: mother and daughter, after father died	Nuclear: lives in Harare with husband and 2 sons
Monica	40 (17-27)	Standard Six	5	M / D	Female-headed: with 6 children – 3 boys, 3 girls; husband in Harare	Female-headed: on her own in co-operative housing attached to work place
More Blessing	31 (9-19)	Grade Three	4/5 / 5	S / M	Female-headed: lived with grandmother in Chiweshe; father died and mother worked on farms	Nuclear: lives with husband with 3 children in low-density suburb. Works as domestic worker

Name	Age	Education	Class	Marital Status	Household Structure
Pardon	34 (11-21)	Grade Seven	4 / 1a	S / M	Extended: with parents-in-law; 2 children; husband worked away
			4 / 5	M	Nuclear: lives with husband and 5 children – 4 girls, 1 boy. Pregnant at time of interview
Phyllis	late 50s (e) (36-46 (e))	Standard Two	5 / 3	M	Nuclear: in Harare with husband and working; one son
					Polygamous household: she is first of 2 wives
Polly	37 (14-24)	Standard Three		S / M	Nuclear: lives with husband and 7 children, 6 boys, 1 girl
Rachel	late 50s (e) (37-47 (e))	Standard Three	1 / 3/4	M	Extendec: with husband and his parents, who moved to Mozambique; 6 children
			3/4		Nuclear: with husband and younger of her children in Chiweshe
Rosy	42 (19-29)	Form Two; some teacher-training; weaving	1a / 5	S / M / D	Nuclear: husband and 1 daughter; with her parents after divorce
			5	D	Female-headed: lives with her mother and 1 son; daughter works away from home
Sarah	27 (4-14)	Grade Three; after Independence progressed to Form Four	3/4 / 6	S / M?	Nuclear: lived with father, brother, sister and stepmother; divorced mother was at her parents home
					Extended: lives with her mother and stepfather, her brother and her son. Has a 'husband' but he rarely visits
Stella	late 50s (e) (37-47 (e))	No formal education; learned basic literacy from friends	4 / 6	M	Nuclear: 9 children – 3 boys, 6 girls
Susan	43 (20-30)	Standard Four	< 4	M	Orphaned: both parents died; children reared themselves; married at 13, lived in Harare and in Keeps (alone with children as husband was in prison)
					Nuclear: with husband and 5 children – 2 girls, 3 boys.

Name	Age	Education	Class	Marital Status	Household Structure
Tecla	Late 50s (e) (34-44 (e))	Standard Three	4 5 / 4/3	M / M	Female-headed: with 5 children – 4 girls, 1 boy; husband worked away / Nuclear: lives with husband
Tendai	39 (16-26)	Grade Six	2 4 / 6	S M / D	Nuclear: with parents and 5 siblings / Female-headed: lives alone in rented rooms; 2 daughters live with their father
Trust	37 (14-24)	Standard Three	2, 3 / 2,3 6	S M / M	Extended; with mother-in-law and children. Moved to Harare in 1978 / Nuclear and extended: husband, 3 children – 2 girls, 1 boy; 1 girl in special school
Veronica	Late 30s (e) (15-25 (e))	Form Two	4,5 / 3	S M / M	Female-headed; alone with children in Keep; moved to Harare / Nuclear: husband and 4 children

Interviews outside of core sample

Name	Age	Education	Class		Marital Status		Home Area	Reason for Interview
Emelda	30 (7-17)		6		S	M	Murewa; Marondera. Emelda and Peter live in extreme poverty; they have 2 children	She and her husband were ex-combatants who I met through a mutual friend
Hope	29 (8-18)	Grade Four	6			D	Marondera; Hope lives in extreme poverty; is divorced with 2 children	She is an ex-combatant and I met her through a mutual friend
Martha							Chiweshe	She was a community development worker in an international development agency; worked on agricultural projects
Michael	Early 40s (e)	N/A	3/4		M	M	Chiweshe	Was an organiser for the guerrillas
Peter	Early 30s (e)	N/A	6		S		Marondera	Is Emelda's husband, they met in Mozambique
Taurai	32 (9-19)	Form Two	1a 3		S	M		Is an ex-comrade who now is engaged in politics; met through mutual friend

Key to Tables

The use of double columns to enter class, marital status and household structure is to indicate possible change over time from the war period (1970–1980) to the time of interview (1993). The use of (e) denotes an estimate was made in the absence of clear information as some women did not know their date of birth. The following notes clarify the use of particular social categories to map out the biographical profiles of the women who participated in this study of the liberation war as experience in Chiweshe:

Name Pseudonyms have been allocated to the women interviewed in Chiweshe.

Age The first entry refers to the age of the woman at time of interview in 1993; the entry in brackets refers to the age of the woman during the war period of 1970–1980.

Education There are two systems of reference used by the women, depending on their age, to describe their level of formal education.[1] Older women refer to the system of education in the reserves up until 1971, when five years of primary education was all that was available: sub-A, sub-B, Standard One, Standard Two and Standard Three. However, state involvement in the rural areas was very limited. Beyond Standard Three, students largely had to seek entry into mission schools to complete their higher primary education (Standards Four through Six). This involved walking long distances or the expensive option of boarding school. Securing even the basic provision of education within the reserves was already costly to families and so many of the women interviewed considered themselves lucky if they had managed to reach Standard Three. Agnes remarks that it was not unusual for girls to be aged 15 before they received any education.

The system changed in 1971, when students automatically received primary education from Grade One to Grade Seven. Younger women in the sample refer to this system. However, not all rural schools were equipped to provide schooling to Grade Seven. The first state secondary school was founded in 1952 in Goromonzi. Moreover, most state schools were located in urban areas. The colonial system effectively created a bottleneck situation, whereby the further an African girl or boy want to proceed with their education the less likely they were to find a place available in school. Bottlenecks developed at the key points of higher primary level, entry into secondary school, progress from Form Two to Form Three at secondary level, movement from Form Four to O-level and from there to A-level.

There were also obvious gendered effects for family decision-making in relation to resources and education. Older women refer to the hostile and degrading attitudes held by communities concerning the education of girls. Those women who had benefited from further education commented upon their concerns of status and reputation when they were younger. They faced accusations of impudence, moral looseness and prostitution. Many families simply saw the education of girls as a waste of money and that any benefits would accrue to her marital home. Younger women in the sample expressed regret and anger that their parents could not afford to keep them in school. This was touched upon in Chapter 5, where marriage was discussed as an economic and social option for young women in the absence of further education.

Class The following categories are used to describe women in relation to class:

1) Professional (in own right) e.g. teacher, nurse, civil servant.
1a) Married to, or daughter of, a professional or a state worker.
2) Business (own or family), e.g. shop, haulage business, poultry enterprise, bottle store (beer), building company.
3) Peasant surplus (sells quantities on markets).
4 Peasant subsistence (for home use and small local sales).
5) Worker (piece-worker for others, farm worker, domestic worker); migrant labour.
6) Trader (informal economic activities).

1   See Zvobgo (1994) for a history of colonial education policy in Zimbabwe.

Categorising women according to class was not a straightforward exercise. How can one capture the diverse economic aspects of women's lives into 'peasant', 'worker', or 'professional'?[2] In relation to the women of Chiweshe, I was faced with many dilemmas in this area, not least the fact that talk of class was not explicitly vocalised by women with the meanings associated with western politics and sociology. Another dilemma involved the question of classifying women according to their husband's occupation or land. The difficulty in the case of Joanne, who is married to a teacher, is that while she may not have enjoyed the same level of education as her husband she may benefit from some reflected status as his wife. In the case of land, Florence may indeed be living and working on a decent-sized holding that produces a surplus, but she has no access to, or control over, resources beyond very basic household maintenance. A woman may in fact be better defined in another class that reflects what she actually has and does: for example, if she has a plot of her own where she grows vegetables for local sale and is involved in informal trading or beer brewing. Such informal market activities may better define a 'peasant' woman than does her attachment to her husband's land. In other cases, however, we can find strong partnerships between husbands and wives in farming their land and making decisions. I would contend that what we often describe as a class affiliation for women is in fact a reflection of the relational context of women's economic activities. That is to say, rural women are often defined in terms of class by virtue of their situation as daughter, mother, wife or daughter-in-law in a peasant household, assumed to be male-headed. I would suggest that typologies of class and household structure are often interrelated in confirming women's class position as well as their often-assumed subordinate position within the household.

In addition to the problem of assigning women to a class by virtue of what they actually own and do, there was the added complication of a generalised crisis of war that destabilises economic certainties; the rich can become poor and the informal economies of wars can enrich marketeers, and some people may be blessed with luck in finding themselves better equipped to survive the uncertainty and impoverishment. The conditions of the Protected Villages undoubtedly impoverished all the families who were fenced inside. To some extent it could be argued that the war levelled economic differences in many cases, as all families faced the difficulties of growing even enough food for consumption. Could it be said that this amounts to a change in class for many people? This question relates to another dilemma in identifying a woman's class; that over her lifetime a woman passes through a number of classes. For example, in her father's home she could be part of a large peasant holding, in her youth she may move to town and become a domestic worker, and later she may marry a teacher and move to a school compound in the rural areas. It could be said that such a woman is of the peasant, working and professional classes over her lifetime.

These limitations notwithstanding, I have attempted to locate women in a class context, both during the war period and in 1993, when the interviews took place. In the case of the former I have referred to family circumstances before and during the Protected Villages in 1974, thus attempting to codify

---

[2] Some of these issues are implicit in Schmidt's (1992) gendering of the peasant option in colonial Zimbabwe, where she uncovers a plethora of economic activities in which women were involved but often invisible in historical accounts. See Abbott and Wallace (1990) for a useful summary of sociological approaches to classifying women and the limitations and merits of these approaches.

the general effects of impoverishment resulting from this transformation of rural life.

Marital Status S: single; M: married; W: widowed; D: divorced
In Zimbabwe there is a co-existence of customary and civil law governing marriage (Armstrong 1987; Batezat and Mwalo 1989; Stewart and Armstrong 1990). Traditionally, marriage is virilocal, that is, the woman moves to her husband's home place but remains tied to the totem or clan of her birth family. Bride price is paid, under customary law, to the bride's family by the prospective husband. This often takes years to pay in full and can be source of family conflict as the wife usually lives with the husband even in the event of unfinished payments. However, any children born into her marriage are members of the husband's totem clan. A woman is often therefore an outsider to the area where she spends much of her life. In Chiweshe, many of the women interviewed were actually born in Chiweshe and married locally so they did not move too far from their families. Civil law only allows for one wife and such legal recognition is often important in civil disputes over inheritance. Women with only a traditional marriage can face difficulties from the husband's family in the event of his death as property often returns to the husband's next brother. Polygamous marriage is a feature of rural society but can only legitimately occur in the context of customary marriage. However, there are also many cases of monogamous marriage where women suspect their husband of having a girlfriend or girlfriends. This is particularly so in the context of migrant labour, where men may be working in towns or for parastatals such as the railways, which often involve considerable periods of time working in other parts of the country. I did come to know of some cases where wives had believed themselves to be in a monogamous marriage, but then discovered that their husbands had other wives in other parts of the country.

Divorce is frowned upon and divorced women are often stigmatised as impudent and loose, particularly by other women. In the event of divorce, a woman has to leave her husband's home and return to her parents. Her children remain with their father. It is not surprising that women often choose to remain in the most difficult and violent of situations rather than face the loss of their children, their home and the demoralising loss of status in returning to their parents. In this impoverished state, women struggle to survive. Some of the divorced women I spoke with referred to boyfriends who came to stay with them now and then. Very few women, even the most critical, referred to this as prostitution. Still, there is no doubting that the presents and cash received from boyfriends are an important source of income for divorced women.

Household Structure The following categories define the structures of the households:

- Nuclear – a situation where wife, husband and children live together in one place
- Female-headed household – a situation where a husband is working away and the wife is alone with the children working the land (migrant labour), where a woman is widowed and living alone with or without children, or where a woman has got divorced and is either back living with her parents or living alone with occasional visits from her children
- Extended family – a situation where wife, husband and children

are living with the husband's parents and siblings in a compound situation; it can also refer to a situation of migrant labour where the husband works away from home but the wife and children are living and working with his parents on their land

• Polygamous household – a situation where there is more than one wife and the families live together in the same compound.

Identifying women within particular household structures holds similar difficulties to those of typifying class affiliation.[3] One example is choosing to define a household as female-headed based on the absence of the husband/father who works away from home. Such a label may hide the fact that real authority over resource decisions still remains with the absent spouse. In another example, a household may be defined as female-headed because the senior woman is a widow, yet in effect she may be under the control of her husband's family who have laid claim to her land and home. Therefore, naming a household does not necessarily give a full appreciation as to the dynamics and relations that shape intra-household realities for women.[4] It is also the case that households cannot be viewed simply as isolated social units, they also exist in a context of wider relations affected by economic relations, kinship and ethnic affiliations.[5] Despite these cautions of interpretation I have placed women in their household contexts both during the war and in 1993. Similarly to class, I note that women's household contexts can change dramatically over a lifetime due to migration, marriage, poverty, divorce and death. The vagaries of this context can be witnessed in the narrative accounts of women's lives.

Florence exemplifies the deficiencies of categorising women's position. Although she is married to a teacher but they have lived apart for many years. He works in Harare and rarely visits his rural home where she now lives alone. Over the years she has had to plant the fields and harvest the crops for her husband. She receives no income or crops from this work, nor does she receive any of her husband's income. She gleans the edges of the fields to gather grain for the house and grows some groundnuts to make peanut butter, which she trades locally. Thus, even though she may fit within the category of comfortable peasant household, she nevertheless lives in poverty.

[3]   Defining the household in an African context has excited various debates concerning shared pots and shared hearths in an attempt to find a baseline understanding women's place in varied household structures. For examples, see Colson (1958), Brydon and Chant (1989), Chambers and Conway (1992), Ekejiuba (1995), Guyer and Peters (1987) and Mackintosh (1979). There is also extensive literature on the issues of gender divisions of labour, intra-household relations and gender planning frameworks that addresses problems of household analysis. For example, see Goetz (1991), Kabeer (1994), Moser (1991), Overholt et al. (1985) and Sen (1990). Social policy approaches to gender and conflict include household analysis to address issues of resources and labour burdens for women in contexts of war (See El Bushra and Piza Lopez, 1994; Byrne, 1995). These studies, however, remain tied to notions of separated spheres such as the personal, household and public in demarcating women's capabilities and vulnerabilities in response to war. Although useful, and indeed essential, to development planning, such categorisations can obscure the relational dynamics within and between these spheres of activity and in so doing fail to apprehend the full extent of problems and possibilities faced by women in surviving war.

[4]   For more on this point, see Peters (1995).

[5]   See Guyer (1986) and O'Laughlin (1995).

BIBLIOGRAPHY

Abbott, P. and C. Wallace (1990) 'Women and Stratification', in P. Abbott and C. Wallace *An Introduction to Sociology: Feminist Perspectives*, London and New York: Routledge.

Agarwal, B. (1994) 'Gender, Resistance and Land: Interlinked Struggles over Resources and Meanings in South Asia', *Journal of Peasant Studies*, Vol. 22, No. 1:81-125.

Al-Ali, N. and N. Pratt (2009) *What Kind of Liberation? Women and the Occupation of Iraq*, Berkeley, CA: University of California Press.

Alexander, J. (2006) *The Unsettled Land: State-Making and the Politics of Land in Zimbabwe, 1893–2003*, Oxford: James Currey.

— (2003) 'Squatters, Veterans and the State in Zimbabwe', in A. Hammar, B. Raftopoulos and S. Jensen (eds) (2003) *Zimbabwe's Unfinished Business: Rethinking Land, State, and Nation in the Context of Crisis*, Harare: Weaver Press.

— (1996) 'Things Fall Apart, The Centre *Can* Hold: Processes of Post-war Political Change in Zimbabwe's Rural Areas', in N. Bhebe and T. Ranger (eds) *Society in Zimbabwe's Liberation War*, Oxford: James Currey, and Harare: University of Zimbabwe Publications, pp. 175-91.

— (1994) 'State, Peasantry and Resettlement in Zimbabwe', *Review of African Political Economy*, Vol. 21, No. 61:325-45.

— (1991) 'The Unsettled Land: The Politics of Land Distribution in Matabeleland, 1980–1990', *Journal of Southern African Studies*, Vol. 17, No. 4:581-610.

Alexander, J., J.A. McGregor and T. Ranger (eds) (2000) *Violence and Memory: One Hundred Years in the 'Dark Forests' of Matabeleland*, Oxford: James Currey.

Armstrong, A. (ed.) (1987) *Women and Law in Southern Africa*, Harare: Zimbabwe Publishing House.

Arrighi, G. (1970) 'Labour Supplies in Historical Perspective: A Study of the Proletarianization of the African Peasantry in Rhodesia', *Journal of Development Studies*, Vol. 6, No. 3:197-234.

— (1977) 'The Political Economy of Rhodesia', in G. Arrighi and J. Saul (eds) *Essays on the Political Economy of Africa*, New York: Monthly Review Press.

Astrow, A. (1983) *Zimbabwe: A Revolution That Lost Its Way?* London: Zed Books.

Auret, D. (1990) *A Decade of Development: Zimbabwe 1980-1990*, Gweru: Mambo Press and the Catholic Commission for Justice and Peace in Zimbabwe.

Bakare-Yusuf, B. (2003) 'Yorubas Don't Do Gender: A Critical Review of Oyeronke Oyeyumi's *The Invention of Women: Making an African Sense of Western Gender Discourses*', *African Identities*, Vol. 1, No. 1. http://www.codesria.org/IMG/pdf/BAKERE_YUSUF.pdf (accessed 13/02/2011).

Barnes, T. (1992) 'The Fight for Control of African Women's Mobility in Colonial

Zimbabwe 1900–1939', *Signs*, Vol. 17, No. 3:586-608.

Barnes, T. and E. Win (1992) *To Live A Better Life: An Oral History of Women in the City of Harare, 1930–1970*, Harare: Baobab Books.

Bartky, S. L. (1988) 'Foucault, Femininity, and the Modernization of Patriarchal Power', in I. Diamond and L. Quinby (eds) *Feminism and Foucault: Reflections on Resistance*, Boston, MA: Northeastern University Press.

Batezat, E. and M. Mwalo (1989) *Women in Zimbabwe*, Harare: Southern Africa Political Economy Series (SAPES) Trust.

Batezat, E., M. Mwalo and K. Truscott (1988) 'Women and Independence: the Heritage and the Struggle', in C. Stoneman (ed.) *Zimbabwe's Prospects: Issues of Race, Class, State and Capital in Southern Africa*, London: Macmillan Publishers Ltd.

Beall, J., S. Hassim and A. Todes (1989) '"A Bit on the Side"?: Gender Struggles in the Politics of Transformation in South Africa', *Feminist Review*, No. 33:30-56.

Bennett, O., J. Bexley, and K. Warnock (1995) (eds) *Arms to Fight, Arms to Protect: Women Speak Out about Conflict*, London: Panos.

Bessant, L. (1985) 'Going into Lines: Centralization and the Perception of Land Shortage in the Chiweshe Reserve, 1940–44', Henderson Seminar Paper, University of Zimbabwe.

— (1987) 'Coercive Development: Peasant Economy, Politics and Land in the Chiweshe Reserve, Colonial Zimbabwe, 1940–1966', DPhil thesis, Yale University.

— (1994) 'Songs of Chiweshe, Songs of Zimbabwe' *African Affairs*, Vol. 93, No. 370:43-73.

Bessant, L. and E. Muringai (1993) 'Peasants, Businessmen and Moral Economy in Chiweshe Reserve, Colonial Zimbabwe, 1930–1968', *Journal of Southern African Studies*, Vol. 19, No. 4:551-92.

Bhebe, N. and T. Ranger (eds) (1995) *Soldiers in Zimbabwe's Liberation War*, Harare: University of Zimbabwe Publications and London: James Currey, and Portsmouth, NH: Heinemann.

— (eds) (1996) *Society in Zimbabwe's Liberation War*, Harare: University of Zimbabwe Publications, and London, James Currey, and Portsmouth, NH, Heinemann.

Bond-Stewart, K. (1987) *Independence is Not Only for One Sex*, Harare: Zimbabwe Publishing House.

Boulding, E. (1988) 'Warriors and Saints: Dilemmas in the History of Men, Women and War', in E. Isakkson (ed.) *Women and the Military System*, London: Harvester Wheatsheaf.

Bourdillon, M.F.C. (1982) *The Shona Peoples*, 2nd edition, Gweru: Mambo Press.

— (1987) 'Guns and Rain: Taking Structural Analysis too Far? Review Article', *Africa*, Vol. 57, No. 2: 263-74.

Bracking, S. (2005) 'Development Denied: Autocratic Militarism in Post-election Zimbabwe', *Review of African Political Economy*, Vol. 32, Issue 104/105, pp. 341-57.

Brownmiller, S. (1976) *Against Our Will: Men, Women and Rape*, New York: Bantam.

Brydon, L. and S. Chant (1989) *Women in the Third World: Gender Issues in Rural and Urban Areas*, Hampshire: Edward Elgar.

Burguieres, M. (1990) 'Feminist Approaches to Peace: Another Step for Peace Studies', *Millennium*, Vol. 19, No. 1:1-18.

Byrne, B. (1995) 'Gender, Conflict and Development, Vol. 1: Overview', BRIDGE Report, Briefings on Development and Gender, Sussex: Institute of Development Studies.

Caute, D. (1983) *Under the Skin: The Death of White Rhodesia*, London: Allen Lane.

Chambers, R. and G. Conway (1992) 'Sustainable Rural Livelihoods: Practical Concepts for the 21st Century', *Discussion Paper 296*, Sussex: Institute of Development Studies.

Chan, S. and R. Primorac (eds) (2007) *Zimbabwe in Crisis: The International*

Response and the Space of Silence, Abingdon: Routledge.

Cheater, A. (1981) 'Women and Their Participation in Commercial Agricultural Production: The Case of Medium-Scale Freehold in Zimbabwe', *Development and Change*, Vol. 12:349-77.

Chimedza, R. (1987) 'Women and Decision-Making: The Case of District Councils in Zimbabwe', in C. Qunta (ed.) *Women in Southern Africa*, London: Allison and Busby.

Cilliers, J.K. (1985) *Counter-Insurgency in Rhodesia*, London: Croom Helm.

Cliffe, L. and C. Stoneman (1989) *Zimbabwe Politics, Economics and Society*, New York: Pinter Publishers.

Cliffe, L., J. Mpofu and B. Munslow (1980) 'Nationalist Politics in Zimbabwe: The 1980 Elections and Beyond', *Review of African Political Economy*, No. 18:44-67.

Clifford, J. (1988) 'On Ethnographic Authority', in J. Clifford, *The Predicament of Culture: Twentieth-Century Ethnography, Literature and Art*, Cambridge, Mass., Harvard University Press, pp. 21-54.

— (1986a) 'On Ethnographic Allegory', in J. Clifford and G.E. Marcus (eds) *Writing Culture: The Poetics of Ethnography*, Berkeley, CA: University of California Press, pp. 98-121.

— (1986b) 'Introduction: Partial Truths', in J. Clifford and G.E. Marcus (eds) *Writing Culture: The Poetics of Ethnography*, Berkeley, CA: University of California Press, pp.1-26.

Cockburn, C. (2007) *From Where We Stand: War, Women's Activism and Feminist Analysis*, London: Zed Books.

Cockburn, C. and D. Zarkov (ed.) (2002) *The Postwar Moment: Militaries, Masculinities and International Peacekeeping*, London: Lawrence and Wishart.

Cohn, C. (2004) 'Feminist Peacemaking: In Resolution 1325, the United Nations Requires the Inclusion of Women in all Planning and Negotiation', *Women's Review of Books*, 21 (5): 8-9.

Cohn, C. and C. Enloe (2003) 'A Conversation with Cynthia Enloe: Feminists Look at Masculinity and Men Who Wage War', *Signs*, Vol. 28, No. 4:1187-207.

Cohn, C., H. Kinsella, and S. Gibbings (2004) 'Women, Peace and Security: Resolution 1325', *International Feminist Journal of Politics*, Vol. 6, No. 1:130-40.

Colson, E. (1958) *Marriage and the Family among the Plateau Tonga of Northern Rhodesia*, Manchester: Manchester University Press.

Connell, R.W. (2000) *The Men and The Boys*, Cambridge: Polity Press.

— (2002) 'Masculinities, the Reduction of Violence and the Pursuit of Peace', in C. Cockburn and D. Zarkov (eds) *The Postwar Moment: Militaries, Masculinities and International Peacekeeping*, London: Lawrence and Wishart.

Couzens Hoy, D. (1986) 'Power, Repression, Progress: Foucault, Lukes, and the Frankfurt School', in D. Couzens Hoy (ed.) *Foucault: A Critical Reader*, Oxford: Basil Blackwell.

Dangarembga, T. (1988) *Nervous Conditions*, London: Women's Press.

Davies, M. (ed.) (1983) *Third World – Second Sex: Women's Struggles and National Liberation*, London: Zed Books.

— (ed.) (1994) *Women and Violence: Realities and Responses Worldwide*, London: Zed Books.

Davis, K., M. Leijenaar and J. Oldersma (1991) (eds) *The Gender of Power*, London: Sage.

Delap, M. (1979) 'The April 1979 Elections in Zimbabwe-Rhodesia', *African Affairs*, Vol. 78, No. 313:431-8.

Diamond, I. and L. Quinby (eds) (1988) *Feminism and Foucault: Reflections in Resistance*, Boston, MA: Northeastern University Press.

Denov, M. and C. Gervais (2007) 'Negotiating (In)Security: Agency, Resistance, and Resourcefulness among Girls Formerly Associated with Sierra Leone's Revolutionary United Front', *SIGNS: Journal of Women in Culture and Society, War and Terror 1*, Special Issue, Vol. 32, No. 4:885-910.

Drinkwater, M. (1991) *The State and Agrarian Change in Zimbabwe's Communal*

Areas, Basingstoke: Macmillan.

Ekejiuba, Felicia (1995) 'Down to Fundamentals: Women-centred Hearth-holds in Rural West Africa', in D. Bryceson (ed.) *Women Wielding the Hoe: Lessons from Rural Africa for Feminist Theory and Development Practice*, Oxford: Berg Publishers.

Ekine, S. (2008) 'Women's Responses to State Violence in the Niger Delta', *Feminist Africa 10*, Special Issue on Militarism, Conflict and Women's Activism, 10:67-83.

El Bushra, J. and E. Piza-Lopez (1994) 'Development in Conflict: The Gender Dimension', Oxfam Discussion Paper 3, Oxford: Oxfam.

El-Bushra, J. and C. Mukarubuga (1995) 'Women, War and Transition', *Gender and Development*, Vol. 3, No. 3:16-22.

Ellert, H. (1993) *The Rhodesia Front War: Counter-Insurgency and Guerrilla Warfare, 1962–1980*, Gweru: Mambo Press.

Elshtain, J.B. (1981) *Public Man, Private Woman: Women in Social and Political Thought*. Princeton, NJ: Princeton University Press.

— (1990) 'The Problem With Peace', in J.B. Elshtain and S. Tobias (eds) *Women, Militarism, and War: Essays in History, Politics and Social Theory*, Savage, MD: Rowman and Littlefield.

— (1995) *Women and War*, 2nd edition, Chicago, IL: University of Chicago Press.

Elshtain, J.B. and S. Tobias (eds) (1990) *Women, Militarism, and War: Essays in History, Politics and Social Theory*, Savage, MD: Rowman and Littlefield.

Enloe, C. (1988) *Does Khaki Become You? The Militarization of Women's Lives*, 2nd edition, London: Pandora Press.

— (1989) *Bananas, Beaches and Bases: Making Feminist Sense of International Politics*, London: Pandora Press.

— (1990) 'Bananas, Bases, and Patriarchy', in J. B. Elshtain and S. Tobias (eds) *Women, Militarism, and War: Essays in History, Politics and Social Theory*, Savage, MD: Rowman and Littlefield.

— (2002) 'Demilitarization or More of the Same? Feminist Questions to Ask in the Post-war Moment?', in C. Cockburn and D. Zarkov (eds) *The Postwar Moment: Militaries, Masculinities and International Peacekeeping*, London: Lawrence and Wishart.

— (2007) *Globalization and Militarism: Feminists Make the Link*, Savage, MD: Rowan and Littlefield.

Feminist Africa 10 (2008), Special Issue on Militarism, Conflict and Women's Activism, African Gender Institute, University of Cape Town, South Africa.

Foucault, M. (1978) *The History of Sexuality: An Introduction*, translated by R. Hurley, Harmondsworth: Penguin.

— (1979) [1975] *Discipline and Punish: The Birth of the Prison*, London: Peregrine Books.

— (1980a) *Power/Knowledge: Selected Interviews and Other Writings 1972–1977*, Edited by C. Gordon, Hemel Hempstead: Harvester Press.

— (1980b) 'Introduction', *Herculin Barbin: Being the Recently Discovered Memoirs of a Nineteenth-Century French Hermaphrodite*, New York: Pantheon.

— (1982) 'Afterword: The Subject and Power', in H.L. Dreyfus and P. Rabinow *Michel Foucault: Beyond Structuralism and Hermeneutics*, Hemel Hempstead: Harvester Press.

Frederikse, J. (1982) *None But Ourselves: Masses Vs. Media in the Making of Zimbabwe*, Harare: Zimbabwe Publishing House.

Giles, W. and J. Hyndman (2001) *Sites of Violence: Gender and Conflict Zones*, Berkeley, CA: University of California Press.

Gluck, S.B. (1995) 'Palestinian Women: Gender Politics and Nationalism', *Journal of Palestine Studies*, Vol. 24, No. 3:5-15.

Goetz, A.M. (1991) 'Feminism and the Claim to Know: contradictions in feminist approaches to women in development', in R. Grant and K. Newland (eds) *Gender and International Relations*, Milton Keynes: Open University Press.

Grant, R. and K. Newland (eds) (1991) *Gender and International Relations*, Milton Keynes: Open University Press.

Greiger, S. (1987) 'Women in Nationalist Struggle: TANU Activists in Dar es Salaam', *International Journal of African Historical Studies*, Vol. 20, No. 1:1-26.

Guyer, J. (1986) 'Intra-Household Processes and Farming Systems Research: Perspectives from Anthropology', in J. Lewinger Moock (ed.) *Understanding Africa's Rural Households and Farming Systems*, Boulder, CO: Westview Press.

Guyer, J. and P. Peters (1987) 'Conceptualizing the Household – Issues of Theory and Policy in Africa – Introduction', *Development and Change*, Vol. 18, No. 2:197-214.

Hamilton, P. (1964) 'Population and Land Use in Chiweshe Reserve', *The Rhodes-Livingstone Journal*, No. 36:40-58.

Hammar, A., B. Raftopoulos and S. Jensen (eds) (2003) *Zimbabwe's Unfinished Business: Rethinking Land, State, and Nation in the Context of Crisis*, Harare: Weaver Press.

Hart, G. (1991) 'Engendering Everyday Resistance: Gender, Patronage and Production in Rural Malaysia', *Journal of Peasant Studies*, Vol. 19, No. 1:93-121.

— (1990) *Famine in Zimbabwe, 1890–1960*, Gweru: Mambo Press.

Isaksson, E. (ed.) (1988) *Women and the Military System*, London: Harvester-Wheatsheaf.

Jabri, V. and E. O' Gorman (eds) (1999) *Women, Culture and International Relations*, Boulder, CO: Lynne Rienner.

Jacobs, S. (1988) 'Women and Land Resettlement in Zimbabwe', *Review of African Political Economy*, Nos. 27/28:33-50.

— (1992) 'Gender and Land Reform: Zimbabwe and Some Comparisons', *International Sociology*, Vol. 7, No. 1:5-34.

Jayawardena, K. (1986) *Feminism and Nationalism in the Third World*, London: Zed Books.

Jeater, D. (1993) *Marriage, Perversion and Power: The Construction of Moral Discourse in Southern Rhodesia, 1894–1930*, Oxford: Clarendon Press.

Johnson, R.W.M. (1964) 'An Economic Survey of Chiweshe Reserve', *The Rhodes-Livingstone Journal*, No. 36:82-108.

Kaarsholm, P. (ed.) (1991) *Cultural Struggle and Development in Southern Africa*, Harare: Baobab Books and London: James Currey and Portsmouth, NH: Heinemann.

Kabeer, N. (1994) *Reversed Realities: Gender Hierarchies in Development Thought*, London: Routledge.

Kadenge, P.G. (1992) 'Zimbabwe's Structural Adjustment Programme: The First Year Experience', Monograph Series, No. 2., Harare: SAPES Trust.

Kandiyoti, D. (1998) 'Bargaining with Patriarchy', *Gender and Society*, Vol. 2, No. 3:274-90.

— (1998) 'Gender, Power and Contestation: "Rethinking Bargaining with Patriarchy"', in C. Jackson and R. Pearson (eds) *Feminist Visions of Development: Gender Analysis and Policy*, London: Routledge, pp. 135-51.

Kazembe, J.L. (1986) 'The Women Issue', in Mandaza, I. (ed.) (1987) *Zimbabwe: The Political Economy of Transition, 1980-1986*, Dakar: Codesria.

Kesby, M. (1994) 'Geographies of Power: State and Patriarchal Spatial Discourse and Practice in Zimbabwe', PhD Thesis, Keele University.

— (1996) 'Arenas for Control, Terrains of Gender Contestation: Guerrilla and Counter-Insurgency Warfare in Zimbabwe, 1972–1980', *Journal of Southern African Studies*, Vol. 22, No. 4:561-84.

— (1999) 'Locating and Dislocating Gender in Rural Zimbabwe: The Making of Space and the Texturing of Bodies', *Gender, Place and Culture*. Vol. 6, No. 1:27-47.

Kriger, N.J. (1988) 'The Zimbabwean War of Liberation: Struggles within the Struggle', *Journal of Southern African Studies*, Vol. 14, No. 2:304-22.

— (1992) *Zimbabwe's Guerrilla War: Peasant Voices*, African Studies Series, Cambridge: Cambridge University Press.
— (2003a) *Guerrilla Veterans in Post-War Zimbabwe: Symbolic and Violent Politics 1980–1987*, Cambridge: Cambridge University Press.
— (2003b) 'Zimbabwe: Political Constructions of War Veterans', *Review of African Political Economy*, Vol. 30, No. 96:323-8.
Lan, D. (1985) *Guns and Rain: Guerrillas and Spirit Mediums in Zimbabwe*, London: James Currey.
Linden, I. (1979) *The Catholic Church and the Struggle in Zimbabwe*, London: Longman.
Lindgren, B. (2003) 'The Green Bombers of Salisbury: Elections and Political Violence in Zimbabwe', *Anthropology Today*, Vol. 19, No. 2:6-10.
— (2005) 'Memories of Violence: Recreation of Ethnicity in Post-Colonial Zimbabwe', in Paul Richards (ed.) *No Peace, No War: An Anthropology of Contemporary Armed Conflict*, Oxford: James Currey, pp. 155-73.
Macdonald, S. (1987) 'Drawing the Lines – Gender, Peace and War: An Introduction', in S. Macdonald, P. Holden and S. Ardener (eds) *Images of Women in Peace and War*, London: Macmillan.
Macdonald, S., P. Holden and S. Ardener (1987) (eds) *Images of Women in Peace and War*, London: Macmillan.
Mackintosh, M. (1979) 'Domestic Labour and the Household', in S. Burman (ed.) *Fit Work for Women*, London: Croom Helm.
Macnamara, E. (1989) *Women in Zimbabwe: An Annotated Bibliography*, Harare, University of Zimbabwe
Mama, A. and M. Okazawa-Rey (2008) 'Editorial: Militarism, Conflict and Women's Activism, *Feminist Africa 10*, Special Issue on Militarism, Conflict and Women's Activism, 10:1-8.
Mandaza, I. (ed.) (1986) *Zimbabwe: The Political Economy of Transition 1980–1986*, Dakar: Codesria.
Mandaza, I. and L. Sachikoyne (eds) (1991) *The One Party State and Democracy: The Zimbabwe Debate*, Harare: SAPES Books.
Manungo, K.D. (1991) 'The Role Peasants Played in the Zimbabwe War of Liberation, With Special Emphasis on Chiweshe District', PhD Thesis, Ohio University.
Marechera, D. (1982) *The House of Hunger*, Harare: Zimbabwe Publishing House.
Marangwanda, T. (1986) 'The "Protected Villages": The Rhodesian Counter-Insurgency Effort and its Effects on the Peasant Population of Chiweshe', MA dissertation, University of Zimbabwe.
Martin, D. and P. Johnson (1981) *The Struggle for Zimbabwe: The Chimurenga War*. London: Faber and Faber.
Mashingaidze, T. M. (2006) 'The Zimbabwean Entrenchment: An Analysis of the Nexus between Domestic and Foreign Policies in a "Collapsing" Militant State, 1990s–2006'. *Alternatives*, Vol. 5, No. 4:57-76.
Maxwell, D. (1993) 'Local Politics and the War of Liberation in North-East Zimbabwe', *Journal of Southern African Studies*, Vol. 19, No. 3:361-86.
May, J. (1983) *Zimbabwean Women in Colonial and Customary Law*, Gweru: Mambo Press.
Mazurana, D. (2002) 'International Peacekeeping Operations: To Neglect Gender is to Risk Peacekeeping', in C. Cockburn and D. Zarkov (eds) *The Postwar Moment: Militaries, Masculinities and International Peacekeeping*, London: Lawrence and Wishart.
Mazurana, D, A. Raven-Roberts and J. Parpart (2005) *Gender, Conflict, and Peacekeeping*, Oxford: Rowman and Littlefield.
McLaughlin, J. (1996) *On the Frontline: Catholic Missions in Zimbabwe's Liberation War*, Harare: Baobab Books.
McGregor, J.A. (2002) 'The Politics of Disruption: War Veterans and the Local State in Zimbabwe', *African Affairs*, Vol. 101:9-37.

Meena, R. (ed.) (1992) *Gender in Southern Africa: Conceptual and Theoretical Issues*, Harare: SAPES Books.

Migdal, J. (1974) *Peasants, Politics and Revolution: Pressures Toward Political and Social Change in the Third World*, Princeton, NJ: Princeton University Press.

Mohanty, C. (1988) 'Under Western Eyes: Feminist Scholarship and Colonial Discourses', *Feminist Review*, No. 30:61-88.

— (1995) 'Feminist Encounters: Locating the Politics of Experience', in L. Nicholson and S. Seidman (eds) *Social Postmodernism: Beyond Identity Politics*, Cambridge: Cambridge University Press.

Molyneux, M. (1985) 'Mobilisation Without Emancipation? Women's Interests, State and Revolution in Nicaragua', *Feminist Studies*, Vol. 11(2):227-54.

Moore, B. (1966) *Social Origins of Dictatorship and Democracy: Lord and Peasant in the Making of the Modern World*, Boston, MA: Beacon Press.

Moore, H.L. (1994) *A Passion for Difference: Essays in Anthropology*, Cambridge: Polity Press.

Moser, C.O.N. (1991) 'Gender Planning in the Third World: Meeting Practical and Strategic Needs', in R. Grant and K. Newland (eds) *Gender and International Relations*, Milton Keynes: Open University Press.

Moser, C.O.N. and F.C. Clarke (eds) (2001) *Victims, Perpetrators or Actors? Gender, Armed Conflict and Political Violence*, London: Zed Books.

Mugabe, R.G. (1983) *Our War of Liberation: Speeches, Articles, Interviews 1976–1979*, Gweru: Mambo Press.

Mungoshi, C. (1989) [1972] *Coming of the Dry Season*, Harare: Zimbabwe Publishing House.

— (1990) 'Mothers of the Sons and Daughters Recognised', *Moto*, No. 94, November:20-1.

Muringai, E. (1990) 'Forced Resettlement of Peasants During the Anti-Colonial Revolution: A Case Study of Peasant Struggles and "Protected Villages" in Chiweshe and Madziwa up to 1980', MA dissertation, University of Minnesota.

Muzondidya, J. (2009) 'From Buoyancy to Crisis, 1980–1997', in B. Raftopoulos and A. Mlambo (eds) *Becoming Zimbabwe: A History from the Pre-colonial Period to 2008*, Harare: Weaver Press, pp. 167-200.

Myrttinen, H. (2003) 'Disarming Masculinities', *Disarmament Forum*, Special Issue on Women, Men, Peace and Security, Geneva, United Nations Institute for Disarmament Research.

— (2005) 'Masculinities, Violence and Power in Timor Leste', *Lusotopie*, Vol. 12, Nos 1-22, pp. 233-44.

Naraghi-Anderlini, S. (2007) *Women Building Peace: What they Do, Why it Matters*, London: Lynne Rienner.

Ncube, W. (1987) 'Released from Legal Minority: The Legal Age of Majority Act in Zimbabwe', in A. Armstrong (ed.) *Women and Law in Southern Africa*, Harare: Zimbabwe Publishing House.

Nhema, A.G. (2002) *Democracy in Zimbabwe: From Liberation to Liberalization*, Harare: University of Zimbabwe Publications.

Nhongo-Simbanegavi, J. (2000) *For Better or Worse? Women and ZANLA in Zimbabwe's Liberation Struggle*, Harare: Weaver Press.

— (2003) 'Gender and Nationalism: The case for ZANLA, in T. Ranger (ed.) *The Historical Dimensions of Democracy and Human Rights in Zimbabwe, Volume Two: Nationalism, Democracy and Human Rights*, Harare: University of Zimbabwe Publications, pp. 77-100.

Nnaemeka, O. (1997) 'Fighting on All Fronts: Gendered Spaces, Ethnic Boundaries, and the Nigerian Civil War', *Dialectical Anthropology*, 22:235-63.

Nordstrom, C. (1997) *A Different Kind of War Story*, Philadelphia, PN: University of Pennsylvania Press.

Nordstrom, C. and A.C.G.M Robben (eds) (1995) *Fieldwork Under Fire: Contemporary Studies of Violence and Survival*, Berkeley, CA: University of California Press.

Nyangura, A. and M. Peil (1991) 'Zimbabwe since Independence: A People's Assessment', *African Affairs* Vol. 90, No. 361:607-20.

O' Gorman, E. (1999) 'Writing Women's Wars: Foucauldian Strategies of Engagement', in V. Jabri and E. O' Gorman (eds) *Women, Culture and International Relations*, Boulder, CO: Lynne Rienner.

— (2011) *Conflict and Development*, Development Matters Series, London: Zed Books.

O'Laughlin, B. (1985) 'Myth of the African Family in the World of Development', in D. Bryceson (ed.) *Women Wielding the Hoe: Lessons from Rural Africa for Feminist Theory and Development Practice*, Oxford: Berg Publishers.

Outshoorn, J. (1991) 'Power as a Political and Theoretical Concept in "Second-wave" Feminism', in K. Davis, M. Leijenaar and J. Oldersma (eds) *The Gender of Power*, London: Sage.

Overholt, C., M.B. Anderson, K. Cloud, and J.E. Austin (1985) 'Women in Development: A Framework for Project Analysis', in C. Overholt et al. (eds) *Gender Roles in Development Projects*, West Hartford, CT: Kumarian Press.

Oyeyumi, O. (1997) *The Invention of Women: Making an African Sense of Western Gender Discourses*, Minnesota: University of Minnesota Press.

— (2002) 'Conceptualizing Gender: The Eurocentric Foundations of Feminist Concepts and the Challenge of African Epistemologies', *JENdA: A Journal of Culture and African Women Studies*, Vol. 2. No 1. http://www.codesria.org/IMG/pdf/OYEWUMI.pdf (accessed 13/02/2011).

— (ed.) (2011) *Gender Epistemologies in Africa: The Gendering of African Traditions, Spaces, Social Identities and Institutions*, New York: Palgrave Macmillan.

Palmer, R. and N. Parsons (eds) (1977) *The Roots of Rural Poverty in Central and Southern Africa*, London: Heinemann.

Pankhurst, D. (1991) 'Constraints and Incentives in "Successful" Zimbabwean Peasant Agriculture: The Interaction between Gender and Class', *Journal of Southern African Studies* Vol. 17, No. 4: 611-32.

Parpart, J.L. and M. Zalewski (2008) *Rethinking the Man Question: Sex, Gender and Violence in International Relations*, London: Zed Books.

Peteet, J. (1991) *Gender in Crisis: Women and the Palestinian Resistance Movement*, New York: Columbia University Press.

Peters, P. (1985) 'Uses and Abuses of the Concept of "Female-Headed Households" in Research on Agrarian Transformation and Policy', in D. Bryceson (ed.) *Women Wielding the Hoe: Lessons from Rural Africa for Feminist Theory and Development Practice*, Oxford: Berg Publishers.

Peterson, V.S. (ed.) (1992) *Gendered States: Feminist (Re)Visions of International Relations Theory*, Boulder, CO: Lynne Rienner.

Peterson, V.S. and A.S. Runyan (1999) *Global Gender Issues*, 2nd edition, Boulder, CO: Westview Press.

Pettman J.J. (1996) *Worlding Women: A Feminist International Politics*, London and New York: Routledge.

Phimister, I. (1986) 'Commodity Relations and Class Formation in the Zimbabwean Countryside 1898–1920', *Journal of Peasant Studies*, Vol. 13, No. 4:240-57.

— (1988) *An Economic and Social History of Zimbabwe 1890–1948*, London: Longman.

Phimister, I. and B. Raftopoulos (2007) 'Desperate Days in Zimbabwe', *Review of African Political Economy*, Vol. 34, No. 113: 573-80.

— (2004) 'Mugabe, Mbeki and the Politics of Anti-imperialism', *Review of African Political Economy*, Vol. 31, No. 131:385-400.

Pierson, R.R. (1987) '"Did your mother wear army boots?" Feminist Theory and Women's Relation to War, Peace and Revolution', in S. Macdonald et al. (eds) *Images of Women in Peace and War: Cross-Cultural and Historical Perspectives*, London: Macmillan.

Pongweni, A.J.C. (1982) *Songs that Won the Liberation War*, Harare: College Press.

Popkin, S. (1979) *The Rational Peasant: The Political Economy of Rural Society in Vietnam*, Berkeley, CA: University of California Pres.

Potts, D. (2006) '"Restoring Order"? Operation Murambatsvina and the Urban Crisis in Zimbabwe', *Journal of Southern African Studies*, Vol. 32, No. 2:273-91.

Raftopoulos, B. (1991) 'Beyond the House of Hunger: The Struggle for Democratic Development in Zimbabwe', Working Paper No. 17, Harare: Zimbabwe Institute of Development Studies.

— (2006) 'The Zimbabwean Crisis and Challenges for the Left', *Journal of Southern African Studies*, Vol. 32, No. 2: pp. 203-24.

— (2009) 'The Crisis in Zimbabwe, 1998–2008', in B. Raftopoulos and A. Mlambo (eds) *Becoming Zimbabwe: A History from the Pre-colonial Period to 2008*, Harare: Weaver Press, pp. 201-32.

Raftopoulos, B. and A. Mlambo (eds) (2009) *Becoming Zimbabwe: A History from the Pre-colonial Period to 2008*, Harare: Weaver Press.

Ranger, T. (1978) 'Growing from the Roots: Reflections on Peasant Research in Central and Southern Africa', *Journal of Southern African Studies*, Vol. 5, No. 1:99-133.

— (1985) *Peasant Consciousness and Guerrilla War in Zimbabwe*, London: James Currey.

— (2004) 'Nationalist Historiography, Patriotic History and the History of the Nation: The Struggle over the Past in Zimbabwe', *Journal of Southern African Studies*, Vol. 30, No. 2:215-34.

Reardon, B. (1990) 'Feminist Concepts of Peace and Security', in P. Smoker, R. Davies and B. Munske (eds) *A Reader in Peace Studies*, Oxford: Pergamon Press.

Richards, P. (ed.) (2005) *No Peace No War: An Anthropology of Contemporary Armed Conflict*, Athens, OH: Ohio University Press and Oxford: James Currey.

Ridd, R. and H. Callaway (1986) (eds) *Caught Up in Conflict: Women's Responses to Political Strife*, London: Macmillan.

Sawicki, J. (1991) *Disciplining Foucault: Feminism, Power, and the Body*, New York: Routledge.

— (1994) 'Foucault, Feminism, and Questions of Identity', in G. Gutting (ed.) *The Cambridge Companion to Foucault*, Cambridge: Cambridge University Press.

Sayigh, R. (1984) 'Review Essay: Look Across the Mediterranean', *Middle East Report*, No. 124:22-6.

Schmidt, E. (1990) 'Negotiated Spaces and Contested Terrain: Men, Women, and the Law in Colonial Zimbabwe, 1890–1939', *Journal of Southern African Studies*, Vol. 16, No. 4:622-48.

— (1991) 'Patriarchy, Capitalism, and the Colonial State in Zimbabwe', *Signs*, Vol. 16, No. 4: 732-56.

— (1992) *Peasants, Traders and Wives: Shona Women in the History of Zimbabwe, 1870–1939*, London: James Currey and Harare: Baobab Books and Portsmouth, NH: Heinemann.

Scott, J.C. (1976) *The Moral Economy of the Peasant: Rebellion and Subsistence in Southeast Asia*, New Haven, CT: Yale University Press.

— (1977) 'Peasant Revolution: A Dismal Science', Review Article, *Comparative Politics*, Vol. 9, No. 2:231-48.

— (1979) 'Revolution in the Revolution: Peasants and Commissars', *Theory and Society*, Vol. 7, Nos 1 and 2:97-134.

— (1985) *Weapons of the Weak: Everyday Forms of Peasant Resistance*, New Haven, CT: Yale University Press.

— (1986) 'Everyday Forms of Peasant Resistance', *Journal of Peasant Studies*, Vol. 13(2):5-31.

— (1990) *Domination and the Arts of Resistance: Hidden Transcripts*, New Haven, CT: Yale University Press.

Scott, L. (1990) 'Women and the Armed Struggle for Independence in Zimbabwe (1964–1979)', Occasional Papers No. 25, Edinburgh University, Centre for African Studies.

Seidman, G.W. (1984) 'Women In Zimbabwe: Postindependence Struggles', *Feminist Studies*, Vol. 10, No. 3:419-40.

Sen, A. (1990) 'Gender and Cooperative Conflicts', in I. Tinker (ed.) *Persistent Inequalities: Women and World Development*, Oxford: Oxford University Press.

Shepherd, L.J. (2008) *Gender, Violence and Security: Discourse as Practice.* London: Zed Books.

Sjoberg, L. and C.E. Gentry (2007) *Mothers, Monsters, Whores: Women's Violence in Global Politics*, London: Zed Books.

Skocpol, T. (1979) *States and Social Revolutions: A Comparative Analysis of France, Russia, and China*, Cambridge: Cambridge University Press.

— (1982) 'What Makes Peasants Revolutionary?' *Comparative Politics*, Vol. 14, No. 3:351-75.

Staunton, I. (ed.) (1990) *Mothers of the Revolution: The War Experiences of Thirty Zimbabwean Women*, Harare: Baobab Books.

— (2009) *Damage: The Personal Costs of Political Change in Zimbabwe*, Harare: Weaver Press.

Stewart, J. and A. Armstrong (1990) (eds) *The Legal Situation of Women in Southern Africa*, Harare: University of Zimbabwe Publications.

Stiehm, J. (1988) 'The Effect of Myths about Military Women on the Waging of War', in E. Isaksson (ed.) *Women and the Military System*, London: Harvester Wheatsheaf.

Stiff, P. (1982) *Selous Scouts: Top Secret War*, Alberton: Galago.

Stoneman, C. (1981) *Zimbabwe's Inheritance*, London: Macmillan.

Sylvester, C. (1986) 'Zimbabwe's 1985 Elections: A Search for National Mythology', *Journal of Modern African Studies*, Vol. 24, No. 2:229-55.

— (1987) 'Some Dangers in Merging Feminist and Peace Projects', *Alternatives*, Vol. 12, No. 4:493-509.

— (1990a) 'Simultaneous Revolutions: The Zimbabwean Case', *Journal of Southern African Studies*, Vol. 16, No. 3:452-75.

— (1990b) 'Unities and Disunities in Zimbabwe's 1990 Election', *Journal of Modern African Studies*, Vol. 28, No. 3:375-400.

— (1991) *Zimbabwe: The Terrain of Contradictory Development*, Boulder, CO: Westview.

— (1994) *Feminist Theory and International Relations*, Cambridge: Cambridge University Press.

— (1995) 'Whither Opposition in Zimbabwe?' *Journal of Modern African Studies*, Vol. 33, No. 3:403-23.

Taylor, J. and S. Stewart (1991) *Sexual and Domestic Violence: Help, Recovery and Action in Zimbabwe*, Harare: Women and Law in Southern Africa.

Tétreault, M.A. (ed.) (1994) *Women and Revolution in Africa, Asia and the New World*, Columbia, SC: University of South Carolina Press.

Tickner, J.A. (1992) *Gender in International Relations: Feminist Perspectives on Achieving Global Security*, New York: Columbia University Press.

— (2001) *Gendering World Politics: Issues and Approaches in the Post-Cold War Era*, New York: Columbia University Press.

Tompkins, T.L. (1995) 'Prosecuting Rape as a War Crime: Speaking the Unspeakable', *Notre Dame Law Review*, Vol. 70, No. 4:845-91.

Urdang, S. (1979) *Fighting Two Colonialisms: Women in Guinea-Bissau*, New York: Monthly Review Press.

— (1989) *And Still They Dance: Women, War and the Struggle for Change in Mozambique*, London, Earthscan.

Utas, M. (2005) 'Victimcy, Girlfriending, Soldiering: Tactic Agency in a Young Woman's Social Navigation of the Liberian War Zone', *Anthropological Quarterly*, Vol. 78, No.2:403-30.

Vansina, J. (1980) 'Memory and Oral Tradition', in J.C. Miller (ed.) *The African*

Past Speaks: Essays on Oral Tradition, Folkstone: Dawson.
— (1985) *Oral Tradition as History*, Oxford: James Currey.
Vera, Y. (1993) *Nehanda*, Harare: Baobab Books.
Vickers, J. (1993) *Women and War*, London: Zed Books.
Weinrich, A.K.H. (1975) *African Farmers in Rhodesia: Old and New Peasant Communities in Karangaland*, Oxford: Oxford University Press.
— (1976/77) 'Strategic Resettlement in Chiweshe', *Journal of Southern African Studies*, Vol. 3, No. 2:207-29.
— (1979) *Women and Racial Discrimination in Rhodesia*, Paris: UNESCO.
Weiss, R. (1986) *The Women of Zimbabwe*, Harare: Nehanda Publishers.
Wolf, E. (1969) *Peasant Wars of the Twentieth Century*. New York: Harper and Row.
Zarkov, D. (ed.) (2008) *Gender, Violent Conflict and Development*, New Delhi: Zubaan.
Zvobgo, R.J. (1994) *Colonialism and Education in Zimbabwe*, Harare: SAPES Books.

Primary Sources

Reports/Documents

Amnesty International (2008) (AFR 34/004/2008) 'Liberia: A Flawed Process Discriminates Against Women and Girls', London.
Catholic Commission for Justice and Peace (CCJP) in Zimbabwe and Legal Resources Foundation (LRF) (1997) 'Breaking the Silence, Building True Peace: Report on the Disturbances in Matabeleland and the Midlands, 1980–1989', Harare: CCJP and LRF.
Council of the European Union (2008) (15671/1/08) 'Comprehensive Approach to the EU Implementation of the United Nations Security Council Resolutions 1325 and 1820 on Women, Peace and Security', Brussels.
General Agricultural and Plantation Workers Union of Zimbabwe (GAPWUZ) (2010) 'If Something is Wrong...: The invisible suffering of farmworkers due to "Land Reform"', report commissioned by GAPWWUZ, Harare: Weaver Press.
Government of Zimbabwe and the United Nations (2010) 'Joint IDP (Internally Displaced Persons) Assessment, Final Report', Harare.
Internal Displacement Monitoring Centre (IDMC) (2008) 'Zimbabwe: Country Fact Sheet', Geneva.
International Alert (2002) 'Gender Mainstreaming in Peace Support Operations: Moving Beyond Rhetoric to Practice', by D. Mazurana and E.P. Lopez, London. See http://www.international-alert.org/pdf/Gender_Mainstreaming_no_covers.pdf.
International Crisis Group (ICG) (2010*)* 'Zimbabwe: Political and Security Challenges to the Transition', *Africa Briefing No. 70*, Harare/Brussels, 3 March.
— (2009) 'Zimbabwe: Engaging the Inclusive Government', *Africa Briefing No. 59*, Harare/Brussels.
— (2008a) 'Zimbabwe: Prospects from a Flawed Election', *Africa Report No. 138*, Brussels, 20 March.
— (2008b) 'Negotiating Zimbabwe's Transition', *Africa Briefing No. 51*, Pretoria/Brussels, 21 May.
— (2008c) 'Ending Zimbabwe's Nightmare: A Possible Way Forward', *Africa Briefing No. 56*, Pretoria/Brussels, 16 December.
— (2007) 'Zimbabwe: A Regional Solution?' *Africa Report No. 132*, Brussels.
— (2005) 'Zimbabwe's Operation Murambatsvina: The Tipping Point?' *Africa Report No. 97*, Brussels.
ICRC (2001) 'Women Facing War: ICRC Study on the Impact of Armed Conflict on

Women', Geneva: ICRC.

Rehn, E. and E. Johnson-Sirleaf (2002) 'Women, War and Peace: The Independent Experts' Assessment on the Impact of Armed Conflict on Women and Women's Role in Peace-Building', New York: UNIFEM.

Sachikonye, L.M. (2003) 'The Situation of Commercial Farm Workers after Land Reform in Zimbabwe', report commissioned by the Farm Community Trust of Zimbabwe, Harare.

Sherriff, A. with K. Barnes (2008) Study for the Slovenian Presidency on *Enhancing the EU Response to Women and Armed Conflict*, Maastricht: ECPDM.

Specht, I. (2006) 'Red Shoes: Experiences of Girl-Combatants in Liberia', Geneva: ILO.

United Nations (2002) 'Women, Peace and Security: A study submitted by the Secretary-General pursuant to Security Council Resolution 1325 (2000)', New York: United Nations.

— (2005) 'Report of the Fact-Finding Mission to Zimbabwe to Assess the Scope and Impact of Operation Murambatsvina', undertaken by the UN Special Envoy on Human Settlement Issues in Zimbabwe, Anna Kajumulo Tibaijuka, New York: United Nations.

United Nations Development Programme–Zimbabwe (2008) 'Comprehensive Economic Recovery in Zimbabwe: A Discussion Document', Harare: United Nations Development Programme.

United Nations Security Council (2000) *Resolution 1325*, 31 October. S/RES/1325 (2000). New York.

— (2008a) *Resolution 1820*, 19 June, 2008 S/RES/1820 (2008).

— (2008b) (S/2008/728) 'Fourth Special Report of the Secretary-General on the United Nations Organisation Mission in the Democratic Republic of Congo', November 2008, New York.

— (2010) (S/2010/164) 'Thirty-First Report of the Secretary-General on the United Nations Organisation Mission in the Democratic Republic of Congo', March 2010, New York.

UN OCHA (2008) 'Zimbabwe Consolidated Appeal', Geneva: United Nations Office for the Coordination of Humanitarian Affairs.

World Bank (2006) 'The Other Half of Gender: Men's Issues in Development', I. Bannon and M. Correia (eds). Washington.

Zimbabwe Women's Bureau (ZWB) (1981) 'We Carry a Heavy Load: Rural Women Speak Out', K. McCalman (ed.), Harare: ZWB.

Zimbabwe Women's Bureau (1992) 'We Carry a Heavy Load: Rural Women Speak Out, Part II, 1981–1991', compiled by Helen L. Vukasin, Harare: ZWB.

Newspaper and Magazine Articles

The Guardian (UK) (2003) 'Living in Fear of Mugabe's Green Bombers', Andy Meldrum, 19 February.

The Herald (1990) 'ZANU (PF) Election Manifesto', 5 March, pp. 2-3.

The Independent (2009) 'UN Warns Sri Lanka over Prison Camps', Andrew Buncombe, 12 September, London.

The Independent (UK) (1994) 'Freedom! But for Women as Well?', David Cohen, 15 April, p. 20.

Moto (1983/84) 'Women in Zimbabwe: The Price of Liberation', Special Issue, No. 17, October, Gweru.

— (1983/84) 'Operation Clean-Up Takes Women's Liberation One Step Back', December/January, pp. 5-9, Gweru.

— (1990) 'She Heroes, Years Later...', Special Issue, No. 94, November, Gweru.

Rhodesia Herald (1974a) 25 July, p. 2.

— (1974b) 'Operation Overload Gets Going', 27 July, p. 3.

— (1974c) 'Update on Operation Overload', 8 August, p. 5.

The Zimbabwean (2009) 'Fresh Violence Rocks Chiweshe', SW Radio Africa, 26 October.
— (2010) 'Villagers Beaten for Wearing Red', Itai Mabasa and Tony Saxon, 19 April.

National Archives of Zimbabwe (NAZ) – Harare

CCJP Rhodesia
MS 311/3. Fasc. 3. 'Alleged Atrocities by the Security Forces 1974'.
MS 311/5. Fasc. 5. 'Responses to the publication of "The Man in the Middle"', 1975.
MS 311/6. Fasc. 6. 'Alleged Atrocities by the Security Forces 1975'.
MS 311/9. Fasc. 9. 'Government's Emergency Powers, Propaganda, Alleged Atrocities 1976–77'.
MS 311/15. Appendices 7, 28. 'Anatomy of Terror' and 'Harvest of Fear: A Diary of Terrorist Activities', Rhodesian Ministry of Information, 1974, 1976.
MS 311/16. Appendix 8. 'Cases of Alleged Security Forces Brutality 1974'.
MS 311/17. Appendices 9-13. 'Justice and Peace Reports on Protected Villages 1974–1978'.
MS 311/20. Appendices 18-19. 'Government's "Hearts and Minds" Psychological Campaign 1974'.
GEN-P/CAT 24480. The Rights and Duties of a Citizen When on Trial', 1974.
GEN-P/CAT 28243. 'Rhodesia: The Propaganda War', CIIR (London) and CCJP (Rhodesia) 1977.
GEN-P/CAT 39657. 'What Are People Saying?', 1978.
GEN-P/CAT 30570. 'Rhodesia after the Internal Settlement', 1978.
GEN-P/CAT 39659. 'An Analysis of The Salisbury Agreement', 1978.
GEN-P/CAT 32114. 'Rhodesia at War: A Story of Mounting Suffering', 1979.
GEN-P/CAT 34235. 'Halfway to the Elections: Some Notes on the Present Situation in Rhodesia', 1980.

General
MS 735. 'The Rhodesian Crisis: 1971–1979', Newspaper Cuttings – The Labour Party (UK).

International Defence and Aid Fund for Southern Africa (IDAF)
MS 589/7/2. 'Reports of Visits to the Protected Villages September 1975-January 1976'
MS 589/7/4. 'Collection of Statement to UN Commission of Human Rights', Ad Hoc Working Group of Experts on Southern Africa, 1977.
MS 589/7/5. 'Christian Care Reports 1974–1975'.
MS 589/7/6. 'Report on ICRC Activities in Southern Africa'.

Newspaper Cuttings
MS 590/1. Rhodesia: General Review, 1967–72.
MS 590/2. Rhodesia: General Review, 1973–74.
MS 590/3. Liberation Movement, 1973–77.
MS 590/9. Urban Areas 1973–74, 1977.
MS 590/13. Rural Areas 1973–74, 1979.

Chiweshe 1890–1923
A3/18/39/12; L2/2/117/19: Chiweshe Native Reserve.

Chiweshe post-1923
S1 542/510. Chiweshe Reserve Centralisation, 1933–41. Chief Native Commissioner.

S1 060/3. Chiweshe Reserve Centralisation of Arable Land and Grazing Lands – Final Reports 1950. Native Commissioner, Mazoe.

S1 060/6. Chiweshe Reserve Firewood: 1949–1950. Native Commissioner, Mazoe.

S1 060/1. Chiweshe Reserve: Publicity and Press Cuttings, 1949–50. Native Commissioner, Mazoe.

S2 259. Mazoe: General 1946–1958. Native Commissioner, Mazoe.

Women

SRG 3/ NAT 35. 'Mainly for Women' In Southern Rhodesia, Fact Paper No. 11, April 1961. Chief Information Officer. Native Affairs Department.

ZG-P /NAT 36. 'African Women and the Changing Pattern of Africa', Information Paper No. 22, 1963, Department of Information Service.

Library and Registry of the Ministry of Local Government – Harare (MLG Archive)

Parliamentary Debates

Rhodesia Parliamentary Debates (1974) Vols 86 and 87: 19th-29th March 1974; 13th-21st June 1974.

Rhodesia Parliamentary Debates (1974) Vol. 88: 26th August-1st October 1974.

Rhodesia Parliamentary Debates (1974–1975) Vol. 89: 2nd October-15th November 1974; 11th January-11th April 1975.

Colonial Administrative Files: Chiweshe Council

Vol. 1 CA/20/1. 'Creation, Representation, Powers, Council Warrants and Amendments, Boundaries and Alterations', Chiweshe Council, 1964–1977.

Vol. 1 CA/20/3. 'Election of Councillors', Chiweshe Council, 1959–1971.

Vol. 1 CA/20/4. 'Councillors, Subsidies, Allowances, Visits', Chiweshe Council, 1965.

Vol. 1 CA/20/7. 'Animal Husbandry, Dipping, Dipping Fees, Thefts, Losses', Chiweshe Council, 1963.

Vol. 1 CA/20/8. 'Schools, Education, Grants Provisions, Management, Maintenance', Chiweshe Council, 1963–1971.

Vol. 1 CA/20/9. 'Hospitals, Clinics, Ambulance Provision, Maintenance', Chiweshe Council. 1965–1971.

Vol. 1 CA/20/10. 'Bottle Store, Beer Halls/Gardens, Liquor Provision, Management, Accounts', Chiweshe Council. 1962–1976.

Vol. 1 CA/20/11. 'By-Laws, Taxes, Rates, Vehicle License Fees', Chiweshe Council, 1960–1977.

Vol. 1 CA/20/14. 'Roads, Bridges, Fencing', Chiweshe Council, 1969–1970.

Colonial Administrative Files: Chiweshe Chiefs

Per 5/Chiweshe. Chief Chiweshe, Administrative correspondence regarding politics of the Chieftancy, Mazoe District, 1933–1993.

Per 5/Negomo. Chief Negomo, Administrative correspondence regarding politics of the Chieftancy, Mazoe District.

Per 5/Makope. Chief Makope, Administrative correspondence regarding politics of the Chieftancy, Mazoe District.

Colonial Administrative Files: Women and Community Development

Vol. I CDV/12/9. 'Annual Reports, Organisation, Administration, Summary of Duties. Community Development Women's Section', 1970–1980.

Vol. II CDV/12/1. 'Organisation, Functions, Policy and Planning', Branch of Community Development Training, 1972–1978.

Vol. II CDV/12/5. 'Community Advisers: Policy', Community Development,

1978–1981.

Vol. III CDV/12/1. 'Organisation, Functions, Policy and Planning', Branch of Community Development Training, 1978–1979.

PER/4/18. 'Provision of District Assistants to Accompany Community Development Assistants (Women) on Patrol', Correspondence between Secretary for Internal Affairs and Provincial and District Commissioners, 1971–1977.

Circular No. 87. 'Creation of Internal Affairs and Community Development Policy', March 1963.

Archive of the Catholic Institute of International Relations (CIIR) – London[1]

Amnesty International (1977) 'Capital Punishment in Rhodesia: A General Background', March. AFR 46/01/77.

Bratton, M. (1978) 'Beyond Community Development: The Political Economy of Rural Administration in Zimbabwe', in the series *From Rhodesia to Zimbabwe*, London: CIIR.

Catholic Commission for Justice and Peace (CCJP) (Rhodesia) (1974) 'Report on the Conducted Tour of Chiweshe Tribal Trust Land on 5th September, 1974'. Ref: 00233R (Arranged by the Ministries of Internal Affairs and Information. D.B. Scholz SJ).

CIIR (1976) 'Civil War in Rhodesia: Abduction, Torture and Death in the Counter-Insurgency Campaign', CCJP (Rhodesia), September.

CIIR (1976) 'Civil War in Rhodesia – Bulletin No. 1', Report from CCJP (Rhodesia) and CIIR (London), November.

CIIR (1977) 'Report on the Publication of "Civil War in Rhodesia"', London: CIIR, March.

CIIR (1977/78) 'Documents Concerning the Prosecution of Members of the Executive 1977/78', CCJP (Rhodesia).

CIIR (London) and CCJP (Rhodesia) (1975) '"The Man in the Middle": Torture, Resettlement and Eviction', Report compiled by the Catholic Commission for Justice and Peace in Rhodesia.

CIIR and ICJ (1976) 'Racial Discrimination and Repression in Southern Rhodesia', Report of the International Commission of Jurists, Geneva, and the Catholic Institute for International Relations, London, March.

House of Commons (1979) '"Free and Fair?": A Report by Observers on Behalf of the British Parliamentary Human Rights Group', London, House of Commons, May.

Ministry of Information (Rhodesia) (1976) '"Harvest of Fear": A Diary of Terrorist Atrocities in Rhodesia', Salisbury: Ministry of Information, Immigration and Tourism (Rhodesia), October.

Riddell, R. (1978) 'The Land Question', in the series *From Rhodesia to Zimbabwe*, London: CIIR.

Zimbabwe Women's Resource Centre and Network (ZWRCN) – Harare

Chigudu, H. (1993) 'Critical Issues for Women in Zimbabwe: The Zimbabwe Women's Resource Centre and Network Response to these Issues', paper presented at a workshop organised by the Global Fund for Women and ZWRCN, January.

Getecha, C. and J. Chipika (eds) (1995) *Zimbabwe Women's Voices*, Harare: ZWRCN.

Ministry of Community Development and Women's Affairs (MCDWA) (1982) 'Report on the Situation of Women in Zimbabwe', compiled by MCDWA and funded by UNICEF, Ministry of Community Development and Women's Affairs.

---

[1] The CIIR archive is now housed at the Institute of Commonwealth Studies Library in Senate House, London.

Primary Sources: Interviews[2]

Transcript Code/Pseudonyms		Date of Interviews (1993)
A	Agnes	21 April; 6 July
B	Alice	23 April; 14 August; 3 November
C	Pardon	26 April; 14 August; 3 November
D	Josephine	27 April; 17 July
E	Florence	28 April; 17 July
F	Anna	8 June; 17 July
G	Rosy	30 October
H	Joanne	23 April; 18 July; 2 November
I	Hilda	13 June; 15 August; 3 November
J	Judith	13 June; 15 August; 3 November
K	Victoria	29 May; 13 July
L	Emily	31 May
M	Veronica	1 June; 14 July
N	Trust	1 June; 14 July
O	Tecla	9 June; 1 August
P	Stella	9 June
Q	Susan	10 June; 4 August
R	Phyllis	10 June; 4 August
S	Margaret	10 June; 4 August
T	Doreen	4 August
U	Dorothy	15 June; 12 August
V	Eva	15 June
W	Monica	15 June
X	Maggie	17 June
Y	Tendai	17 June; 8 July; 10 August
Z	Sarah	8 July; 12 August
AA	Gladys[3]	1 July; 11 November
AB	Polly	1 July; 17 August; 11 November
AC	Ellen	1 July; 16 August; 11 November
AD	Salvation Army Group	7 July
AE	Rachel	4 September; 4 November
AF	Mercy	29 August
AG	Mary	22 October; 21 November
AH	More Blessing	5 November
AI	Lorine*	January, 1994
AJ	Farasia*	January, 1994
AK	Lucia*	January, 1994
AL	Juliet*	January, 1994
AM	Mrs Moyo (Salvation Army HQ)	12 October
AN	Fr Fidelis	14 October
AO	Everjoyce Win (WILDAF)	16 October
AP	Selina Mumbengegwi (WAG)	21 October
AQ	Taurai	1 November
AR	Peter	1 September
AS	Emelda	1 September
AT	Hope	20 March
AU	Martha	6 June
AV	Michael	13 June

[2] Appendix 2 provides tabulated profiles of the interviewees while preserving anonymity.
[3] Gladys was a serving MP at time of interview.
* I am grateful to Ishmael Magaisa, then from the Department of Sociology, University of Zimbabwe, for conducting each of the four interviews marked with an asterisk.

INDEX

Printed and bound by CPI Group (UK) Ltd, Croydon, CR0 4YY

09/06/2025

14685775-0001